# DOING THINGS WITH THINGS

# Doing Things with Things
## The Design and Use of Everyday Objects

Edited by

ALAN COSTALL
*University of Portsmouth, UK*

and

OLE DREIER
*University of Copenhagen, Denmark*

ASHGATE

Published by
Ashgate Publishing Limited
Gower House
Croft Road
Aldershot
Hampshire GU11 3HR
England

Ashgate Publishing Company
Suite 420
101 Cherry Street
Burlington, VT 05401-4405
USA

Ashgate website: http://www.ashgate.com

**British Library Cataloguing in Publication Data**
Doing things with things: the design and use of everyday
objects – (Ethnoscapes)
1. Material culture 2. Technology – Social aspects
3. Knowledge, Theory of 4. Knowledge, Theory of, in children
1. Costall, Alan II. Dreier, Ole
306.4'6

ISBN-10: 0 7546 4656 4
ISBN-13: 978-0-7546-4656-3

**Library of Congress Cataloging-in-Publication Data**
Doing things with things: the design and use of everyday objects / edited by
Alan Costall and Ole Dreier.
p. cm. -- (Ethnoscapes)
Includes index.
ISBN: 0-7546-4656-4
1. Material culture--Philosophy. I. Costall, Alan. II. Dreier, Ole. III.
Series: Ethnoscapes (Unnumbered)

GN406.D65 2006
302--dc22

2006007245

Printed and bound in Great Britain by Antony Rowe Ltd, Chippenham, Wiltshire.

# Contents

*List of Contributors* *vii*
*List of Figures and Tables* *ix*

Introduction 1
*Alan Costall and Ole Dreier*

**Part I Intentionality and the Functionality of Things**

1. The Case of the Recalcitrant Prototype 15
*Beth Preston*

2. Use Plans and Artefact Functions: An Intentionalist Approach to Artefacts and their Use 29
*Pieter E. Vermaas and Wybo Houkes*

**Part II Things in the World of the Child**

3. Autism and Object Use: The Mutuality of the Social and Material in Children's Developing Understanding and Use of Everyday Objects 51
*Emma Williams and Linda Kendell-Scott*

4. Object Use in Pretend Play: Symbolic or Functional? 67
*Ágnes Szokolszky*

5. Culture, Language and Canonicality: Differences in the Use of Containers between Zapotec (Mexican Indigenous) and Danish Children 87
*Kristine Jensen de López*

**Part III Transformation and Things**

6. The Cognitive Biographies of Things 113
*David de Léon*

7. The Woman who used her Walking Stick as a Telephone: The Use of Utilities in Praxis 131
*Hysse Birgitte Forchhammer*

8. Politics of Things: The Interplay of Design and Practice in a Design Workshop with Children 147
*Estrid Sørensen*

**Part IV Organisation and Things**

9. Working with Material Things: From Essentialism to Material–Semiotic Analysis of Sociotechnical Practice 167
*Finn Olesen and Randi Markussen*

10. Words and Things: Discursive and Non-Discursive Ordering in a Networked Organisation 193
*Steven D. Brown and David Middleton*

11. Learning to Do Things with Things: Apprenticeship Learning in Bakery as Economy and Social Practice 209
*Klaus Nielsen*

12. Urban Makings and the Formalisation of Informal Settlements 225
*Gustavo Ribeiro*

*Name Index* *239*
*Subject Index* *241*

# List of Contributors

Steven D. Brown, Department of Human Sciences, Loughborough University, England. s.d.brown@lboro.ac.uk

Alan Costall, Department of Psychology, University of Portsmouth, England. alan.costall@port.ac.uk

David de Léon, Cognitive Science, Lund University, Lund, Sweden. david.deleon@sonyericsson.com

Ole Dreier, Department of Psychology, University of Copenhagen, Denmark. ole.dreier@psy.ku.dk

Hysse Forchhammer, Neurological Department, Glostrup University Hospital, Glostrup, Denmark. hybf@glostruphosp.kbhamt.dk

Wybo Houkes, Department of Philosophy, University of Eindhoven, The Netherlands. W.N.Houkes@tm.tue.nl

Kristine Jensen de López, Department of Communication, Aalborg University, Denmark. kristine@hum.aau.dk

Linda Kendell-Scott, University of Winchester, England. linda.kendell-scott@winchester.ac.uk

Randi Markussen, Dept. of Information and Media Studies, Aarhus University, Denmark. rmark@imv.au.dk

David Middleton, Department of Human Sciences, Loughborough University, England. d.j.middleton@lboro.ac.uk

Klaus Nielsen, Institute of Psychology, Aarhus University, Denmark. klausn@psy.au.dk

Finn Olesen, Dept. of Information and Media Studies, Aarhus University, Denmark. finno@imv.au.dk

Beth Preston, Department of Philosophy, University of Georgia, USA. epreston@uga.edu

Gustavo Ribeiro, Royal Danish Academy of Fine Arts, School of Architecture, Copenhagen, Denmark. gustavo.ribeiro@karch.dk

Ágnes Szokolszky, Deparment of Psychology, University of Szeged, Hungary. szokolszky@t-online.hu

Estrid Sørensen, Institute of Technology Studies, Technical University, Berlin, Germany. estrid@gmx.net

Pieter E. Vermaas, Department of Philosophy, Delft University of Technology, The Netherlands. p.e.vermaas@tbm.tudelft.nl

Emma Williams, Department of Psychology, University of Surrey, England. e.i.williams@surrey.ac.uk

# List of Figures and Tables

## Figures


| | | |
|---|---|---|
| Figure 4.1 | Photographs of the experimental objects | 76 |
| Figure 4.2 | Ranking of the fitness of the substitute objects | 77 |
| Figure 4.3 | Frequency of action types | 80 |
| Figure 5.1 | Illustration of the semantic differences expressed in Danish and Zapotec | 97 |
| Figure 5.2 | Imitation of the UNDER spatial relation to the Initial-Canonical oriented basket | 99 |
| Figure 5.3 | Imitation of the UNDER spatial relation to the Initial-Inverted oriented basket | 100 |
| Figure 5.4 | Responses by language group to the I/LÁANI configuring linguistically-guided object manipulation for the Initial-Inverted basket | 103 |
| Figure 6.1 | The shelf (to the left of the door), sink and plate rack (far left of picture) and corner of fridge (far right side of picture). Part of the dining room can be seen through the kitchen door | 116 |
| Figure 6.2 | Basic categorisation of the shelf | 117 |
| Figure 6.3 | A schematic history of the shelf | 121 |
| Figure 9.1 | A reproduction of one of the very first medicine lists of the EMM to be used for measuring out medicine at the ward. | 183 |
| Figure 9.2 | A medicine list in harmony with the situated needs of the nurses | 186 |
| Figure 12.1 | Tung Pattana Boardwalk (Photo: Jørgen Andreasen) | 231 |
| Figure 12.2 | Tung Pattana Boardwalk (Photo: Jørgen Andreasen) | 231 |


## Tables


| | | |
|---|---|---|
| Table 4.1 | Target and substitute objects | 75 |
| Table 5.1 | The three main response types to the imitative and the linguistically-guided task by language group | 98 |
| Table 6.1 | Summary of main cognitive differences between using the box and using the shelf. | 124 |

# Introduction

Alan Costall and Ole Dreier

It has been claimed that the natural sciences have abstracted for themselves a 'material world' set apart from human concerns, and the social sciences, in their turn, constructed 'a world of actors devoid of things' (Joerges,1988, p. 220). A dualism between people and things has certainly been institutionalized in the very distinction between the natural and human sciences. Yet, the situation is more complicated and in some respects even worse than that. There is great diversity among the human sciences in their focus on objects. At one extreme, archaeology would seem obliged by its very nature to take into account human tools and artefacts. At the other extreme, mainstream psychology with its emphasis upon internal mental structures, and commitment to stimulus-response thinking, has presented us with a world not just devoid of things but also of agents.

As psychologists critical of the neglect of the material conditions of human thought and action, we were keen to bring together a number of researchers in the human sciences who have been taking *things* more seriously, and whose work interconnects in several distinctive and important ways. This book stems from two interdisciplinary meetings we organized at the University of Copenhagen. In addition to the discussions held at these meetings, the later drafts of the chapters were circulated among all of the contributors to make the individual contributions speak more directly to each other and to common issues. We are grateful to Benny Karpatschof and Kurt Keller, who also took part in the workshops, for their insightful commentaries on the following chapters. We would also like to thank the Danish Research Council for the Humanities for funding the workshops; the Department of Psychology, Copenhagen University for hosting the meetings and providing a visiting professorship for Alan Costall which led to our joint project.

This book reflects a growing interest within the human sciences about how people relate to objects. However, the standard approaches assume that the meanings of things can be *localized* – within the things themselves, *or* within our heads, *or* within our 'discourse'. Furthermore, most of the recent work in this field has also been concerned with how people cope with new technologies, with an emphasis as much on the novelty of these technologies as upon their highly technical nature. In contrast, the contributors to the present book mainly focus on everyday objects and how these objects enter into our activities over the course of time. Indeed, even though we have included some chapters concerned with the use of 'high-tech' objects, these also approach such objects as parts of ongoing everyday activities. The chapters also reflect a distinctive and coherent combination of different theoretical approaches, including actor network theory, ecological psychology, cognitive linguistics, and science and technology studies. What unites the contributors to this book is not just their rejection of the standard notion of objects and their properties as inert, inherently meaningless, and quite alien to ourselves. All of the contributors emphasize the need to understand the relations between people and objects in terms of process and change.

## I. Intentionality and the Functionality of Things

The first two chapters address a fundamental issue taken up again in many of the later chapters. Although any particular object lends itself to a limitless number of possible uses, many of the objects we encounter nevertheless present us with their own unique meaning: an apple, for example, is 'for eating', even though it can be thrown, or used as a paperweight, or even as a target for archery. Both Beth Preston and also Pieter Vermaas and Wybo Houkes critically examine the standard philosophical accounts of the 'proper function' of artefacts (notably, Ruth Millikan's writings) and present alternative analyses. As a whole the discussion is framed in terms of three supposedly distinctive roles for human agents with regard to artefacts – designer, maker, and user. While Preston argues that the intentions of the designer are not sufficient for establishing proper function, Vermaas and Houkes defend such an intentionalist approach to artefacts and artefact use.

The standard view of artefacts assumes that the design, making and use of artefacts are quite distinct and separate activities. In her chapter, 'The case of the recalcitrant prototype', Beth Preston points out that while users often use artefacts creatively for purposes other than their designers had in mind – and, in so doing, also modify them – standard theories of how artefact functions are established privilege the intentions of designers. The use of artefacts is then said to rest on their 'proper function' as opposed to a contingent, occasional 'system function'. Preston argues that a distinction between proper function and system function is necessary in order to prevent the proper functions of artefacts from proliferating in an uncontrolled and incoherent way. At the same time, however, this distinction makes the view that artefact function is established by designers' intentions problematic. To resolve this dilemma, Preston proposes that a history of selection and reproduction, rather than the intentions of designers, establishes the (direct and derived) proper functions of an artefact. In accounting for how artefacts get their functions neither proper function nor system function then require an appeal to intentions.

Pieter Vermaas and Wybo Houkes present an action-theoretical view of artefacts in their chapter on 'Use plans and artefact functions: an intentionalist approach to artefacts and their use'. They reject the strong emphasis on functionality in the standard view of artefacts, and endorse a version of intentionalism by describing artefact design and use primarily in terms of plans: that is, structured sequences of considered actions. Users, they argue, may take artefacts simply as a means of attaining their own desired ends and thus be primarily interested in their own plans for realising those ends without even supposing that artefacts have functions. This question about what something is *for*, should, on their view, be understood in terms of how and for what goals that thing could be used. In designing, designers construct what Vermaas and Houkes call 'use plans' for the artefacts they are designing. The concept of proper use may now be maintained by claiming that use plans for artefacts constructed by designers hold a privileged position relative to other plans. Consequently, the proper use of an artefact is the use that follows a plan that is approximately identical to the use plan developed by its designers.

A further distinction can also be made between good (rational) and bad (irrational) use, which is independent of the distinction between proper and non-standard use, allowing us to recognise the rationality of non-standard uses of artefacts. Vermaas and Houkes argue that action plans are incomplete 'lightweight plans' with respect to both the necessary skills involved and the circumstances of their realisation. Furthermore, they see the functions of an artefact as corresponding to those dispositions of the artefact that serve to explain why the use plan for the artefact achieves its goal.

The arguments and differing views of these two chapters set the stage for the rest of the book. In fact, designing, making, and using artefacts – and the relationships between them – are addressed in various ways in all the other chapters, for example, in relation to the significance of multi-purpose artefacts and the transformation of artefacts in ongoing activities.

## II. Things in the World of the Child

How do young children come to develop a sense of things having a proper function – an inherent, 'impersonal' meaning – and how might this depend upon the particular cultural context? These questions are only beginning to be addressed by developmental psychologists. Indeed, the way children relate to things more generally has been neglected within psychology. In part, this has been the legacy of the developmental theorist, Jean Piaget. Despite treating the interactions between children and objects as the foundation of development ('sensori-motor' intelligence'), Piagetian theory, along with most of cognitive psychology, posits abstract thinking ('formal operations') as the culmination of the developmental process. Even the social-cultural theory of Vygotsky, widely regarded as a radical alternative to Piagetian theory, itself posits a process of decontextualization, through a developmental transition from the interpersonal to the intrapersonal (Wertsch, 1996).

In one important respect, matters have become even worse within developmental theory in recent years. In going beyond Piaget, many developmental psychologists now stress the importance of domain specific knowledge, and regard the developing child as a 'theorist', forming and elaborating theories restricted to highly specific domains. In particular, 'the Theory of Mind' approach, which has been dominant within developmental psychology for the last decade, has largely removed the issue of children's use of objects from the research agenda, not only because of its emphasis upon 'mind', but also because of its explicit separation of children's understanding of other people from their understanding of things.

Autism, according to this approach, is a disorder stemming from a specific failure to understand other minds, and, furthermore, one that affects the child's ability to relate to other people, but not to things. In their chapter, on 'Autism and object use', Emma Williams and Linda Kendell-Scott present evidence of extensive delay and disruption for autistic children in their dealings with things, not least in the 'proper' use of objects (the topic of the chapters in Section 1 of this book). As they point out, even if the Theory of Mind account were correct, such disruption in object use should have been expected, given the way we normally come to learn about novel objects, by being introduced to them by other people, noticing other people using them, and entering into the standard practices in which things have their place. However, Williams and Kendell-Scott argue that the fundamental division between people and things, assumed by the Theory of Mind approach, is untenable: the widespread failure to use things *properly* in commonly understood ways must itself set powerful obstacles to relating to other people and communicating with them.

The unwordliness of psychological theory is further challenged by Ágnes Szokolszky. Her chapter on 'Object use in pretend play' is concerned with the impressively resourceful way in which young children can incorporate objects into their play activity, make-believing these things are something they are not. At one of the workshops on which this book is based, Szokolszky used the example of her young son announcing, somewhat unpromisingly, that his discarded sock was a 'gun'. But her son then held the sock taut between his two hands, and 'aimed' it at her. The fact that things lend themselves to so many pretend uses (and indeed practical uses) has encouraged theorists to suppose that the ability to engage in imaginative play with objects is purely 'cognitive,' and little, if anything, to do with the play object itself. Yet it is just not true that we can do *anything* with *anything*. The fact that any object could in principle be used in an infinite variety of ways, does not mean that their functionality is completely unconstrained. Socks may lend themselves to being used as pretend guns, but they do not make good pretend houses, nor even swords.

The puzzle for researchers of cognitive development has been that pretend play seems to be highly anomalous. After all, one might suppose that the developing child should be concerned with finding out how things *really* work, rather than delighting in treating them in such 'unrealistic' ways. Ágnes Szokolszky's research has nicely demonstrated that young children are well aware of the suitability – the 'affordances' – of different objects for particular kinds of play event, such as using those objects as a pretend pillow. Her conclusion, therefore, is that children are not 'escaping' from reality when they engage in pretend play, but rather they are, in an important sense, getting things *right*. They are exploring the various action possibilities of objects, over and above their proper functions.

These two chapters on object use and autism, and pretend play, were informed by a broadly 'ecological' framework (Gibson, 1979; see also Costall, 1995). Kristine Jensen de López's research is situated within the new perspective of 'cognitive linguistics,' an approach that takes the human body as a fundamental source of linguistic meaning. Her chapter compares how Zapotek and Danish speaking children comprehend spatial relations. Zapotek, a Mayan language, describes the spatial relationships between objects in terms of body parts (head, stomach, etc), rather than the prepositional forms used in Danish and English. When the children in her study were asked to imitate the experimenter's actions of putting items *in*, *on*, or *under* a basket, there were striking differences between the two groups of children. Even when the experimenter had placed the item *on* or *under* the basket, the Danish children were much more likely to put the object *in* the basket than were the Mayan children. Kristine Jensen de López proposes, however, that these differences cannot solely be understood in terms of linguistic differences, but also in terms of how things are normally used differently in the two groups. The human body itself is configured differently according to these different uses of objects. In the Mayan culture, objects are routinely used in multiple ways, as when a basket is turned upside down to serve as a cage to confine a chicken about to lay its eggs.

Each of the chapters in this section is concerned with the question of the proper function of objects, and raises the further questions (already addressed in the first section) of how the proper function of an object is to be construed theoretically, and how children (at least under certain cultural conditions) come to develop a sense that objects have such a privileged, proper meaning. Proper function is defined culturally, and its definition depends on the ways of designing and using things within a particular culture.

## III. Transformation and Things

From the perspective of the human sciences, an emphasis upon the importance of *things* in human affairs can often seem like a retreat into reductionism and materialistic determinism. However, in the present book, objects are far from considered in isolation, but, instead, as participating in human activities. The three chapters in this section are concerned with things in transformation: how things are incorporated into our activities over the course of time, and, how, in that process, they come into new relations with other things and other people, and thus take on new significance.

As we have already noted, much of the existing research on how people relate to things has concerned information technology and, furthermore, information technologies relatively new to the users. It has also typically focused on team-work. Seldom has the research taken a longer-term historical perspective, tracing the processes by which the material resources for various practices themselves both become shaped and, in turn, shape those practices (but see Hutchins, 1995). And, most importantly, there has been little research pitched at the level of everyday engagements with 'low-tech' objects used primarily by single individuals.

David de Léon has been studying people in the course of preparing and cooking meals in their own homes. As he explains in his chapter on the 'Cognitive biographies of things', there is no single locus of order in such activities, but a continual interplay between the human agents and the things they are using. Order is 'bounced', as it were, between agent and the objects in this process, as in the deliberate acts of 'maintenance', where time is set aside to rearrange things so that they can support the next phase of the activity. But this can also come about unintentionally, as when frequently used objects end up being conveniently close to hand precisely because they are likely to have been recently used, and thus left drying, for example, on the plate rack.

The chapter focuses on the history of a spice rack over the course of almost thirty years, and how it was transformed over this period according to the circumstances and interests of its main user. Initially, the collection of spices was very small and not even kept in a rack but in a box; as it grew larger, it was then set out on a deep shelf, and then, finally, on an extensive set of shallow, one-jar deep, shelves.

The 'cognitive congeniality' of any object, should be regarded not as an intrinsic property of that object, but, as David puts it, concerns 'the *combination* of techniques, procedures, and / or habits, with particular artefacts and task environments, in relation to specific tasks'. For example, only if the spice jars are removed one at a time can the shelves serve to 'remind' the user about where a jar that has just been removed needs to be returned. Furthermore, from a much broader temporal perspective, this *thing*, the spice rack, far from being a pre-existing, fixed resource for cookery, has itself been undergoing continual transformation and elaboration within the activities of cookery.

Hysse Birgitte Forchhammer's chapter, 'The woman who used her walking stick as a telephone,' also takes up the issue, raised in Section 1, of the proper function of things. Her research explores the many different ways that the aids provided to stroke patients fail to be used 'as intended' – as a result of poor design, unanticipated changes in the circumstances of the user, and the fact that such aids can serve to trap the user into an identity of a disabled person. However, her chapter also presents many examples of improvisation, as when one woman used a walking stick to communicate with her neighbour, by tapping on the ceiling. The analysis she presents not only ranges across the different levels of definition of function (the 'mass' or impersonal, the interpersonal, and the individual), but has, as she points out, also important practical implications for the design of disability aids.

Many of the contributors to this book highlight the multiple ways a single object can be used, in improvisation and in pretend play. And, as Kristine Jensen de López argues in her chapter, there are cultural differences in the extent to which things are supposed to have a single, privileged function. Yet certain objects even in Western culture are distinguished by their multifunctionality. One kind of multifunctionality is exemplified by the Swiss army knife with its numerous blades and gadgets, but this is no more than a concatenation of specific tools with definite functions. The computer is an example of multifunctionality in a much more interesting sense. Now the digital computer was envisaged, from the outset, as a 'general purpose machine', that is, a machine whose function was to be constrained solely by the computer program and not by the machine itself. Even so, the computer has still managed to enter into our lives in a whole diversity of ways unanticipated by its original designers, not least as a resource for play.

Estrid Sørensen's chapter, 'The politics of things', is about the 'open' nature of computer technology, and describes the design and use of virtual reality software for groups of young children to create their own micro-worlds. What constitutes the design, she argues, is not just the computer interface provided by the software but also the surrounding pedagogical practices. Although Sørensen is specifically concerned with an open-ended design, it is never the case that a design can completely *prescribe* practices, any more than rules fully define their application. Thus, it is necessary in general, Sørensen argues, to study the continual interplay between design and practices, and how this interplay leads to orderings *in* practice and *of* practice (Mol & Law, 1994). Fluidity and regionality are examples of such orderings. By drawing upon two instances from her study of the design workshop, Sørensen shows that these two orderings may either co-exist harmoniously or conflict in ongoing practices.

Sørensen traces the transformation of designs in ongoing practice through the introduction of new objects, the children's ideas, their discussions, and division of labour. In that sense, Sørensen proposes that we should regard design as politics, in which a design is proposed, picked up, continued, and either changed or left unchanged. Studies of such continuing processes of design in practice may lead to a better understanding of how best to design for ongoing, open-ended practices within both the school setting and beyond.

## IV. Organisation and Things

The chapters in this book are primarily about how things are used by individual users or informal groups. The four chapters in the final section, however, examine the active role of things in the organisation of practices and in the practices of organisations, and bring out the wider cultural, social, organisational, economic, and educational aspects of things and how they are used. In most theoretical approaches to things, classification is assumed to be the most natural way of understanding objects. Yet, 'sorting things out' (Bowker & Star, 1999) is not the only way we engage with objects. Once we consider things, not as isolated objects or artefacts, but as already involved in ongoing practices, we can no longer take their classification for granted. Classificatory practices are themselves rather special kinds of activities, often subservient to other ends in practice. Indeed, the relevant 'properties' of things, and the proper functions of those things, are transformed within those practices.

Furthermore, once we situate things within practices, the stability of things and the stability of practices can be seen as inseparable, and as mutually affording each other. Things are involved in both maintaining and changing the order of social practices. They are ordered and reordered, and they are arranged and rearranged in and for particular social practices (Dreier, 2005, Schatzki, 2002). Thus, in order to make sense of the human practices of organisations and of organising, it is necessary to include the various *things* involved.

In their chapter, 'Working with material things: From essentialism to material-semiotic analysis of sociotechnical practice', Finn Olesen and Randi Markussen describe their field study of socio-technical practice in a hospital ward concerning the introduction of a an electronic module for dispensing medication. Their approach is based in science and technology studies, in which people and things are regarded as intertwined in heterogeneous sociotechnical arrangements. Rather than regarding things as somehow *pre-given objects* with definite known qualities, they are studied as *dynamic elements* in a continuous flow of activity. Similarly, design itself should be understood as an evolving process in an ongoing practice. A practice (even one involving conflict) may attain stability for some time, due to a dynamic, interdependent evolution of things and humans which stabilises particular relations between them. This was the case for the medication list in their study, so that it became a 'stable actor' within the hypercomplex, sociotechnical arrangements of the ward.

Following Haraway (1997), Olesen and Markussen maintain that social relationships may become congealed into and located within objects as 'decontextualized things'. Material and semiotic dimensions of reality are thus interwoven, and material artefacts, such as the medication list, also comprise 'fictional' constructions (compare the chapters by Szokolszky and Forchhammer). Olesen and Markussen are engaged, as they put it, in an investigation into the 'mundane philosophy of things' in everyday practice. They criticize the notion that a thing is the sum of its properties since properties are not inherent to the object, but ascribed to it through a process of classification and comparison with other, similar things. In the case of the electronic medication module this becomes very evident in practice, since there was a struggle over its definition and use, and thus no single classification scheme was able to unify the competing classifications and exhaust the essence of the thing.

Despite the intentions of its original designers, the electronic medication record does not in fact function as a 'classification machine' that ensures widespread order within the organization. It can only be understood in terms of how it is embedded in the ongoing practices in the ward, such as the closely linked practices of writing and reading and measuring medication. Olesen and Markussen's chapter serves to expand a conception of writing as a practice linking people and things in the material fabric of the world and things.

This theme is also central to Steven D. Brown and David Middleton's chapter, 'Words and things: Discursive and non-discursive ordering in a networked organization'. They focus on the active role of email archives in a company producing a complex product in a process distributed across different parts of the world, and upon the relationship between words and things within the unfolding organisational practices. In part, they are attempting to move critically beyond a background of discursive psychology and studies of communication in the work place which, they argue, consider things simply as formulated and described by speakers. Within that standard approach, the social is the standard against which to consider the role of things, and the things themselves are thus regarded as external to sociality.

However, instead of just asking how we *talk* about things, Brown and Middleton argue that we should also ask how things become fit objects for talking *about*, and how things make us talk with each other in particular ways, perform activities in particular ways, manage in particular ways, and so forth. In accordance with this alternative point of view, they ask how the archival practices concerning the emails in the company order the socialities of its organisational practice. Organisational order, they contend, is produced not only by discursive but also by non-discursive means.

Brown and Middleton consider the archives as a means of creating and maintaining order and stability in the practice of the organisation by creating interdependencies between persons and things. Furthermore, this organisational order stretches across different times and places, drawing together a large number of people, materials and activities around the entire world. The creation of schedules requiring everyone to adhere to the same strict programme of events is a distinct feature of this ordering across times and places by means of the archives. We might add that the creation of schedules leads to the creation of sequences (Abbott, 2001), that is, a sequential order (Dreier, 2005). A further means of creating and maintaining order across places is the modularisation of the complex process of production across diverse production sites, ordered into a coherent process of production by means of the scheduling and sequencing accomplished through the email archives. That, in turn, has created new problems of order in the organisational practice of the company.

In his chapter, 'Learning to do things with things – Apprenticeship learning in bakery as economy and social practice', Klaus Nielsen also examines ongoing practices in which things and people participate in dynamic, transforming and changing ways. However, since doing things with things is mostly something we have to *learn* to do, his research has been examining how the arrangement of education in work practices mediates the way we learn to do things and thus come to do things with things. For this purpose, he adopts a social practice theory of learning as situated in particular ongoing practices and in particular arrangements of learning and education (Dreier, 2003; Lave, 1993).

In his interviews with apprentice bakers about their training, Nielsen found they were concerned with economic issues rather than 'learning'. Yet, according to the apprentices, all issues relating to economy were neglected in the training provided at the trade school. While learning in school is arranged by dissecting the topic into elements to be learned sequentially as accumulated discrete categories and skills, practical considerations about the organisation of work and economical considerations led to a quite different arrangement of learning in the bakery itself. Here 'economy' is to be understood in both the sense of market economy and also the maximisation of efficiency in the use of time, materials, resources, and so forth. According to the ideal of school learning, however, such economic issues, so central to apprenticeship, are dismissed as incidental, and a distraction from the proper business of learning. In contrast, in the bakery, these economic issues are an essential part of what needs to be learnt. The apprentices, journeymen and masters alike emphasized this positive, enabling influence of economy on learning in the educational arrangement in the bakery. It is also the case that the form taken by this learning process – the sequence of close initial supervision gradually leading towards increased 'individual autonomy' – was clearly economically motivated.

However, as Nielsen explains, there are aspects of the economic realities of the actual work situation that are far from benign. The craft of baking is challenged from two sides. There is the deskilling of the baker apprentices promoted by the growing industrialisation of baking (Braverman, 1974; Projektgruppe Automation und Qualifikation, 1987). Second, there is the issue of 'commodity aesthetics' (Haug, 1971), since the bakers have to learn to adopt the perspective of the potential customer, and place a higher priority on the 'look' of the product, than how it actually tastes. Indeed, as Nielsen pointed out at one of the workshops that gave rise to this book, the bakers are now required even to dress up in special clothing in order to *look* more like bakers.

A recurrent theme in this book concerns the need to understand things not in isolation but in relation to the human activities in which they are involved, and the different, even conflicting, meanings things can have for the people involved with them. Another main theme has concerned the need to think of design not as a separate stage prior to the use of things, but as a continuing process within the context of their actual use. Gustavo Ribeiro's chapter, 'Urban makings: formalisation of informal settlements in Thailand' is about changes in the landscapes and infrastructures of small third-world low-income settlements such as the development of walkways or bridges, either with or without the assistance of architects and other experts external to the local community. As far as the first- and third-world experts are concerned, such developments should be regarded primarily as 'sites for social activities' with the paradoxical consequence that the material products of such construction projects – the things themselves – are regarded as merely incidental to the business of empowering and unifying communities in the process of planning and construction.

Ribeiro draws a telling contrast with his earlier studies on the creation of urban landscapes and patterns of urban change in Latin American shanty-towns. Here, simply by moving between one place to another across open ground in the course of their daily lives, the people created beaten tracks on the ground which came to define a network of footpaths; these, in turn, became the source of the layout of the shanty towns that were eventually constructed on the previously open sites. The formations of physical environments/structures and of social relations are inseparable aspects of the organisation and change of ongoing everyday practices. Ribeiro contrasts such long-term, unplanned, urban making through 'direct action' with 'mediated urban making' brought about through the intervention of external actors and the introduction of formal planning procedures. Such 'mediated urban making' creates a form of practice in which experts are positioned in such a way that they come to frame the practice they are involved in making solely in terms of organisation and education (much in the way that, as Brown and Middleton in their chapter argue, things in social theory can become relegated to mere subjects of talk).

Ribeiro points to a serious consequence of the definition of the process of construction not just as educational but also as ceasing with the creation of the 'final structure'. The project-mediated form of making downplays the importance of the maintenance of the constructed object through use, and the incorporation of physical intervention into the daily life of the community. It thus threatens the very sustainability of any project. Such externally imposed organisation of projects complicates and distorts the interrelations between the material and social aspects of practices so that the material landscapes themselves tend to be reduced to mere 'sites of the social' (Schatzki, 2002). Ribeiro argues that the role of material transformations in daily social practices must be brought to the fore, and the understanding of the role of projects must be re-anchored in such ongoing daily practices.

Finally, Ribeiro also addresses the issue of stability and change that has also been raised in many of the earlier chapters. Compared to consolidated urban areas, squatter settlements have an inherent power to change and adapt. In contrast to the 'permanence and persistence' of urban structures, we are presented with changes – 'instead of morphology, patterns of use'. Such settlements are transitory, and any stability that might arise must be understood as an accomplishment of ongoing practices.

## Conclusion

The beaten paths studied by Ribeiro in his research on shanty towns provide a vivid example of the kind of understanding of things presented in this book – things not as fixed and independent of human beings, but as themselves transformed, even coming into being, within ongoing human practices, and which, in turn, transform those practices. We learn much more about both people *and* things by studying them as worldly, though not just as in the world, but as incorporated in *practices* in the world (Holzkamp, 1996). However, there also needs to be an emphasis upon process, upon change. Stability is not the 'natural' state of things. Objects cannot be understood as static entities with fixed categories. Even stability must be understood as processual, one stable pattern giving rise to another. So stability is never final but open to further unanticipated change. Things are never entirely resolved, once and for all.

## References

Abbott, A. (2001). *Time matters. On theory and method.* Chicago: University of Chicago Press.

Bowker, G.C. and Star, S.L. (1999). *Sorting things out: Classification and its consequences*. Cambridge, MA.: MIT Press.

Braverman, H. (1974). *Labor and monopoly capital. The degradation of work in the twentieth century*. New York: Monthly Review Press.

Costall, A. (1995). Socializing affordances. *Theory and Psychology*, *5*, 467–481.

Dreier, O. (2003). Learning in personal trajectories of participation. In N. Stephenson, L.H. Radtke, R.J. Jorna & H.J. Stam (Eds.), *Theoretical psychology. Critical contributions* (pp. 20–29). Concord, ON: Captus Press.

Dreier, O. (2005). The social practice of psychotherapy. Theory, structure, critique. In A. Gülerce, A. Hofmeister, I. Staeuble, G. Saunders & J. Kaye (Eds.), *Contemporary theorizing in psychology: Critical perspectives* (pp. 162–170). Concord: Captus University Publishers.

Haraway, D. (1997). *Modest_Witness@Second_Millennium. Female Man© _Meets_ OncoMouse™– Feminism and Techno science.* New York: Routledge.

Haug, W. F. (1986). *Critique of commodity aesthetics : appearance, sexuality, and advertising in capitalist society.* (R. Bock, trans.) Minneapolis: University of Minnesota Press, c1986.

Holzkamp, K. 1996. Manuskripte zum Arbeitsprojekt 'Lebensführung'. *Forum Kritische Psychologie 36*, 7–112.

Hutchins, E. (1995). *Cognition in the wild.* Cambridge, MA: MIT Press.

Joerges, B. (1988). Technology in everyday life: Conceptual queries. *Journal for the Theory of Social Behaviour, 18,* 221–237.

Kirsh, D. (1995). The intelligent use of space. *Artificial Intelligence, 73*, 31–68.

Lave, J. (1993). The practice of learning. In S. Chaiklin & J. Lave (Eds.). *Understanding practice. Perspectives on activity and context.* New York: Cambridge University Press.

Mol, A. & Law, J. (1994). Regions, networks and fluids: Anaemia and social topology. *Social Studies of Science, 24*(4), 641–671.

Projektgruppe Automation und Qualifikation (1987). *Widersprüche der Automationsarbeit.* Berlin: Argument Verlag.

Schatzki, Theodore R. (2002). *The site of the social. A philosophical account of the constitution of social life and change.* University Park, PA.: Pennsylvania State University Press.

Wertsch, J.V. (1996). The role of abstract rationality in Vygotsky's image of mind. In A. Tryphon & J. Voneche (Eds.), *Piaget-Vygotsky: The social genesis of thought* (pp. 25–43). Hove, East Sussex, UK: Psychology Press.

# PART I
# Intentionality and the Functionality of Things

# Chapter 1

# The Case of the Recalcitrant Prototype

Beth Preston

In the presumed absence of a creator god, the functions of biological organs are not functions any agent intended them to have. Consequently, theories of biological function must start from the assumption that function can be established without appeal to the intentions of intelligent agents. But the opposite assumption operates with regard to artifact function. The intentions of human agents are commonly regarded as a necessary condition for establishing function. Although it is difficult to show that the intentions of any particular agent are required, it does seem that without human designers, makers, and users in general, there would be no human artifacts, let alone artifact functions (McLaughlin 2001, p. 48). But many theorists also regard the intentions of the designer, specifically, as a *sufficient* condition for establishing function. In other words, if an agent intends an artifact she designs to have a specific function, then that is the function it has, at least initially. It is this latter claim I wish to examine here. I shall show that regarding designers' intentions as sufficient generates serious problems for a theory of artifact function. Moreover, there is a viable theory of artifact function that does not appeal directly to the intentions of designers as sufficient conditions. Thus there is ample reason to reject the claim that designers' intentions are sufficient. But I shall begin by explaining why this claim has so much appeal for function theorists in the first place.

## Proper Function and System Function

There are three distinguishable roles human agents may play with regard to artifacts – designer, maker, and user. As commonly understood, the designer specifies the characteristics of the artifact to be made; the maker does the actual construction work; and the user subsequently puts the artifact to use. These roles are not mutually exclusive. A single individual may play any combination or all of them with regard to a specific artifact. But they can also be played by completely different individuals – indeed, by individuals who do not communicate or are unaware of each others' existence, and whose intentions are thus independent.[1] Unfortunately, writers on

1 The distinction between these roles does not appear to be contingent on the historical mode of production. Plato (1992, 272/*Republic* 601c–602a) distinguishes between 'the one who knows' how an artifact should be (the designer), the maker who is instructed by the one who knows, and the user. He then argues that in fact the user has the most knowledge about

artifact function typically use terms like 'creator,' 'producer,' or 'maker' in a way that is ambiguous with regard to the designer and maker roles. But as we shall see, it is clear that in fact it is the intentions of designers in particular that are in question in theories of how artifact functions are established. Thus sorting out this issue depends on distinguishing these roles.

On the other hand, an important feature of these roles, and one that will come into play in the course of the argument, is that many activities are borderline or fuzzy with regard to classification in terms of them. For example, designers often make scale models, or make and try out specific parts of the artifact during the design process in order to see whether certain materials are suitable, or certain devices safe and effective, or whatever. More importantly for present purposes, users often use artifacts creatively. This may involve using something for a novel purpose – using a screwdriver to remove staples, for instance. Or it may involve some modification of the artifact to suit it for the novel purpose – filing down a key to make it more effective as a cutting instrument, for instance. Similarly, makers often construct creatively, departing from the instructions of designers in order to improve the artifact, or to continue construction in the absence of specified materials or needed tools. For example, cooks continually tinker with recipes to suit them to their own tastes, or substitute ingredients when specified ingredients are unavailable, prohibitively expensive, and so on. Phenomena like these show that although the roles of designer, maker, and user are distinguishable – even clearly and unequivocally distinguished in many cases – they are not rigorously distinct.

There is another important feature of these roles I will be leaving out of account in this paper. It is also possible – indeed, common – for groups rather than individuals to fill these roles. This is clearly the case for users, who typically form loose communal groups. But production, too, is typically collaborative, even in non-industrial contexts, and design is often collaborative, perhaps particularly in industrial contexts. Moreover, there are important social and communicative relations among the individuals or groups filling the various roles. For example, designers may seek user input or maker advice during the design process, or users or makers may offer or even demand this. In short, these roles as actually practiced are thoroughly social in character. This raises a different problem for the intentionalist view of artifact function because it requires an account of collective intentions. But I will abstract from this important issue in framing my argument, because the question of whether designer intention is sufficient for the establishment of artifact function does not depend on whether the intention in question is individual or collective, but only on what relation it bears to the artifact. So when I speak of 'the designer,' for instance, I will be referring to the role in abstraction from the concrete collective or individual ways in which it may be carried out in practice.

---

the artifact, and should instruct the maker, i.e., the user should also be the designer. But the very fact that an argument was called for here shows that the roles of user and designer were not routinely identified.

It is also important to distinguish between *proper* functions and *system* functions (also sometimes called causal role functions). A *proper* function is what a thing is supposed to do – usually understood in the case of artifacts as what it is designed to do. A *system* function is a contingent purpose a thing may serve on occasion without having been designed to do so. For example, the proper functions of spoons are stirring and transporting food. Among the system functions a spoon may serve are use as a percussive musical instrument, as a unit of measure for cooking ingredients, as a dibble for transplanting seedlings, as an opener for cocoa tins, and so on. Biological traits also have both proper functions and system functions. For example, the human hand has the proper functions of grasping and gripping, but it can be used in various ways as a weapon.

The best-known account of how system functions are established comes from an early paper on functional analysis by Robert Cummins (1975). According to Cummins, a function is established in terms of the capacity or disposition a thing has to perform a specific role in the context of a system. A system is a configuration of components interacting in an orderly way such that the performance of the whole can be explained in terms of the performances of the components. In the case of biology, the system is usually the whole organism, or one of its subsystems, such as the circulatory system. In the case of artifacts the system is usually a suite of related artifacts and the practices involved in using them. For example, the proper function of beer is as a beverage for humans. But there is a practice among home gardeners of pouring beer into saucers and then setting them out in the garden as slug traps. The system function of the beer in this context of organized social practices and artifacts is slug bait.

It is important to note that this account of how system functions are established does not require an appeal to the intentions of intelligent agents. A function is established solely in virtue of having a role in a containing system, whether or not that role was ever intended by anybody. This is an important positive feature of Cummins' account in its application to biological function, where an appeal to intentions is ruled out. But it also suggests an account of artifact function that does not require an appeal to intentions. In this connection it should be noted that Cummins' account can allow for indirect appeal to intentions of agents in the case of artifacts. For example, in the case of beer as slug bait there are in fact intentions of beer users involved in sustaining the relevant gardening practices. But the important point is that were these practices the practices of a race of intentionless garden robots, the beer would still have the system function of slug bait. It is the system and the role of the artifact in the system that is essential.

The best known account of how proper functions are established comes from the work of Ruth Millikan (1984, 1993) – indeed, 'proper function' is her term. On Millikan's theory, proper functions can be established either *directly* or *derivatively*. A thing has a specific performance as its *direct* proper function if it is reproduced from ancestors which successfully engaged in that performance, and which survived and proliferated because of this (1984, p.28), i.e., if there is a selection history for the performance. Thus the human hand has the direct proper functions of grasping and gripping because the successful use of their hands for these purposes contributed to the ability of our ancestors to survive and reproduce. Similarly, the direct proper functions of a spoons are stirring and transporting food, since historically it is in virtue of such successful stirring and transporting that spoons have been maintained and reproduced.

When something has a direct proper function that it accomplishes by producing some other thing, the produced thing inherits a *derived* proper function from the producing thing, even though it has not itself undergone selection for this function (1984, pp.41-3). Thus if a chameleon contains a mechanism the direct proper function of which is to change the chameleon's skin color to camouflage it from predators, the skin coloration this mechanism produces on any particular occasion has the derived proper function of camouflaging the chameleon. Similarly, if a spark plug has the proper function of initiating combustion by producing a spark, the spark has the derived proper function of initiating combustion.

As in the case of system function, this account of direct and derived proper functions does not require any appeal to intentions of agents. Direct proper functions and the derived proper functions that depend on them are established by a history of selection and reproduction. In the biological realm selection and reproduction are causal processes so an appeal to the intentions of directing intelligent agents is neither required nor desired. In the case of artifacts, the intentions of human agents in fact implement both selection and reproduction indirectly. But if a race of intentionless robots were responsible for the same history of selection and reproduction, the artifacts would have the same direct and derived proper functions. It is the selection history that is essential, not the intentions of the agents or the robots involved.

The relationship between proper functions and system functions is a controversial one in the recent philosophical literature on function. They are regarded by some as rival theories, one of which is wrong and must be discarded. Davies (2001) argues, for instance, that all proper functions are really system functions. Attempts are made by others to unify these two concepts of function either by subordinating one of them to the other (Walsh and Ariew 1996) or by subordinating both to an overarching conceptual framework (Kitcher 1993). Yet other, more pluralistically minded theorists insist that these are distinct concepts of function with different domains or ranges of application (Godfrey-Smith 1993, Millikan 1989, Preston 1998). I hold this last, pluralist view, and I assume it for the purposes of this paper. The central point to be borne in mind is that on the pluralist view proper function and system function are distinct but equally important conceptions of function, applicable to distinct but equally important functional phenomena. In this connection it should also be noted that on the pluralist view, as well as on some of the other views, system functions may become proper functions over the course of time. For example, if breweries start to make and market beer specifically for use as slug bait, and it is regularly bought and used by gardeners for that purpose, it will acquire slug bait as a proper function in addition to its original proper function as a beverage.[2] But what I have to say does not depend on settling any of these issues. The basis for my argument is just that *if* you recognize a theoretical distinction between proper function and system function, *then* holding the view that artifact function is established by designers' intentions is problematic.[3]

## The Recalcitrant Prototype

Because direct proper functions are established through an historical process of selection and reproduction, the first instance of what will later become a functional trait itself has no proper function. For example, suppose a chance mutation causes a single moth to have a color that is particularly good as camouflage from predators. This first moth – I shall refer to it as the prototype moth – has an advantage in survival and breeding, as do its offspring which (let us say) inherit the camouflaging coloration. On Millikan's theory, the mutated color of the prototype moth does not have the direct proper function of camouflaging it from predators; that is only the *effect* it has at this initial stage. Only after some indeterminate number of generations of selection and reproduction can we say the coloration has the direct proper function of camouflaging these moths from predators.

Some theorists (e.g., McLaughlin 2001) regard this inability to ascribe proper functions to apparently fully operational prototypes as a serious failing of Millikan's theory and other theories like it. But there are a couple of considerations that take the edge off this criticism. First, even if prototypes do not have proper functions, if the operations they perform fit successfully into roles in existing systems, they have system functions (Millikan 1989, 175). For example, the coloration of the prototype moth in our example above has a camouflaging, protective role in the predator-prey system. Similarly, a can opener of novel design that succeeds in opening cans plays a successful role in our food storage and retrieval system. It is important to note

2 My arguments for the pluralist view, as well as further discussion of the ways system functions and proper functions are related to each other, may be found in Preston (1998).

3 It should also be noted here that there may be cross-cultural and developmental differences in the way proper functions and system functions of artifacts are handled or evaluated. For example, modern industrial culture in the West has resulted in a material culture oriented towards special purpose artifacts. There are dedicated devices for opening paint cans, for instance, even though a screwdriver or a knife or a dozen other things readily available to the average painter work perfectly well. In other cultures this is not the case, and this suggests that in these cultures system functions may be more important to people, both practically and in terms of what they might value. Similarly, within cultures there may be developmental differences with regard to the perception of proper function and of the possibilities for system functional (non-proper) uses stemming from the fact that children have to learn *that* artifacts have proper functions, and not just what proper functions various artifacts have. It is clearly very important to investigate these cross-cultural and developmental aspects of artifact function. But since nothing in my argument depends on them, I will have to leave these aspects aside for the purposes of this paper.

that not all prototypes will have such a system function, though. Having a system function depends on having a current capacity to fill a system-defined role. So if a mutation produces a prototype trait which does not fit into such a role, or which does not fulfill it successfully, the prototype will have no system function. For example, if the sole predators of our moths are bats hunting entirely by echolocation, there will be no role in the predator-prey system for the new coloration to play. On the other hand, if the predators are sighted and the new coloration does nothing to camouflage the moth from them, the new coloration will not have the relevant capacity. In either case, the new coloration will fail to have a system function. And of course this can happen with artifacts as well – imagine a machine invented by a visionary medieval machinist to open cans, although there are none to open; or a modern prototype can opener which simply does not work.

So appealing to system function to solve the prototype problem will still leave some prototypes with neither direct proper functions nor system functions. This is acceptable to some (although by no means all) theorists in the case of biological function, where some mutations produce changes that are indifferent or harmful to the possessor from the point of view of selection, and to which we might therefore be reluctant to assign any kind of function at all. But in the case of artifact prototypes, even the anachronistic or non-working ones were intended by their producers to have a function, so there is a strong impetus to ascribe that intended function to them. Moreover, there is a strong impetus to ascribe *proper* function rather than merely system functions to prototypes because the intentions of their producers are construed as establishing what the prototype is *supposed* to do, whether or not it actually does it. So most theorists will simply not be satisfied with the appeal to system function in the case of artifact prototypes.

There is a specific application of Millikan's theory of proper functions which offers an alternative. Millikan holds that intentional states of agents have direct proper functions – desires have the direct proper function of getting themselves fulfilled, for example. Some desires are desires to accomplish this result by producing something else. For example, I may desire to open cans by producing a machine to do the job, and this machine then has the derived proper function of opening cans (1984, 49; 1999, 205). This is true even if it is a unique prototype – a can opener of completely novel design, for instance. And it is true even if the prototype does not work. Thus an artifact may have its proper function established either directly by a selection history that does not require an appeal to intentions, or derivatively through its producer's intentions, or in both ways in parallel. If in both ways, the direct and derived proper functions usually coincide. But where they do not, there is no problem in principle with an artifact having more than one proper function, or even conflicting proper functions (1999, 205). For example, as a matter of selection history beer is brewed as a beverage for humans. This is its direct proper function. But suppose I buy up a brewery with the express intention of brewing beer for use by gardeners as slug bait. The beer I brew now has both its original direct proper function (beverage), and a new derived proper function (slug bait) layered over it. But the most important point here is that when the concept of derived proper function is applied to intentional states in this way, it renders the intentions of producers sufficient for establishing proper functions of artifacts.

Millikan's theory of *derived* proper function thus provides for prototypes to have proper functions if they derive those functions from a producing mechanism. For example, the chameleon already contains a mechanism with the direct proper function of changing its skin color to camouflage it from predators. So any skin coloration this device produces, even if it is unique in the history of chameleons, has the derived proper function of camouflage. Similarly, and most importantly for our purposes, because all intentional states of agents have direct proper functions on Millikan's view, all prototype artifacts produced as a consequence of those intentions have derived proper functions. This will still leave some biological prototypes without a function, but as we noted above, this may be acceptable in the biological domain. And it will yield what seems like the intuitively right result for artifact prototypes. So Millikan provides a theoretical underpinning for the common idea that the intentions of designers are a sufficient condition for the establishment of artifact function. Even theorists who do not necessarily subscribe to Millikan's theory of proper function agree with her leading intuition here (Dipert 1993, McLaughlin 2001, Vermaas and Houkes 2003). For if the intentions of designers are not a sufficient condition for the establishment of function, prototype artifacts will have no proper functions – there will be nothing they are *supposed* to do. So the view that designers' intentions are sufficient seems eminently well motivated. When someone designs an artifact, they do so with some purpose for it in mind, and intuitively that just *is* what it is for – *its* purpose. This intuition is reinforced by the theoretically generated problem of prototype artifacts that have as yet no selection history, and thus no possible source of proper function *other* than derivation from their designer's intentions. However, in the next section I shall show that regarding designers' intentions as sufficient for establishing proper function causes other difficulties for the theory of artifact function – difficulties that are far more serious than the prototype problem their sufficiency so neatly resolves.

## Why Designers' Intentions are not Sufficient

Regarding designers' intentions as a sufficient condition for function privileges the intentions of the originating agent in relation to the intentions of subsequent users. Millikan says specifically that 'artifacts have as derived proper functions the functions intended for them by their makers... *not* their users' (1999, p.205, my emphasis). It is important to realize that in this context 'maker' primarily means 'designer.' The maker and the designer may be the same individual, of course, in which case the point is moot. Or the maker may be a different individual but have the same intentions towards the artifact as the designer – the maker may be following detailed and informative instructions from the designer, for instance. But the problem is that making – constructing, strictly speaking – can be a mechanical or uninformed process where the maker has no relevant intentions towards the artifact. The maker may not know what the thing is designed to do, or she may be in a distracted state of mind – think of someone working on a production line, for example. On the other hand, a designer can hardly fail to have relevant intentions towards the artifacts she designs. So what is primarily at stake here is the relationship between the intentions of designers and the intentions of users. But what is supposed to underwrite or justify this distinction between the intentions of designers and the intentions of users, and the privileging of the former with regard to the establishment of artifact functions?

To put the problem in better perspective, consider the role of users in instituting system functions of artifacts. I may use a can opener as a paperweight, or a table knife as a screwdriver, or a highjacked airliner as an incendiary bomb. I certainly intend these artifacts to have the functions mentioned. So why are these functions not the *proper* functions of these artifacts? Why are the user's intentions not efficacious in the same way the designer's intentions would be if he were to design a paperweight or a screwdriver or an incendiary bomb from scratch? Millikan rules this out, but she does not give any reason for her stipulation. It might seem that she can sidestep this issue because she defined derived proper function in terms of production relations in the first place. I must have a desire to open cans by *producing* (as opposed to utilizing) a machine to do the job for that machine to have the derived proper function of opening cans. But this just shifts the problem rather than removing it. A definitional stipulation should not be arbitrary or *ad hoc* with regard to the phenomena under investigation.

One obvious possibility is that the intentions of designers might have some special cognitive structure or characteristic that sets them apart from the intentions of users. In his action theoretic account of artifacts Randall Dipert (1993) focuses on the cognitive processes employed by designers of artifacts. On Dipert's view, there is a characteristic and distinctive process from which the artifact derives its function and other features. Specifically, there is a 'deliberative history' in the course of which the creating agent contemplates the overall function of the artifact as her goal, considers alternative means for achieving it, and forms a complex set of intentions in the form of a construction plan. When executed, this plan imposes artifactual features on the resulting object, chief among them the artifact's purpose or function (1993, pp.150-53). The artifact may fail to fulfill this function (1993, pp. 143–50). But the artifact *has* the intended function; it is only failing to live up to it. Taking 'screwdriver' as a functional predicate, for instance, you say of a broken or defective screwdriver that it doesn't work, or is a bad screwdriver, not that it is *not* a screwdriver. In short, the intentions of the designer (or designer/maker – Dipert uses the ambiguous term 'creator' throughout) are sufficient to establish the proper function of an artifact in virtue of the plan construction and execution the designer undertakes.

The problem is that system functional uses of existing artifacts are often the outcome of exactly the same sort of planful deliberation. You want to pry a large rock out of your lawn; you don't have a crowbar; you consider available artifacts like steel fence posts and wooden rake handles until you find the one that best suits your purposes. You may even modify it to better suit your purposes – pounding the end of the steel fence post flat with a sledgehammer so as to get it under the rock more easily, for instance. But if designers' intentions in the form of a deliberative history are sufficient for establishing function, and if users must employ relevantly similar deliberations in order to use artifacts in a system functional way, then why are the intentions of users not also sufficient for establishing a proper function? It seems that cognitive characteristics cannot be the criterion that distinguishes designers' intentions from users' intentions and underwrites the privileging of the former over the latter in the establishment of proper function.

Another obvious possibility is that production is *creative* in a way that use is not. Designing and making brings something new into the world, whereas use merely operates with what is already there. But here we encounter a problem analogous to the one we noticed in Dipert's case. On the one hand, use is in fact often very creative. It endows existing artifacts with new, if transient, system functions by using them in novel ways. And in some cases a system function instituted in this way by users ultimately becomes a new proper function. For example, the original proper function of aspirin tablets was to lower fever and alleviate pain, but they are now so commonly prescribed to prevent blood clots in cardiac patients as well that they are most reasonably regarded as having acquired the additional proper function of preventing heart attacks. You might be tempted to say that creative system functional uses are cases of 'virtual' design in order to distinguish them from routine, standard use. But on the one hand, this only concedes the creativity of use and institutes an *ad hoc* move to assimilate creative use to design. And on the other hand, it prompts the corresponding observation that production is often not very creative, especially in contexts where what is being designed and produced is a variation on a standard type. Much design work only changes the form of an artifact, for instance, with little or no effect on function. Consider the constant redesign of soft drink bottles, for instance. And much design work is oriented towards the enhancement of an existing function rather than the institution of a new one. Consider the streamlining of automobiles, for example. In short, both design and use have a creative dimension, and both also have a pedestrian, routine dimension. So creativity cannot be the criterion that distinguishes design from use either.

A third possibility is that design and production involve intentional modification of materials in forming the artifact, whereas use does not. But in fact many common use activities involve or result in modification of artifacts, e.g., maintenance (polishing, washing, sharpening) and repair (mending, patching, rebuilding). These modifications can be quite extensive, and are typically intended. More importantly, many artifacts are intentionally and necessarily modified in the very process of use, for example, perfume and other cosmetics, food artifacts, solvents and other cleaning agents – in general, anything that gets used up, as opposed to just used. On the other hand, there are cases of design and production that involve little or no modification because prototypes can be produced by utilizing existing artifacts as components. For instance, Les Paul is said to have put together his first electric guitar by using an acoustic guitar, a telephone mouthpiece, and a radio as an amplifier (Bacon and Day 1993, p.8). This case does involve some modification in the sense that the telephone mouthpiece had to be attached to the guitar and wired into the radio.

But the modifications were very minor. The basic form and function of the guitar, the mouthpiece and the radio were not changed, just connected up in a novel way. So neither the fact of intentional modification nor the extent of the modification provides a plausible criterion for distinguishing cases of design and production from cases of use.

The intentions of users do not seem to be significantly different from the intentions of designers and producers in any relevant way, then. So if the intentions of designers are sufficient for establishing a proper function, it seems the intentions of users must be sufficient as well. This conclusion reflects the fact, noted already at the beginning of this paper, that the roles of designer, maker, and user, while distinguishable, are not rigorously distinct. Moreover, we can now see that if you want to hold both that there is a distinction to be had between proper function and system function, and that the intentions of designers are sufficient for the establishment of proper function, you also must hold that design and use are rigorously distinct. If not, system functions are rapidly and exhaustively assimilated to proper functions, and that distinction is effectively lost for theoretical purposes. Similarly, it will not do to say that creative use is really a kind of design. This moves the line between design and use, so that the only activities that count as use are pedestrian employments of artifacts for their unequivocally proper purposes. But then the distinction between proper function and system function is erased, because the intentions of designers (a group that now includes creative users) establish proper functions, and use is defined in terms of the exercise of proper functions as well, so it is proper function all the way down, so to speak. In other words, this is just another way of conceding that if the intentions of designers are sufficient for the establishment of proper functions, so are the intentions of (creative) users, and no matter which way you do it, the consequence is the loss of the distinction between proper function and system function.

But conceding that users' intentions are also sufficient and accepting the consequences has ramifications that must be laid out in full detail. First, all intended functions of artifacts, whether initiated by designers or by users, are derived *proper* functions if we allow the sufficiency of users' intentions. Thus all functions of artifacts, no matter how transiently performed, are what the artifact is supposed to do. For example, suppose I use my safe deposit box key as a screwdriver to tighten the screws on my garage door lock. This is now a derived proper function of that key, a function it is supposed to perform, completely on a par with its function of unlocking my safe deposit box. In short, we no longer have any theoretical mechanism for marking the distinction between functions an artifact is designed to perform and can therefore be criticized for not being able to perform, and functions an artifact may serve on occasion even though it was not designed to do so and thus cannot be criticized for failing to do so. But this distinction is a salient feature of the phenomenology of artifacts and their use (Vermaas and Houkes 2003). So it would be a signal failing in a theory of artifact function if it were not able to capture this distinction.

Second, not being able to maintain the distinction between proper functions and system functions allows the proper functions of artifacts to proliferate in an uncontrolled and disorganized way. Typically the proper functions of artifacts are regarded as the proper functions of types of artifacts. It is this fact that Millikan's theory of direct proper function is designed to capture – in virtue of spoons having been historically selected and reproduced for stirring food, all spoons have this as a direct proper function. It is not clear whether the derived proper functions of particular artifacts would have to be regarded as establishing proper functions for their type or not. But let us suppose that they do not. Then each exemplar of a type of artifact would have a different, although slightly overlapping, set of proper functions. One spoon, having been used on one occasion as a musical instrument and on another as a weapon, would have the corresponding proper functions; whereas another indistinguishable exemplar of the same type, having been used once or twice as a screwdriver, would have that proper function instead. In short, the proper functions of indistinguishable exemplars of the same type of artifact would be different depending on their own particular history of use. On the other hand, let us suppose that *every* exemplar of a type of artifact has every proper function derived by any of them. Then spoons, for example, would have not only the proper functions intended by their designers, but all the functions any spoon user ever intended for any particular spoon, and these are surely legion. This would be especially problematic if, as is often held, artifact kinds must be defined in whole or in part in terms of proper function. Uncontrolled proliferation of proper functions would make such function-based classificatory systems for artifacts unstable, counterintuitive, or outright unworkable.

So we are faced with a choice. If we follow Millikan and most other theorists in holding that designers' intentions are sufficient for the establishment of proper function, we will be able to ascribe proper functions to prototypes, even to prototypes that never work as they were intended to work. But we will have to grant that users' intentions are also sufficient, and then we will lose the distinction between proper function and system function for artifacts altogether, and suffer with an uncontrolled proliferation of proper functions of artifacts in consequence. On the other hand, we can deny that the intentions of either designers or users are sufficient by themselves to establish the proper functions of artifacts, and we can rely on the theories of direct proper function and system function, neither of which requires an appeal to intentions, for our account of how artifacts get their functions. This option preserves the phenomenologically crucial distinction between proper function and system function, and the ways of talking about and thinking about artifacts that depend on it. But we will not be able to ascribe any functions at all to prototypes that do not work.

In my view, the second option is clearly preferable. It captures more of the important features of the phenomenology of our dealings with artifacts. It absolves us of the thankless task of trying to draw an implausibly sharp line between design and use. And we can blunt the counterintuitive edge of not being able to ascribe proper functions to prototypes by noting that our talk about prototypes can just as easily be interpreted as merely attributing a purpose to the designer, who believes, hopes, or expects her device will work in a certain way. But this human purpose is not necessarily and without further ado the proper function of the artifact. To suppose otherwise gives an unfortunate, quasi-theological flavor to the philosophical enterprise of understanding agents, artifacts, and their relationships.

## Conclusion

If designers' intentions are regarded as *sufficient* conditions for the establishment of function, it is unreasonable to deny sufficiency to users' intentions as well. But this move threatens the theoretical distinction between system function and proper function, and results in an uncontrolled proliferation of proper functions. An account of artifact function in which designers' intentions are not sufficient can be constructed by combining Millikan's account of direct proper function with Cummins' account of system function, and it does not generate these problems. So it is deserving of adoption as a viable alternative to the more traditional intentionalist accounts. The presence of a few functionless prototype artifacts among us seems a small price to pay.

## References

Bacon, T. & Day, P. (1993). *The Gibson Les Paul Book*. San Francisco: GPI Books (Miller Freeman, Inc.).

Cummins, R. (1975). Functional analysis. *The Journal of Philosophy*, *72*, 741–65.

Davies, P. S. (2001). *Norms of nature: Naturalism and the nature of function*. Cambridge, MA: The MIT Press.

Dipert, R.R. (1993). *Artifacts, art works, and agency*. Philadelphia: Temple University Press.

Godfrey-Smith, P. (1993). Functions: consensus without unity. *Pacific Philosophical Quarterly*, *74*, 196–208.

Kitcher, P.E. (1993). Function and design. *Midwest Studies in Philosophy*, *18*, 379–397.

McLaughlin, P. (2001). *What functions explain: Functional explanation and self-reproducing systems*. Cambridge, UK: Cambridge University Press.

Millikan, R.G. (1999). Wings, spoons, pills, and quills: A pluralist theory of function. *The Journal of Philosophy*, *96*(4), 191–206.

Millikan, R.G. (1993). *White queen psychology and other essays for Alice*. Cambridge, MA and London: The MIT Press.

Millikan, R.G. (1989). An ambiguity in the notion 'function.' *Biology and Philosophy*, *4*, 172–76.

Millikan, R.G. (1984). *Language, thought, and other biological categories*. Cambridge, MA and London: The MIT Press.

Plato. (1992). *Republic*. 2nd edition. [translated by G.M.A. Grube, revised by C.D.C. Reeve] Indianapolis/Cambridge: Hackett Publishing Company.

Preston, B. (1998). Why is a wing like a spoon? A pluralist theory of function. *The Journal of Philosophy*, *95*(5), 215–54.

Vermaas, P.E. & Houkes, W. (2003). Ascribing functions to technical artefacts: A challenge to etiological accounts of functions. *British Journal for the Philosophy of Science* 54, 261–289.

Walsh, D.M. & Ariew, A. (1996). A taxonomy of functions. *Canadian Journal of Philosophy*, *26*, 493–514.

Chapter 2

# Use Plans and Artefact Functions: An Intentionalist Approach to Artefacts and their Use

Pieter E. Vermaas and Wybo Houkes

Artefacts are the means as well as the products of intentional human action. Users intentionally manipulate artefacts such as toasters and screwdrivers for attaining their goals; designers intentionally create artefacts that users can manipulate for attaining these goals. Many philosophers therefore seek to describe artefacts in terms of the intentions of their designers and users: what distinguishes a toaster from a screwdriver has something to do with the intentions with which humans have designed or are using them. In addition, many philosophers feel that a philosophy of artefacts primarily ought to understand artefacts as objects with functionality. After all, when we describe artefacts we routinely do this in terms of their functions. We, for instance, classify artefacts in functional terms, such as 'toaster' and 'screwdriver'. Also when users manipulate artefacts in ways that are different to the use for which they was designed, we express this in terms of functions: if a screwdriver is used to extract small objects from cracks, we say that the user manipulates the screwdriver not as a 'screwdriver', but as a 'lever'. The combination of an emphasis on intentions and on functionality constitutes what we call the 'standard view' of artefacts: artefacts are understood primarily as functional objects, and their functionality is strongly connected to the intentions of users and, first and foremost, designers.

In our contribution to this volume we sketch this standard view and then present an alternative view of artefacts. This alternative endorses the intentionalism that underlies the standard view, but renounces its strong emphasis on functionality. Our alternative intentionalism primarily addresses artefact use and design and describes them in terms of plans, i.e., structured sequences of considered actions, rather than in terms of (only) functions.

Our alternative view is motivated in part by recent criticism of the standard view. Beth Preston, for instance, argues in her contribution to this volume that intentions of designers cannot be sufficient to determine the functions of artefacts, and advocates a non-intentionalist understanding of the functionality of artefacts.[1] It is, however, our position that the intentionalist intuitions behind the standard view are viable.

1 Beth Preston's theory of functions can be found in Preston (1998).

We have developed our alternative view to demonstrate this viability and to defend intentionalism as a sufficient, if not necessary, approach to understanding artefacts and their use and design.

We start by describing some relevant parts of the current situation in the philosophy of artefacts. We introduce the standard view of artefacts, sketch Preston's criticism of intentionalism and present two problems we have with the standard view. In the next section we go on to describe our alternative view by conceptualising artefact use in terms of plans. We show that this use need not be understood in terms of the functionality of artefacts, and in this sense our plan theory is a development of the intentionalist approach that, in comparison to the standard view, de-emphasises functionality. Then, we discuss the limitations of planning – in phenomena that we call 'embodiment' and 'situatedness' – and counters objections to a plan view, put forward by Lucy Suchman. Next, we shift our attention from use to artefact design and to artefacts themselves. We describe design on the basis of our plan theory, and then draw conclusions about how to understand artefacts and their functionality. And we defend intentionalism against the criticism and problems raised. Finally, we consider the consequences of our plan view and comment on the view held by James Gibson and John Searle that the observation of objects is primarily the observation of the uses of those objects.

## The Standard View of Artefacts and their Use

Artefacts are intimately and rather obviously connected to human intentional action. Their use is often deliberate, as when we choose a tool to achieve a certain task or wonder how to use a newly bought household appliance. Moreover, it seems artefacts can be distinguished from 'natural objects' because they are the products of intentional action. Spelling out this connection between artefacts and intentionality has been a major task of the philosophy of artefacts so far. Straightforwardly defining artefacts as the products of intentional action is too simple-minded, as this would grant the status of artefacts to waste products such as soot and radiation, and to other 'by-products' of our actions, such as footprints. More refined definitions have been proposed, which refer to a specific type of intentional action, usually called 'design'. The common core of these philosophical efforts can be called 'intentionalism': general conceptualisations of artefacts, artefact use and design should be built on the notion of intentional action. Nevertheless, this intentionalism usually is incorporated in those conceptualisations by referring to intentions, a certain type of mental states of intentional agents, rather than to the actions themselves.

Many authors combine this assumption with an emphasis on functionality, to produce what we call the 'standard view' of artefacts. On this view, design is described as an activity aimed at providing means to certain ends, artefacts themselves as these means, and use as the manipulation of these means to an end. That artefacts play a role as means to an end is expressed by ascribing a function to them – or even categorising artefacts in 'functional kinds': a toaster is an object with the function of toasting bread; a screwdriver is by its very name a means to drive screws into various materials. If this emphasis on functionality is combined with the above-mentioned appeal to intentions, the central task for a philosophy of artefacts becomes to explain artefact functions in terms of the intentions of designers and users.

There is a further phenomenon that seems relevant to a philosophy of artefacts. Virtually all artefacts can be used for many different purposes (see also Hysse Forchhammer's contribution to this volume). Screwdrivers, for example, can be used to extract small objects from cracks or to remove staples from stacks of paper. All of these uses employ dispositions[2] of the object, such as its rigidity. On the standard view, the distinction between the function of an artefact and its other dispositions should be made in terms of intentions, for example by analysing the function as a 'privileged' set of dispositions intentionally produced or selected by the designer of the artefact for attaining a certain purpose. This difference between the function and a non-privileged disposition of an artefact shows in a number of ways. For one thing, it leads to a distinction between proper and improper use, as employing the function of an artefact versus employing its other features respectively; adding the connection between functionality and intentions, proper use is use in accordance with the designer's intentions. This terminology – or the analogous distinction between 'proper' and 'accidental' functions – is not just a figment of the philosophical imagination: Many warranties include a clause that excludes damage caused by 'improper' use.

Summing up this brief presentation, we have identified the following elements of what we call the standard view of artefacts:[3]

(1) Artefacts are best understood as objects with a function.
(2) The function of an artefact is a set of dispositions of the artefact; this set is intentionally selected or created by a designer.

---

2 'Disposition' is used by philosophers to indicate anything that an object does when acted upon in a certain way; this concept is therefore considerably broader than its everyday counterpart, which primarily applies to people and their mannerisms (e.g., 'of a sunny disposition') and to possibilities for human action (as in the phrase 'at one's disposition'). Examples of 'philosopher's dispositions' are the disposition of solid objects to cast a shadow in bright daylight and of a thin layer of ice to crack when someone steps on it.

3 The following quotes all illustrate aspects of this standard view: 'An object *o* is an artefact made by an agent *Ag* only if it satisfies some type-description *D* included in the intention $I_A$ which brings about the existence of *o*.' (Hilpinen 1992, p.61); 'Roughly, an artefactual property is an intentionally-added property that is intended to get us to believe (in certain ways) that the object possesses certain tool properties [i.e., properties that were intentionally modified or deliberately left alone]' (Dipert 1995, p. 129); '[…] if the desire is to produce a certain result by means of making, for example, a certain tool […] then a derived proper function of the tool (token) […] is to produce this result. Thus, it happens that artefacts have as their derived proper functions the functions intended for them by their makers […]' (Millikan 1999, p. 205).

(3) Alternative, or improper, use of an artefact is best understood as employing another set of dispositions – the artefact's 'accidental functions'; users are under normative pressure to use an artefact as intended by the designer of an artefact, that is, to use it for its (proper) function.

One may doubt the claim, inherent to the standard view, that *designers* select or create the set of dispositions that makes up the functions of an artefact. In her contribution to this volume, Beth Preston develops this doubt into an argument against the standard view. Preston argues that designers' intentions are not sufficient to determine artefact functions. Briefly summarising her exposition: if the designers' intentions were sufficient, users' intentions would also be; after all, there is little or no distinction between creative use on the one hand and design or production on the other. But if users' intentions are also sufficient to determine artefact functions, the distinction between proper and accidental use collapses, and the classification of artefacts in terms of their proper functions becomes impossible: there would be no reason to call a screwdriver 'screwdriver' instead of 'staple remover'. Preston concludes this argument with a call for a 'non-intentionalist' theory of technical functions, i.e., a theory that does not define functions in terms of designer's intentions, analogous to the one that has been developed for the functions of biological items.[4] In terms of the elements of the standard view, she denies (2) and (3), while maintaining (1).

As we have said in our introduction, we regard the intentionalist approach that underlies the standard view as viable and have developed an alternative intentionalist view. We present this view in the next sections and defend it against Preston's and other criticisms. This does, however, not imply that we are not critical to the standard view ourselves. We wish to point out two problems of this view, which in part motivate our alternative view. The first arises because, as we have noted, the standard view appeals to intentions of agents, rather than to their actions. This leads to a definition of artefact functions in terms of the intentions of their designers: a screwdriver has the function to drive screws iff its designer intended it as a driver of screws.[5] The problem is that this definition gives rise to a proliferation of functions, given additional designer intentions: if a designer intended the screwdriver also as a cheap Christmas present or regards it as a means to earn money, then on the given definition 'to be a cheap gift' and 'to earn money' are functions of the screwdriver – on a par with its function to drive screws into materials. Moreover, it becomes difficult to isolate the relevant intentions when artefacts are designed by teams of designers. We aim at avoiding this problem by conceptualising artefacts in terms of intentional actions. A second problem of the standard view is that it maintains that artefacts are to be understood primarily as objects with functions. For designers it most probably is important to understand artefacts in terms of functions: in design methodology, for instance, designing is often defined as a process that starts with specific required

4 E.g., Neander (1991), Millikan (1984) and Preston (1998).

5 Millikan's definition of derived proper function quoted in footnote 3, comes close to this possibility.

functions and that ends with a physical description of an artefact that can perform these functions.[6] But for users this understanding may be unnecessarily full. Users may take artefacts simply as *means* for attaining desired ends, without making the additional step of expressing this as that artefacts have functions. This second problem is addressed in our view by describing artefact use and design primarily in terms of plans, i.e., structured sequences of considered actions, by which users can attain goals, and only secondary (and optionally) in terms of functions. Hence, in terms of the elements of the standard view, we deny (1) while maintaining (2) and (3).

## A Plan View of Artefact Use

Before presenting our alternative view, we give a hypothetical but illustrative example of the use of an everyday artefact. Then we discuss how our view can accommodate the difference between proper and improper use (element 3 of the standard view) but undermines the idea that artefacts are best understood in terms of functions (element 1). Later, we extend the alternative view to also artefact design and to the conceptualisation of artefacts themselves, and show how it can counter the criticism of Beth Preston, and stop the proliferation of functions due to additional designers' intentions.

Suppose Anna has a craving for a piece of toast and decides to use her trusty toaster. She takes the machine from the cupboard and plugs it in. Then she puts two slices of bread in the toast rack and pushes down the switch. The toaster has a small dial that determines when it will switch off. According to the manual, users should determine which setting of the dial ('1' to '5') goes with their preferred 'level of browning' of the toast, put the dial at that level and then wait until the toaster switches off and the toast rack lifts. Yet what Anna usually does is turn the dial to some higher-than-desired setting (say, '5'). Then, she uses either her experience with this type of bread or frequent checks of the 'level of browning' to determine when she wants the toasting to stop. At that moment, she turns the knob to the lowest setting, causing the toaster to switch off and the toast rack to lift. In other words, Anna uses the dial as a glorified on/off-switch.

By the standard view, with its appeal to intentions, this case would be described as a series of decisions or intention-formations: Anna's decision to use a toaster, to push down the switch, to turn the dial to a higher-than-desired setting, etc. With each decision, a new intention is formed, which is subsequently realised, after which another decision is taken and a new intention formed on the basis of the current situation. The individual decisions are rational and the intentions consequences of valid 'practical reasoning' only as long as the alternative with the highest utility is chosen.[7] Yet this description of artefact use turns out to be inadequate on closer

6 See, e.g., Gero (1990) and Roozenburg and Eekels (1995).

7 The processes of decision-making and intention-formation are described in the voluminous literature on rational choice theory and theories of practical reasoning. Some

inspection. Turning the dial of the toaster to a setting indicating a longer-than-desired toasting time may be irrational *in isolation*, given the possibility to turn the dial to the optimal setting. Yet a natural objection in this case is that the rationality of this action should not be considered in isolation but as part of Anna's course of action. And as part of that course, turning the dial to a non-optimal setting appears to be rational – or so we maintain.[8]

It appears to be more accurate to describe this case and artefact use in general as the realisation of a plan. As a first approximation, a plan can be characterised as a series of considered actions, execution of which is supposed to achieve a certain goal. We call the process of constructing a plan 'deliberation' and the process of executing it 'realisation'. Anna's plan to use her toaster consists of a number of steps: plugging it in, pushing down the switch, turning the dial clockwise, waiting and observing, and turning the dial counter-clockwise. In general, when settling on a course of action, one considers alternative plans, not alternative actions within plans – although, of course, it is possible to reconsider steps of plans while realising them.

On this view, artefact use can be schematically represented as a 'sequence' of actions:[9]

*U.1* The user wants to bring about some state of affairs $\phi$, and believes it does not obtain.

*U.2* The user either chooses from a set of available alternatives a use plan *P* for bringing about $\phi$ that involves the intentional manipulation of objects $O_1$, $O_2$, etc., or he constructs a novel use plan *P* by deliberation.

*U.3* The user believes that the physical circumstances support realising *P* and that he possesses the necessary skills.[10]

*U.4* The user intends to carry out *P* and acts accordingly.

*U.5* The user observes $\phi'$ as the outcome of *P* and compares $\phi'$ with $\phi$.

---

introductions to these fields are Raz (1978), French (1986) and Audi (1989).

8 This is only one example of theories of practical rationality having to conform to intuitions concerning rational actions. It may be possible to account for the rationality of Anna's dial turning by considering a succession of intention formations; we do not *refute* this traditional action-theoretical account. Yet a description in terms of courses of actions and plans seems more natural. A more sophisticated version of this argument can be found in Pollock (1995), §5.2.

9 This representation of artefact use is a simplified version of the one presented in Houkes *et al.* (2002), §1.

10 Two remarks are in order. First, the beliefs mentioned in *U.3* are, of course, used to assess the relative utilities of the available alternatives or to construct a novel use plan in *U.2*. These steps only serve to reconstruct them explicitly. Secondly, the beliefs mentioned are oversimplified. In many cases, plans will be chosen or constructed on the basis of comparative and considerably less apodictic beliefs, such as 'I believe I'm better at carrying out *P* than *P*′, although I'm not quite sure under the present circumstances'.

*U.6* The user believes that $\phi$ has been brought about or not. In the latter case, he may decide to repeat the realisation of *P* or to repeat the entire *U*-sequence. If he repeats *U* he may reconsider his intended state of affairs $\phi$, select another use plan *P′*, or do both.

This sequence can be illustrated by means of the toaster example. Anna deliberates on a way to obtain toast, given her desire for toast and lack thereof. As said above, this deliberation cannot be understood as merely a sequence of intention-formations, but is rather the adoption of a single plan consisting of a sequence of intentional actions for attaining the goal. This plan can be chosen from a (small) set of available alternatives – using a toaster, buying readymade toast, putting slices of bread in an oven, etc. – on the basis of Anna's beliefs about her skills and circumstances. In most circumstances, using a toaster in an established, instead of newly devised, way probably has the highest utility of the listed alternatives because it combines a high chance of success with a small amount of time spent and little chance of overtaxing Anna's skills. Once Anna has settled on a plan, she executes it, and judges whether the result is satisfactory. Suppose the toast comes out distastefully and evidently burnt. Then she may repeat the execution of the plan with a different slice of bread, change her plan (e.g., turn the knob at an earlier point or put slices of bread in an oven), or abandon altogether her intention to eat toast.

We call this the 'plan view' of artefact use. And although it is as yet a view of only artefact use – not of design, which is of central importance to the standard view – two conclusions can already be drawn. The first is that a detailed description of the use of artefacts need not mention the functions of the artefacts involved. Our plan view will in the end also include a characterisation of the functions of artefacts, but this is motivated by our description of *design*, not that of use. In the design context it makes sense to introduce functions. But in the context of use of especially everyday artefacts[11] functions may be taken as redundant. In that sense, we deny the first element (1) of the standard view.

Another conclusion is that our view accommodates the distinction between proper and improper use, which was introduced in the previous section. As step *U.2* in the 'use sequence' shows, use plans may be either constructed by the user herself or drawn from a set of available alternatives. Some of these alternatives have obviously been constructed by others, often by designers and sometimes by fellow users. Use plans constructed by designers are expressed in the user manuals of artefacts and communicated to potential users by various other means (e.g., explicit instructions, television ads, features of the artefact (so called *use cues*), product demonstrations). Use plans constructed by fellow users are usually communicated orally among users and by explicit hands-on demonstrations. The concept of proper use can now be explained by maintaining that use plans for artefacts constructed by designers hold a privileged position in the set of available alternative plans. Proper use of an artefact

11 The concept of function is most probably helpful when the use of professional equipment such as aeroplanes is described.

is then use that follows a plan approximately identical to the use plan developed by designers, i.e., their goals are identical and there is an approximate similarity of included actions.[12] Improper use, on the other hand, is use that follows a plan constructed by the user herself. And use that follows plans developed by fellow users may be seen as filling up a spectrum between proper and improper use.

If we explain proper use in this way, one can draw on the intrinsic normativity of plans to make a distinction between proper use and what could be called 'rational' use. To illustrate the normativity, suppose someone undertakes the same actions when writing poems for profit as another who writes poems for fun, such as jotting down some lines in the weekends, occasionally reading the results to family and friends, and sending the most successful ones to a magazine once a year. Although this is a rather good plan for writing poems for fun, it is exceptionally bad as a plan for writing poems for profit – if there is a good plan for doing so. Plans are subject to many standards. One of the most straightforward ones is that plans should be likely to lead to the desired state of affairs, or at least more likely than other plans. This standard of 'appropriateness' of a plan can be formulated in terms of a calculation of utilities of several available plans.[13] Some other standards include 'means-end coherence', which requires the person who executes a plan to obtain necessary means (such as slices of bread for making toast) and construct relevant sub-plans, and 'belief coherence', which means that a plan should be based on beliefs held by the person realising it (such as *U.3* in the sequence presented above).[14] These standards on plans allow for a distinction between good (rational) and bad (irrational) use, which is independent from the distinction between proper and non-standard use. Users may assume that proper use is always rational use as well – designers are on the basis of their technical knowledge and skills, supposed to construct good use plans. And it is probably safe to say that most of such use plans are indeed rational. But even use plans by designers can be or become irrational, as is illustrated by the designed use of asbestos plates to make walls fire-resistant. And improper use plans developed by users themselves are often rational, as was illustrated by Anna's use of the toaster. One may now interpret the 'normative pressure' put on

12 The identity conditions for plans are hard to spell out in detail. Making toast with a toaster and making it by putting slices of bread on a hot roof are obviously different plans, although they are aimed at the same goal; writing poems for fun and writing them for profit are different plans, although they may include the same actions. And in many cases, two different sets of actions may count as the same plan. Is driving a car and checking the tyre pressure before starting the car a different plan than checking the tyre pressure when the car has been started? Or even different than checking this pressure only when one thinks there might be something wrong with the car? This leniency in the identity conditions of plans also affects the notion of proper use. Suppose the car manual says that one has to check the tire pressure before starting the car. It seems implausible to maintain that this by itself is sufficient to characterise checking the tire pressure after starting the car as *improper* use of the car. Yet this intuition may be based largely on certain connotations of the term 'improper', such as 'potentially harmful' or 'damaging to the artefact'.

13 Cf. Pollock (1995), §5.3 for a method of evaluating plans by calculating utilities.

14 These standards are taken from Bratman (1987), §3.2.

users (element (3) of the standard view) as a pressure to follow use plans that are rational. This interpretation does change the purport of the pressure since, as we have said, rational use plans need not cover all use plans constructed by designers and does cover many use plans constructed by users themselves. Specifically users are on this interpretation not pressured to follow irrational plans of their designers, a consequence one may easily accept.

So the plan view accounts for the phenomenon of (im-)proper use in a rather sophisticated way, perhaps outperforming the standard view in this respect. Yet this account still presupposes that one can make a distinction between the designers of artefacts and their users. Preston's criticism of the standard view seems to show that such a distinction cannot be properly made. However, on the basis of our plan view of the design of artefact we are able to differentiate designers from users of artefacts, as we show when we present our view of artefact design.

## Objections to Planning

Before turning to design and artefact functions, we first consider an obvious objection to the plan view: does it not overemphasise the role that deliberation actually plays in our dealings with artefacts? In this section, we argue that there *are* limitations to planning, but that these limitations – which we call embodiment and situatedness – can be incorporated in the plan view of artefact use. A secondary aim of this section is to counter arguments to the effect that a plan view is fundamentally mistaken. Arguments to this effect have been put forward by Lucy Suchman, whose primary purpose is to show that the 'planning model of agency' is incapable of describing interactions between agents and has led to seriously flawed models of human-machine interaction. She proposes to replace these theories with an appeal to 'situated action', a notion inspired by the phenomenological tradition of Merleau-Ponty and the early Heidegger, as interpreted by Hubert Dreyfus.[15]

It may seem impossible to specify the limitations of planning and deliberation in general. For one thing, some people tend to think a lot before they act, whereas others prefer to act quickly and think later. Moreover, in some cases, such as kicking a stone to let off steam, deliberation makes little sense, whereas in others, such as constructing a nuclear power plant, it seems one can hardly deliberate enough. We think that, nevertheless, there are two general limitations to planning.

Once again consider the use of a toaster. Above we gave a rudimentary reconstruction of this example of artefact use in terms of a use plan: Anna gets the toaster, plugs it in, puts slices of bread into the toast rack, pushes down the switch, etc. Most steps of this

---

15 Suchman only refers to Heidegger and Merleau-Ponty as cited by Hubert Dreyfus; cf. Suchman (1987, pp. 53–54). The theme of 'situated intentionality' is developed in Dreyfus' (1991) influential commentary on the First Division of Heidegger's *Being and Time* and many of Dreyfus' later papers. We do not go into Suchman's proposed alternative here, besides noting that her notion of 'situatedness' differs from the one presented in this paper – in fact, it includes both embodiment and situatedness in our sense.

plan can themselves be constructed as a number of steps, e.g., the 'sub-plan' of getting slices of bread. Yet for other steps, such a construction would be contrived. Anna does not, for instance, deliberate on how to push down the switch. In any plan, one necessarily reaches a point at which deliberation ends, because further deliberation becomes strongly counterproductive – no one will deliberate for a week on what to eat – or because further sub-planning is infeasible, e.g., for simple bodily movements. Furthermore, one does not, in general, plan everything one is supposed to do in advance, even if this would be possible in principle. To allow for mistakes in deliberation or the beliefs on which it is based, to accommodate changes in the situation and other eventualities, plans are usually not complete. In the toaster case, for instance, Anna probably does not deliberate on where to put the toaster – she takes a decision while realising the plan. The first limitation – which we call 'embodiment' – is based on a principled incompleteness of planning: it is impossible to specify all included actions in all details. The second limitation – which we call 'situatedness' – is based on incompleteness in practice: plans seldom specify all actions regarding a situation.

Our plan view can accommodate both phenomena – without reducing them to aspects of planning. Let us start with the former, the limitation of embodiment. One way to spell out this embodiment is to acknowledge that in realising plans, we necessarily draw on mental and motor skills. Even for the simplest plans, containing only one step, this is the case. Throwing a ball to someone is realised by taking one action, but this action combines several motor skills. Most cases of artefact use ultimately appeal to elementary motor skills without explicitly referring to them: a user manual of a toaster that specifies how the user should hold her hand when pressing the switch of the toast rack would be odd indeed. And this 'skill gap' is not closed by deliberation on the part of the user either. So some details of artefact use are not determined by the communicated plan or autonomous deliberation by the user; skills take over at some point. This goes not just for elementary motor skills, which are involved in virtually every plan, but also for more sophisticated skills, such as operating the gears and clutch of a car (which one does not expect to be explained in the car manual).

The importance of skills for artefact use can be represented in the use sequence presented in the previous section: the user of an artefact has a belief about his skills (as part of *U*.3) and stops deliberating as soon as he thinks he knows 'how a certain thing is done'. If he in fact possesses the skills he thinks he has – i.e., has 'embodied' these skills – and if these skills are the ones presupposed by the designer of the artefact, this decision to stop deliberating and start drawing on skills is a rational one; otherwise, it is not. The rationality of this decision depends both on the executor of the plan and on the nature of the task. In the case of a toaster, little harm is done if it turns out one does not in fact know how to stop the toasting process; but if one uses a parachute, it may be best to double-check whether one knows the ropes before drawing on possibly non-existent skills.[16]

16 Skills are related to, but different from what 'ingrained' action patterns – which can also be described on our plan view. In toasting bread or putting on clothes, most users

This phenomenon of embodiment is different from that of situatedness, to which we now turn. Apart from their incompleteness regarding skills, plans are also incomplete in practice, to make them more readily executable. Sometimes one is, for instance, not sure about the circumstances in which a plan is realised, or about the stability of these circumstances. In those cases, it makes little sense to construct an elaborate plan for using an artefact – even if one is so inept that ample deliberation is required to realise the plan. Plans may turn out to be worthless in later situations. What is more, cognitive resources may be wasted on attempts to continue acting along the lines of the original plan. Hence, it makes more sense to construct a 'lightweight plan', which specifies only the starting actions and a broad route that leads to the goal state.[17]

This practical, rather than principled incompleteness makes plans more adaptable to the situation in which they are realised. Suppose one decides to use a toaster and includes in one's use plan a step of turning the knob to the level '3' (out of five levels), only to find that one's spouse has bought a new, more sophisticated toaster with ten levels. Then one has to revise one's plan before using this toaster. If, on the other hand, one uses a toaster by turning the dial to the maximum level and turning it back once the toast is sufficiently browned, there is no need to revise the plan. Hence, the second, less detailed plan is more flexible and more 'situated', i.e., more responsive to the details of the situation in which it is realised.

This responsiveness can be accommodated in the plan view. As was argued in the previous section, plans are based on beliefs that the agent has about herself, the artefact, and the environment. These beliefs enter into the standards for rational planning; in this way, we plan our actions in a context-sensitive way. A plan to make fire with a cigarette lighter in the middle of a storm may be purposeful, but it is nevertheless a bad plan. Moreover, additional information can lead to quick revisions of a plan, given sufficient sensitivity to the context. Previous planning may even, through focussing mechanisms, be helpful in acquiring relevant beliefs about the environment, which can then be used to revise or complete the plan. In this way, planning and situatedness may support each other.

Suchman's arguments against planning conclude impotence from limitations.[18] She, for instance, considers the example of a canoeist who has to navigate a series of

---

probably go through a more or less fixed routine. Both the goal and the method of attaining it with a certain artefact are so familiar that the execution of the corresponding use plan has become rote. The difference between routine and skilled use shows in the drawbacks of the former. Routine users can easily make mistakes when confronted with an unfamiliar aspect of the standard situation ('breakdown') or with a slightly different specimen of the artefact. Furthermore, routine use may be sub-optimal from the start – many users standardly use artefacts in an inefficient way.

17 A similar point about the practical importance of lightweight planning is made in Leudar and Costall (1996), who use a 'dialogical' notion of plan different from ours. We lack the space for a critical comparison of these two approaches.

18 It is important to note, moreover, that Suchman uses a different definition of 'plan' than ours. According to Suchman, a plan is a series of considered actions that can be mechanically

rapids and concludes that: 'When it really comes down to the details of responding to currents and handling a canoe, *you effectively abandon the plan* and fall back on whatever embodied skills are available to you'.[19] In our plan view, the canoeist example is an extreme case in situatedness and embodiment – responsiveness to the particular circumstances, by means of exercising exceptional skills, is of the essence to realise the goal state. Yet even here, constructing a lightweight plan – a choice for a point to enter the rapids, or a rough outline of a route – makes sense. Moreover, most cases of artefact use are far less adventurous; and if they are, they resemble rock climbing more than wild-water canoeing: the circumstances in which we most often use artefacts are relatively stable and do not require exceptional skills.

An analogous argument builds on situatedness alone. Suchman notes that '[...] we constrain and direct our actions according to the significance that we assign to a particular context. How we do that is the outstanding problem. Plans and goals do not provide the solution for that problem, they simply restate it'.[20] Our analysis of situatedness points out that planning does not take place in a void, but is based on beliefs. This may not solve the problem, and it does show that planning must be balanced with other cognitive strategies, but it does more than 'restate' the problem: it indicates the conceptual resources that can be used to describe the context-sensitivity of human action. Hence, we conclude that Suchman's arguments fail to show that planning in the sense described here is not just limited, but ineffective.[21]

Summing up, in this section, we have offered a sketch of an integration of the phenomena of embodiment and situatedness within our plan view. Much work is still to be done to show exactly how an appeal is made to skills in the context of constructing a plan and how deliberate actions merge seamlessly with situated actions. Furthermore, situatedness and embodiment are surely far richer phenomena than described here. But it has at least been shown in what way embodiment and situatedness can be accounted for in our plan view, namely by imposing limitations on the practical and principled possibilities of planning. By explicitly stating these limitations, general arguments against the role of planning in human action lose their bite.

---

implemented (1987, p. 52) – all cognitive resources are spent on planning, and none on execution. Hence, any kind of incompleteness discredits plans as generative mechanisms. But surely this notion of 'plan' is overly strict, although it may be close to that used in cognitive science and the planning approach in AI; see, for instance, the highly influential Miller *et al.* (1960). Our notion is more liberal; for this reason alone, it is already less likely to be vulnerable to Suchman's criticisms.

19 Suchman 1987, p. 52; emphasis added.

20 Suchman 1987, pp. 47–48.

21 David de Léon (private communication) has suggested that Suchman's arguments can also be taken to show that plans are not the generative mechanism of actions – although they may play a part in subsequent reconstructions of our actions (1987; p. 39). Yet such an alternative view should be supported by independent arguments against planning as a generative mechanism. As indicated, we do not think Suchman supplies valid arguments. Thus, her alternative lacks an argumentative foundation.

## A Plan View of Artefact Design and of Artefact Functions

We have now presented our plan view of artefact use and we have developed it by accommodating the phenomena of embodiment and situatedness. In this section we continue by presenting our view of artefact design and of artefact functions. Since our approach is action-oriented, we first extend the plan view to the process of designing. We take this as a process that aims primarily at the development of use plans, and, subordinately, at designing objects.

Because we describe the use of artefacts as the realisation of use plans, it seems natural to describe the design process that leads to those artefacts as the construction of such plans. The concept of a 'use plan developed by designers' was introduced earlier to account for the distinction between proper and improper use. Focusing on the role of this plan, designing can be represented by the following sequence of actions:[22]

*D.1* The designer wants to contribute to a user's goal of bringing about a state of affairs $\phi$.
*D.2* The designer believes that the state of affairs $\phi'$ is the closest consistent and viable approximation of $\phi$, and intends to contribute to bringing about $\phi'$.
*D.3* The designer believes that if the users follow an appropriate use plan *P* that involves the manipulation of objects $O_1$, $O_2$, etc., this will contribute to bringing about $\phi'$, and intends to construct this plan *P* and to communicate it to the users.
*D.4* The designer intends to contribute to producing the objects $O_i$, $O_j$, etc., that do not yet exist by designing[23] them, and acts accordingly.
*D.5* The designer intends to communicate *P* to the users, and acts accordingly.
*D.6* The designer believes that $\phi'$ can or cannot be brought about by the users to whom *P* is communicated. This belief is based on the observation that some users go through a sequence of actions *P′* and bring about $\phi''$, and on a comparison of $\phi''$ with $\phi'$.
*D.7* The designer decides that his goal to contribute to bringing about $\phi'$ has been achieved or not. In the latter case, he may decide to repeat the entire *D* sequence, settle on another plan (return to *D.3*), redesign at least one of the objects $O_i$, $O_j$, etc., (return to *D.4*) or re-attempt communication (return to *D.5*).

By means of this description we can define 'artefact' and 'artefact function'. By step *D.3*, the use plan *P* that is constructed by the designer involves the manipulation of objects. Some of these objects, denoted by $O_i$, $O_j$, etc., may not exist. Hence,

22 This representation of designing is a simplified version of the one presented in Houkes *et al.* (2002), §2.

23 'Designing' is here used in the broad sense of describing the objects in words, pictures, gestures or some combination of these, along with instructions for producing the objects.

they should be produced if users are to carry out the designed plan. In step *D.4*, the designer contributes to the production of these objects by describing them and the way in which they can be manufactured. We now define artefacts as objects that are designed and manufactured as part of the construction of a use plan. The definition of a function is somewhat more involved.[24] The whole plan *P* has the purpose of bringing about a state of affairs $\phi'$ and the plan is supposed to generate a transition from an initial state of affairs to $\phi'$. An explanation of this capacity of *P* singles out dispositions of the objects $O_1$, $O_2$, etc., used in *P*, by referring to those dispositions as the ones that contribute to *P*'s capacity to bring about $\phi'$. These singled-out dispositions are the functions of those objects.

Let's get back to the toast to illustrate all this. By our description, the original designer of the toaster did not start by intending to make an object that can toast bread. Instead the designer started with the intention to help people with a taste for toasted bread by constructing a plan with which these people can acquire toast (step *D.1*). The designer may adjust or refine this desire, for instance, by requiring that the size of the toast fall within certain limits (step *D.2*). After that the designer actually develops the use plan as a series of actions he or she thinks the prospective users can carry out. These actions involve using an object that heats bread, and since this object did not exist in the pre-toaster era, the designer describes this object as part of the construction of the use plan (*D.3* and *D.4*). Finally, the designer checks the resulting plan by, among other things, explaining it to some of the considered users and determining whether they manage to acquire toast with the plan (*D.5* and *D.6*). We guess the toaster was an immediate success, but if not, the designer would have returned to some of the steps in the design sequence to improve on the design of the plan or the toaster (*D.7*). Based on the definition given above, the toaster that is designed and manufactured as the result of this plan is an artefact. The disposition of the toaster to slightly roast the surfaces of slices of bread is its function, because that disposition (in contrast to other dispositions such as that to generate an awful smell if cheese falls in) is referred to when it is explained why toasted bread can be generated by the plan.

On the basis of this plan view of artefact design and the proposed definitions we can address Beth Preston's criticism of intentionalism and show how to avoid the additional problems of the standard view discussed above.

Firstly, we can make a clear distinction between users and designers of artefacts. Users primarily realise use plans for attaining the goals associated with these plans. Designers develop use plans that prospective users can carry out for attaining the associated goals, and designers check whether they have achieved this by communicating the developed use plans to users and by observing if these users do attain the associated goals with the plans. By the use sequence (step *U.2*) given in above it is acknowledged that users themselves may also construct use plans, but this does not automatically turn them into designers: users usually do not communicate

24 In Vermaas & Houkes (2003) we discuss existing theories of artefact functions and present our own, plan-based, theory.

the plans they construct to other users and do not check whether these plans are (still) successful if others carry them out; designers are by the design sequence (steps *D.5* and *D.6*) required to do so. Some users may actually communicate a use plan they have constructed to fellow users but this does not undermine the principled distinction between users and designers. It merely proves that the class of users can be broken up in subclasses: passive users that carry out existing use plans (users that drive screws with screwdrivers); creative users that construct their own use plans (Anna with the toaster), and innovative users that construct their own use plans and communicate them to other users (Anna if she starts to inform other toast consumers of her use of the toaster). And if those latter agents also check whether their newly constructed and communicated plans have the intend results, they stop to be innovative users and become designers on our plan view (Anna, if she also checks whether those other toast consumers achieve their required 'level of browning' with Anna's use plan).

Secondly, we can avoid the proliferation of functions due to additional intentions of designers. On our view, the functions of an artefact correspond to the set of dispositions of the artefact that are singled-out or 'highlighted' by the explanation of why the use plan for the artefact leads successfully to its associated goal: the functions of an artefact correspond to the set of dispositions that contributing to this success. This determination of the functions of an artefact is independent of the specific intentions that the designer of the artefact had: the function of the toaster is still its disposition to slightly roast the surfaces of slices of bread, regardless of whether the original designer of the toaster, in addition to his or her intention that the toaster has this disposition, wanted to earn money with it, or become known as a great benefactor of mankind.

Thirdly and finally, we can defend intentionalism, if not the standard view, against Preston's criticism. Our determination of functions is different from the simple creed that designers' intentions determine functions. In that sense Preston's criticism does not to apply. Moreover, on our plan view we can, as argued above, make a clear distinction between designers and users. Hence, if we define the proper functions of an artefact as those dispositions of the artefact that are highlighted by the designer's explanation of the success of the use plan of the artefact, we do not fall prey to the conclusion that users by their (explanations of) improper use of artefacts also determine proper functions of artefacts. Instead we can define accidental functions of an artefact as those dispositions of the artefact that are highlighted by the explanations of the success of use that follows a plan constructed by the users themselves, and maintain that these functions are in general different to the proper functions. One can quarrel about whether the dispositions of artefacts highlighted by explanations of the use plans developed by users and communicated to fellow users are to be characterised as proper or accidental functions. These plans may earn the same status as the use plans developed by designers, especially when the can be taken as rational. On the other hand, if such a use plan is clearly irrational, people may not be inclined to call it proper use nor the dispositions highlighted proper functions. So, in terms of the examples, to drive screws is the proper function of a screwdriver and to pierce is an accidental function if a user incidentally uses a screwdriver for making a hole in plasterboard. And to open tins of paint may be taken as a proper function even though screwdrivers are not designed for this use.

## Artefacts and their Functions

Our definitions have some surprising consequences for the understanding of artefacts. First, objects produced by intentional agents outside the context of constructing a use plan are not considered artefacts. Hence, objects made absent-mindedly, such as a little pile of sand swept together at the beach during a lively conversation, or a fancy but useless alloy designed just because nobody thought it was possible to make it, do not count as artefacts. Secondly, artefacts exist relative to a particular designed use plan. In that sense one can take them as relational, i.e., as being a particular type of artefact with respect to that plan. This would mean that the toaster is a toaster relative to the toasting plan, and not relative to any other plan, say to warm one's hands with it. Many artefact names reflect this relativity to some extent. We return to this in a moment. Plan-relativity does not extend to artefactuality as such, which would be counterintuitive. In a way, designed objects are more intrinsically artefacts than they are toasters or screwdrivers: once an object is designed and manufactured as the result of the construction of a use plan, it becomes an artefact independently of which use plan one is considering, as long as it is clear that it was constructed to play a role in *some* use plan. Thirdly, functions of artefacts are also relative to use plans. A screwdriver, for instance, has the function to drive screws relative to the use plan to install or remove screws, and the function to lever relative to the plan to remove little items from cracks.

On our plan view, artefacts can still be taken as objects with functions. But artefacts are better understood as objects subsidiary to actions included in use plans. Functions are defined relative to these use plans. In the context of designing it is helpful to speak about functions because a function of an artefact or, more generally, of an object, refers to those dispositions of the artefact or object, respectively, that the designer puts into action to create a use plan. The use plan as a whole is supposed to bring about some state of affairs. The designer can, roughly speaking, construct this plan by choosing actions with specific effects for which it holds that when the actions are carried out sequentially, their effects result in this state of affairs. The designer then has to devise the individual actions with their specified effects. One of the means the designer has for doing this is choosing an object or artefact with certain dispositions that give rise to a specified effect when employed. The chosen dispositions are then by definition the functions of that object or artefact, respectively.

In the context of artefact use, one can introduce functions in the same way as for artefact design. Everyday language reflects this. Names of some artefacts are functional, such as toaster, screwdriver, shoe polish, and computer. However, everyday language does not confirm that function is an all-pervading concept.

Many artefacts are not named by the functions that can be ascribed to them: bread is not called 'hunger-killer,' paper is not called 'sign-carrier', nitro-glycerine is not 'explosion-fluid', and compact discs are not called 'music-carriers'.[25] Moreover, if we discuss in everyday life how artefacts can be used, we need not mention functions. An inquiry about the use of a strange artefact on display in a shop can be formulated as 'what is the function of this thing?' And the answer can be 'Its function is to absorb fluid and smearing it over a surface.' But it can also be formulated as 'what is this thing for?' and answered by 'it is for applying paint'. If our plan view of artefact use is right, users are primarily interested in goals they can achieve with artefacts, and in the plans they have to realise for doing so. The question 'what is this thing for?' should then be interpreted as the question 'how and for what goals can one use this thing?' And the answer should be taken as 'you can use it for achieving goal $\phi$ by carrying out plan *P*'. One advantage of this latter answer is that it provides users with the information they need, whereas the answer in terms of the function generally does not. Consider a coffee percolator. Telling somebody unfamiliar with percolators that it has the function to make coffee with does reveal the goal that can be achieved by this artefact, but does not tell much about how to achieve it. Saying that the coffee maker is for making coffee by putting a filter in the percolator, filling the filter with an amount of grained coffee, and finally pouring boiling water on that grained coffee, is more informative.

Yet functional lingo is of some help in communicating use plans. By naming the functions of artefacts, designers (or fellow-users) provide some information to users about how they may use the artefact. This communication works better if the functional description is unambiguous, i.e., if the artefact is used in use plans relative to which it has mostly the same function. So, if our plan view holds, then artefacts that have functional names are mainly artefacts that have one dominant use. Examples are toasters, corkscrews, and coffee makers. Artefacts that have different functions relative to different plans are, on other hand, mainly not named functionally.[26] Examples are concrete, boards, flour, and compact discs.

This discussion on functions has some bearing on the view, taken in other contributions to this volume, that the observation of objects by agents is primarily the observation of the uses those objects have for the agents, instead of the observation of the objects' physical and chemical properties. One finds this view defended in – otherwise quite different – works by James Gibson and John Searle. According to Gibson's ecological approach to visual perception,[27] objects and substances

25 In everyday language there are also cases of artefacts with non-functional names that became functional. An iron, for instance, was most probably named after the material used. But one now can say that ironing is its function.

26 Some functional names are ill chosen, if artefacts have acquired new functions. The Dutch fire brigade (to give an example of a social artefact) has, for instance, recently launched an expensive advertising campaign to inform people that it does more than extinguishing fires. Changing its name to a non-functional one would probably be even more costly, in many respects.

27 Gibson (1979), especially chapters 3 and 8.

have '*affordances*'. Gibson defines an affordance of an object or substance in the environment of an animal – this animal may also be a human being – as that 'what it *offers* the animal, what it *provides* or *furnishes*, either for good or ill.'[28] These affordances are taken to be properties of the object or substance concerned and can be perceived directly by the animals. An open environment, for instance, affords locomotion to pedestrian animals, water affords drinking, bathing and drowning, fire affords the cooking of food substances and the glazing of clay, and scissors afford cutting.[29] Searle, on his turn, remarks that we more easily learn to perceive things as functional objects than as material objects stripped of functionality. So we learn to see full bathtubs as objects with the function to bathe in instead of 'enamel-covered iron concavities containing water,' and money as an object with the function to store value instead of 'cellulose fibers with green and gray stains.'[30]

It is not our intention to evaluate the tenability of the view that agents can (learn to) perceive immediately the uses of objects, which belongs to the philosophy of perception rather than that of artefacts. Instead we wish to point to an ambiguity in the formulation of this view. By our plan view of use, there is a difference between perceiving the function of an object and perceiving how an object can be used. The latter means that observers perceive an entire use plan by which the object can be used; whereas the former means that observers perceive merely the function the object has relative to a plan. For most of the examples Gibson and Searle give, this ambiguity does not surface. Perceiving that water has the affordance to be drunk or the function to quench thirst, leads rather straightforwardly to the plan to quench thirst by swallowing the water. Perceiving a full bathtub as affording bathing or as having the function to bathe in leads similarly to the plan to step in the tub and start washing. But for the fire example by Gibson, the ambiguity starts to play up. Perceiving that a fire has the affordance to glaze clay, may lead to the conclusion that fire has 'glazing clay' as a function relative to a use plan that has glazed clay as its goal. But this perception does not yet inform the observer how to use the fire for glazing clay. In the case of artefacts that can have more than one function, the ambiguity is also clearly present. By looking at a pile of iron beams one may perceive that they afford building a duplicate Eiffel tower or that they have this function. But this certainly does not reveal how to use those beams for actually building such a tower. This ambiguity can of course be removed by just choosing one of the options available. If one takes the position that observers of objects perceive whole use plans as, one could argue, Gibson is doing, the view becomes more daring: when observing beams, observers indeed perceive the plans by which they can be used, for instance, to construct towers. And if one takes the position that observers of objects perceive only their functions as, one could argue, Searle is tending to, the view becomes more mysterious: how can one perceive that fire has the function to

28 Gibson (1979, p. 127), his emphasis.

29 Gibson (1979, pp. 36–40).

30 Searle (1995, pp. 4–5, 14). Presumably, Searle regards only dollar bills as real money.

glaze clay without having knowledge of the use plans to glaze clay relative to which fire has this function?

## Conclusions

In this chapter, we defended an intentionalist approach in the philosophy of artefacts. We identified a standard view of artefacts and artefact use and design, which describes artefacts in terms of their functionality and builds a strong connection between artefact functions and designers' intentions. We showed that this standard view could be criticised, but that its intentionalism can be salvaged by an alternative, which we called the plan view. We first described artefact use in terms of use plans and countered criticisms to a plan view by showing that purported limitations to our theory, which refer to skills and situated action, can be accommodated within it. Then we went on to extend our view to artefact design and artefacts. Designing was described as the construction of a use plan and possibly some subsidiary objects. We refer to these objects as 'artefacts' and ascribe functions to them via explanations of use plans. Function-talk turns out to be useful in the context of designing, but of limited use in the context of using. In the latter context, it mainly serves to communicate to users part of the designed use plan of artefacts designed for a single purpose. In this way, we have described artefacts and their use and design in terms of plans and thus salvaged the intuitively plausible intentionalist approach in the philosophy of artefacts.

## Acknowledgements

We would like to acknowledge the participants of the two 'Doing Things with Things' meetings for valuable and pleasant discussions and we would like to thank Beth Preston, David de Léon, Gustavo Ribeiro, and the Editors for their helpful comments. Research for this chapter was part of the program 'The Dual Nature of Technical Artefacts', which is supported by the Netherlands Organisation of Scientific Research (NWO).

## References

Audi, R. (1989). *Practical reasoning*. London: Routledge.

Bratman, M. (1987). *Intentions, plans and practical reason*. Cambridge, MA: Harvard University Press.

Dipert, R.R. (1995). Some issues in the theory of artefacts: Defining "artefact" and related notions, *The Monist*, *78*, 119–135.

Dreyfus, Hubert L. (1991). *Being-in-the-world. A commentary of Heidegger's* Being and Time, *Division I*. Cambridge, MA: MIT Press.

French, S. (1986). *Decision theory: An introduction to the mathematics of rationality*. Chicester, UK: Horwood.

Gero, J.S. (1990). Design prototypes: A knowledge representation schema for design, *AI Magazine*, *11*(4), 26–36.

Gibson, J.J. (1979). *The ecological approach to visual perception*. Boston: Houghton Mifflin Company.

Hilpinen, R. (1992). On artefacts and works of art, *Theoria*, *7*, 58–82.

Houkes, W., Pieter E. Vermaas, P. E., Dorst, K., & de Vries, M. J. (2002). Design and use as plans: An action-theoretical account. *Design Studies*, *23*, 303–320.

Leudar, I. & Costall, A. (1996). Situating action IV: Planning as situated action, *Ecological Psychology*, *8*, 153–170.

Miller, G.A., Galanter , E. & Pribram, K.H. (1960). *Plans and the structure of behavior*. New York: Holt, Rinehart, and Winston.

Millikan, R.G. (1999). Wings, spoons, pills, and quills: A pluralist theory of function, *Journal of Philosophy*, 96, 191–206.

Neander, K. (1991). The teleological notion of 'function', *Australasian Journal of Philosophy*, 69, 454–468.

Pollock, J.L. (1995). *Cognitive carpentry: A blueprint for how to build a person*. Cambridge, MA: MIT Press.

Preston, B. (1998). 'Why is a wing like a spoon? A pluralist theory of function', *The Journal of Philosophy*, *95*, 215–254.

Raz, J. (Ed.) (1978). *Practical reasoning*. Oxford: Oxford University Press.

Roozenburg, N.F.M. & Eekels, J. (1995). *Product design: Fundamentals and methods*. Chichester: John Wiley & Sons.

Searle, J.R. (1995). *The construction of social reality*. New York: Free Press.

Suchman, L.A. (1987). *Plans and situated action*. Cambridge: Cambridge University Press.

Vermaas, P.E. & Houkes, W. (2003). Ascribing functions to technical artefacts: A challenge to etiological accounts of functions. *British Journal for the Philosophy of Science* 54, 261–289.

Vermaas, P.E. & Houkes, W. (2006). Technical functions: A drawbridge between the intentional and structural natures of technical artefacts, *Studies in the History and Philosophy of Science*, *37*, 5–18.

# PART II
# Things in the World of the Child

Chapter 3

# Autism and Object Use: The Mutuality of the Social and Material in Children's Developing Understanding and Use of Everyday Objects

Emma Williams and Linda Kendell-Scott

When comparing human interaction to interactions amongst other animal species, social scientists have tended to centre their attention solely on language. Such a narrow focus results from a tendency to limit conceptions of the 'social' to only person-to-person interactions, as if we lived in a 'a world of actors devoid of things' (Joerges, 1988, p. 220). Recently, a number of researchers (Costall, 1995; Tomasello, 1999; Preston, 2000; Williams & Costall, 2000) have begun to question this restriction, contending that it is problematic for a number of reasons: it fails to recognise the far-reaching impact that commonplace artefacts (such as eating utensils) can have in shaping everyday human activity, including interactions with other people; it ignores the fact that we encounter objects in a social context; and neglects the role that other people play in introducing children to the 'proper' use of objects. Schiffer (1999) takes this argument a step further, proposing that the most defining attribute of human beings is not in fact language (though this is obviously important), but rather our daily interactions with innumerable kinds of things:

> ... the terms 'interpersonal' interaction and 'social' interaction which permeate publications in the social sciences, are misnomers, for nearly always artefacts – at the very least body paints, clothing and ornaments – accompany individuals in every interactional setting. Humans ... interact not with other humans *per se,* but with artefacts and humans compounded with artefacts ...What is singular about *homo sapiens* is the constant intimacy of people with countless kinds of things – our immersion in the material medium (p. 3-4).

Western Psychology, in particular, has been taken to task for underestimating the psychological significance of objects (Costall, 1995; Williams & Costall, 2000). Not only does traditional Psychology in the West neglect our relations to things, but to the limited extent that it even touches upon them they have been regarded as existing primarily in a physical, asocial realm, as distinct from the socio-cultural domain of people. In addition, many psychologists appear to be convinced that the *only* real 'object' of study is, not what people actually do and the material conditions of this action, but the internal structures and processes underlying human agency. Hutchins (1995) describes this as an over-reaction to behaviourism:

> Behaviorism had made the claim that internal mental structure was either irrelevant or nonexistent – that the study of behavior could be conducted entirely in an objective characterization of behavior itself. Cognitive science's reaction was not simply to argue that the internal mental world was important too; it took as its domain of study the internal mental environment largely separated from the external world. Interaction with the world was reduced to read and write operations conducted at either end of extensive processing activity (p. 371).

In other words, people's actions in the material world are regarded as important only to the extent that they provide clues to the 'hidden' mental activity that is going on. The 'theory of mind' approach, which has proliferated in developmental psychology from the 1980's onwards, exemplifies this emphasis on invisible internal cognitive structures. It assumes that people's minds are the sum of their beliefs, desires, emotions and intentions and that our awareness of the existence of these internal thoughts and wants enables us to explain and predict what people will do in specific situations (Astington, 1994). According to exponents of 'Theory of Mind', individuals who are unable to impute mental states to either themselves or other people, such as those suffering from autism, will experience severe difficulties in understanding and engaging successfully with other people (Leslie, 1987; Baron-Cohen, 1995).

## Psychological Theories of Autism and the Material-Social Divide

The most influential models of autism have been derived from the 'Theory of Mind' approach (e.g., Leslie, 1987; Baron-Cohen, 1995; Hobson, 1993). Baron-Cohen, Leslie and Frith (1985) proposed that autism derives from an impairment in a specific cognitive mechanism (a 'Theory of Mind' mechanism) required for second-order representations, which in turn are necessary for understanding the mental states of other people (for further information relating to this theory see Baron-Cohen, Tager-Flusberg, Cohen, & Volkmar, 1993). Baron-Cohen (1995) has recently expanded his model to take into account joint attention deficits in autism, arguing for the failure of a cognitive mechanism required to engage in shared attention, which is developmentally more primitive than the 'Theory of Mind' module, but which in turn is necessary for the development of a theory of mind. Both these models of dysfunction do not explicitly deal with our understanding of objects, as they focus on the evolution of social understanding, or even more specifically with the development of cognitive structures inside the head of the individual, which result in the understanding that other people also have things going on inside their heads. Nevertheless, their logic would predict that those activities which do not call on the use of secondary representation, such as the proper use of everyday objects, ought to be completely intact.

Contrary to this widely accepted conclusion, we propose that, given the considerable evidence from sociocultural theory and research suggesting that learning to use objects in normally developing children is an inherently social process (Leontiev, 1981; Volpert, 1985; Valsiner, 1987), it would seem reasonable to suppose that children who have trouble in relating to other people would also have extensive difficulties entering into the appropriate use of cultural tools. Our aim in this Chapter is to challenge both the notion of a rigid separation between the material and the social, and the downplaying of the psychological significance of the material world. In order to do this we first consider an important body of socio-cultural research and theory which highlights, on the one hand, the role that other people play in introducing children to objects and, on the other, the part that artefacts themselves play in structuring human activity in conventional ways. Drawing on this work, we call into question the characterisation of autism as a disorder that combines difficulties in relating to other people with 'intact' relations to objects. In contrast, we suggest that, given the evidence of the reciprocal nature of the interactions between people and objects, impairment in interpersonal relations should itself entail corresponding disruptions in the use of objects. We present evidence from a qualitative investigation of everyday object use in young children with autism in support of this proposition.[1] In this Chapter, we will use the term 'everyday object' to refer to material items that are regularly used in mealtime and washing routines and which can be manipulated by the hand, such as a toothbrush and cutlery. Our findings suggest that, as a consequence of disruptions experienced in relating to other people, children with autism have more limited opportunities to pick up the social conventions surrounding the use of everyday objects than children without this condition. They may also have difficulty in picking up the notion of 'properness' itself – an understanding of the fact that most artefacts have a single, definite, culturally selected, function. The results also suggest that the tendency of children with autism to relate idiosyncratically to objects may add an additional obstacle to their ability to acquire the proper use of everyday objects from other people.

## The Social Mediation of Object Use

Not all Psychology neglects the role of objects in our social life. Within developmental psychology there is an important body of 'socio-cultural' theory and research, largely drawing upon the tradition of Soviet psychology, that does challenge any rigid separation of the social and the material in children's developing understanding of their surroundings. Proponents of this approach argue that our dealings with people and with objects do not occur in mutual isolation (Leontiev, 1981; Volpert, 1985; Valsiner, 1987). And this is true not only for adults but all the more so for infants and young children.

---

1 Full details of the study can be found in Williams, Kendell-Scott and Costall, (2005) 'Parents' experiences of introducing everyday object use to children with autism', *Autism* 9, 495–514.

According to Valsiner (1987), a number of factors dovetail to ensure the cultural canalisation of infants' use of everyday artefacts: direct and indirect guidance by caregivers (and older siblings), the child's own eagerness to participate in the activities of the adults around them, and the nature of the object itself. Valsiner carried out a small number of longitudinal case studies in which mothers and their infants were videotaped interacting during mealtime sessions. The infants were followed from the age of 7 or 8 months to 2 years, during which time they were visited by the investigators every 2–4 months. Mothers were observed using a number of different techniques aimed at channelling their child's attention and skill in using the implements they were given in culturally appropriate ways. This included structuring the wider setting in such a way as to promote desired actions, whilst discouraging undesirable ones. For example, in teaching their child to use a spoon or fork correctly, the parent usually placed the infant in a high-chair, restricting their freedom of movement, and moved distracting objects out of the way. Only then was the cutlery presented, at the appropriate orientation, to the child. Brief and intermittent periods of joint action tended to occur in the early stages of an infant learning to use a particular implement. Either the mother placed her hands over those of the child, who was holding the object, and physically guided their action, or they performed a sub-part of an action, such as loading a spoon or fork, leaving the child to do the rest. As the children became more adept at using the cutlery, the mothers were more likely either to verbally prompt the child, for example if they became distracted from the task in hand, or to use verbal encouragement when the child was performing the correct action.

Valsiner (1987) proposed that only short and episodic periods of intensive instruction by the parent may be required, as the child's interest in what other people are doing and their willingness to copy them would ensure that the child's actions will, eventually, be canalised even without direct intervention: 'If a child misses being explicitly taught a specifically relevant skill, this child may acquire it himself on the basis of observation and trying' (p.179).

It is important to note that the participants in Valsiner's study were white middle-class Americans and, therefore, the observations he made cannot necessarily be generalised to other cultures. However, there is evidence to suggest that, whilst there are cultural differences in the extent of adult mediation and in the specific cultural messages which are conveyed to infants about objects, adults in all cultures comment and instruct at least occasionally (Bakeman, Adamson, Konner & Barr, 1990; Tomasello, 1999).

Social influence, however, does not simply occur *around* objects, but *through* them. Our world has already been shaped by human activity, and is full of things designed by people to be used in specific human activities, by people who share a common body shape, needs & cultural history. Artefacts such as a child's toothbrush provide a means by which the child appropriates new action schemes, and in so doing enters into the shared practices of society (Volpert, 1985). Furthermore, the child's eating behaviour is not only shaped through the direct and indirect guidance of the more culturally experienced people around them, but also through the very form of the artefacts commonly used at mealtimes (Leontiev, 1981; Valsiner, 1987; Preston,

2000; Williams & Costall, 2000). Their design reflects society's expectations for children to become socialised eaters. Preston (2000) argues that appropriate eating behaviour at the table is organised systematically with regard to the proper functions of the tableware: 'Take cutlery in Western culture. Forks, spoons and knives have a specific set of eating functions which are proper to them, and these functions govern the behaviour we call table manners' (p.41). According to Valsiner (1987), the cultural canalisation of children's actions starts from 'the coding of some suggestive cultural messages into the form and function of objects' themselves (p.173). Objects intended specifically for children are not simply scaled down versions of those used by adults, but are often specifically constructed in such away as to further constrain and guide the infant's activity. For example curved cutlery, 'Anywayup' beakers, and 'Doydy' cups, whose lip is slanted in such a way as to require less tipping by the child to get the liquid into the mouth.

## Autism and the Conventional Use of Everyday Objects

In the light of the body of 'socio-cultural' research and theory that clearly challenges any rigid separation of the social and the material in children's developing understanding of their surroundings, it would seem highly unlikely that the problems associated with autism, whatever its underlying 'cause', would be restricted, in any clear cut way, to a particular 'domain' of the child's life, such as his or her relations with other people. If the child's relations with people are disrupted, then their understanding and use of objects should also be impaired – and *vice versa.* However, in spite of this there is little published evidence concerning the problems, if any, experienced by parents in training a child with autism to use them. In our review of the literature we were able to identify only one empirical study (Ungerer & Sigman, 1981) which bears on the subject of everyday object use in children with autism, with the remaining, limited, information coming from case study reports.

As part of an investigation into the relationship between play and language, Ungerer & Sigman (1981) assessed the ability of 16 children with autism (Mental age=24.8 months; Chronological age=51.7 months) to use the objects they encountered in their daily environment appropriately. At the time of the study all the children were inpatients at a neuropsychiatric institute. Their primary nursing staff were asked to complete a checklist consisting of 62 objects commonly found in the home and residential hospital setting, including eating utensils, items used in grooming, books, telephones and pencils. For each object listed, the staff were asked to record whether the child could use it spontaneously, whether they could use it if verbally prompted, or whether, even with verbal prompting they were unable to use the object according to its designated function. Of the 62 objects surveyed, the children were able to use, on average, just under 60% appropriately either on their own or with verbal prompting. A mean of 25% were reported as never having been used appropriately, even with a verbal cue. The children's ability to use the remainder could not be assessed, either because they were unavailable for use by the child or because the primary caretaker was unable to give any information regarding them. Methodological problems with this study, however, make it difficult to draw precise conclusions with regard to how proficient children with autism actually are in their use of everyday objects. Firstly, it is not clear to what extent verbal prompting was required for the child to use the object in an appropriate manner, as the children's ability to use the objects on their own or only with a verbal cue were not analysed separately. Secondly, no comparative data were collected from a comparison group of typically developing children or children with learning difficulties of an equivalent developmental age.

Case study reports appear to present a less positive picture of the acquisition of everyday object use by children with autism than that suggested by Ungerer and Sigman (1981). Asperger (1944, p. 39) notes the difficulties experienced by parents in getting their children to eat normally at the meal table. Park (1983) also describes the difficulties her daughter with autism had with using spoons and cups. Her ability to use these things was much delayed and she had to be intensively trained in order to use them appropriately. Although she did spontaneously use a spoon at 15 months, this occurred only once, after which she refused even to hold a spoon until she was over two-and-a-half. The use of other everyday objects, such as taps and light switches, also had to be extensively trained, using the hand-over-hand method, with periods of retraining required when her daughter encountered an unfamiliar version of the same object. A striking feature of some self-reports and adult recollections of highly functioning children with autism is the extreme affective responses provoked by certain commonplace artefacts (Bemporad, 1984; Volkmar & Cohen, 1985; Grandin and Scariano, 1986). Whilst some everyday objects appear to be a source of deep fascination (Bosch, 1970), others give rise to unusual fears (Darr & Worden, 1951). Such evidence indicates that children with autism may experience some difficulty entering into the conventional uses of objects.

## A Comparative Study of Everyday Object use in Children with Autism

We decided to conduct a comparative investigation of the acquisition of everyday object use in children with autism, children with Down syndrome and typically developing children[2] with two main aims in mind. Firstly, we wanted to carry out an empirical investigation that examined systematically the notion that object use is socially mediated, in order to complement the findings obtained from the case studies conducted by Valsiner (1987). Secondly, we wanted to investigate whether disturbances in relating to other people, such as those experienced by children with autism, would have a disruptive effect on their ability to pick up the social conventions surrounding those objects used in everyday routines. In addition, the

2 In autism research it is standard practice to include 2 comparison groups, consisting of typical children and learning disabled children, in order to determine what aspect of any behaviours identified are attributable to the autism and what simply reflects general difficulties in learning (Burack, 1997).

findings obtained from the little research that has been conducted in this area to date are difficult to interpret, due to fundamental methodological flaws.

Semi-structured interviews were administered, asking the parents (10 in each group) to describe their child's current use of objects traditionally used during mealtime and washing routines, the process by which their child learnt to use these objects appropriately, and any problems they encountered in attempting to guide their child's actions. The groups of children were individually matched for general developmental age (23 months) using the second edition of the Bayley Scales of Infant Development (BSID II; Bayley, 1993). Each child with autism was matched to one child with Down syndrome and one typically developing child.

Following transcription a detailed examination of the interview transcripts was undertaken following the guidelines outlined by Giorgi (1985), which combine phenomenological and content analysis. In this approach, although some presuppositions of the investigators may serve to structure the findings, the participants' own descriptions of their experiences form the primary basis for understanding the particular phenomenon under investigation. In this study these were the parents' own descriptions of their experiences in introducing their children to the appropriate use of everyday objects, and in monitoring that usage once it was established (for further applications of this methodology, see Hétu, Riverin, Lalande, Getty & St-Cyr, 1988 and Yardley, Todd, Lacoudraye-Harter & Ingham, 1992). The process of analysis consisted of the following three stages:

*Stage 1*

All statements referring to the following themes were identified and isolated from the rest of the transcript: problems experienced by parents in introducing their children to, and maintaining, the appropriate use of an object; specific parental strategies designed to introduce children to the proper use of an object; and any means identified by the parents by which they thought their child had come to use a particular object in a conventional manner. Once identified, the statements were broken down into the smallest unit that allowed for the sense of the statement to remain intact[3] (Yardley *et al.*, 1992). This process yielded approximately 1,500 statements in total.[4]

3 The origin of the interview data (i.e. which parent-child pair and which group the participants were allocated to) was recorded by each statement, using a letter and number system in order to preserve confidentiality. In addition the context was preserved in square brackets where this was essential to making sense of a statement.

4 Reliability in terms of isolating statements from the transcripts was checked by having a second investigator code approximately 30% of the transcripts (3 from each group), yielding a mean percentage agreement of 85% (range, 77–90%).

*Stage 2*

Progressive categorisation was undertaken to structure the data and a series of inter-rater comparisons employed to ensure that the category definitions arrived at reflected the nature of the statements assigned to them as closely as possible. Based on the themes identified by the list of statements isolated from the transcripts, a first classification scheme was arrived at through the consultation of the two authors. Two of the main categories (parental strategies and problems in introducing objects) were pre-selected as the interview schedule had been designed to elicit information relating to these topics. The other main categories, non-parental influences and child role, as well as all the subcategories emerged directly from the statements made by the parents. Following Yardley *et al.* (1992), flow-charts were compiled which outlined the rules used to classify each particular statement into its appropriate subcategory.

*Stage 3*

The statements within each subcategory were then represented by 'summary statements', presented in the form of comparative tables, which indicated the number of parents in each group who had reported them.[5]

The findings below are presented under the headings 'the social mediation of object use' and 'cultural canalisation of everyday object use'. This division is an analytical, rather than conceptual, one. Its purpose is simply to present clearly for the reader both the influence of other people on object use and the role played by the object itself in shaping the child's activity. It should not be taken as implying a rigid distinction between relations to people and relations to objects, which are viewed as interdependent.

## The Social Mediation of Object Use

Valsiner's (1987) contention that the social canalisation of the motor functions of the developing child towards culturally-specific ways of using objects is over-determined, in the sense that there is more than one route via which a child can come to use an everyday object in a conventional manner, was clearly supported by the findings from the study. Almost without exception, the parents in the typical and Down groups spontaneously reported that their child's object use was shaped, not only through conscious instruction by them, but also indirectly through the child's exposure to other people's (particularly family members and peers) conventional use of particular everyday objects:

5 Only summary statements based on the accounts of *at least* four parents from any of the groups, or ten parents overall (i.e. a third of the total sample) were included in the summary tables.

> In the highchair he would sit with just his food on a tray, a plate and a cup, and we would sit at the table with a mat and stuff. And quite often he would reach from his highchair for a coaster and bring the coaster onto his highchair, and put his cup on the coaster to show that he was copying us ... (child 6, typical).

> He loves eating and he loves being part of a group and loves to be seen to be the same as everybody else, and so because everybody else in the nursery and his school are using a fork he has a good bash (child 10, Down).

According to all these parents, their children showed signs of actively participating in the pick up of the conventions surrounding object use. This was demonstrated by their interest in, and copying of, other people's actions on objects, their desire to use a particular object when they saw someone else doing so, and their initiation of the introduction of an object themselves by asking their parent for it.

In stark contrast to the parents in both comparison groups, those who had children with autism reported more problems in introducing appropriate object use, less active involvement on the part of their child and, the use of more intensive teaching methods. They described their children as lacking interest; both in what other people are doing with objects, and in reproducing these actions: 'There can be a whole load of children around the table, and they will be tucking into lovely food. She will not be motivated by any of them. She will do her own thing' (child 10, autism); 'It seems to me L. [sibling] does things by example. She would just look at what you are doing, and she will just copy it because that's the way it should be done, because an adult does it ... but with B. [child with autism], you have to teach him how to do something.' (child 9, autism). In addition, half of the parents of children with autism reported that their child refused to eat at the table with other family members. This means that even if the child was motivated to copy other people's use of various eating utensils, the opportunity is simply not there:

> He wouldn't eat his yoghurt if anyone was in the room. I had to show him the bowl outside the room, put the bowl in here, and he would see me put it in here and then we would have to go ... the whole family would have to stay out of the room until he had finished (child 5, autism).

In addition, only one parent of a child with autism made a positive statement indicating that her child watched what other people did with objects, and this was only after the child had spent several weeks participating in an intensive training programme, which involved the explicit modelling of actions to the child. Finally, no parent mentioned that his or her child was motivated to use an object by seeing someone else do so, or that they ever initiated the introduction of an object themselves.

Parents of children with autism predominantly reported using physical methods of instruction, and needing to successively repeat verbal prompts and demonstrations, as well as emphasising the importance of structured intervention by the school.[6] These are all consistent with a failure of more indirect means of social transmission.

Whereas the redundancy typically present in the socialisation of object use means that the task of shaping children's utensil use usually takes the form of episodic instruction by an adult (or older sibling), rather than that of an intensive instruction session, the absence of such over-determination in the case of children with autism leaves their caregivers reliant on more structured, 'intensive', teaching methods if they are to achieve success. The greater, conscious, effort needed on the part of parents who have children with autism to shape the developing motor functions of their child toward objects in culturally specific ways is made particularly clear in the comparisons they draw between their child with autism and that child's non-autistic sibling. For example:

> I don't remember having to teach him [older brother] particularly you know, there must have been a little bit there, but not that I remember [but] everything with J. had to be taught, and reminded to go carefully. And remind him when he was putting it to his mouth [spoon]…it was literally saying over and over again (child 4, autism).

In contrast, several parents of typically developing children remarked on the ease by which their child seemed to pick up the conventional use of everyday objects. Some referred to the progress as a 'natural' one: 'I don't think it is a strategy [getting the child to use an object appropriately]. I think it is something that comes naturally' (child 8, typical); 'he is generally very good at wanting to go on to the next thing, as it were, and we just sort of leave it to be quite a natural progression'. (child 6, typical). Other parents remarked that their child seemed to acquire the ability to use a particular object 'spontaneously': 'well I never had to show him how to put it to his mouth, he just understood that it needed to go into his mouth'(child 1, typical); 'you start with a spoon, and … then you give him a fork when it is a more appropriate thing to eat the meal with, and then you just … you know …one day they are just using a knife…' (child 10, typical).

An alternative, although not necessarily mutually exclusive, explanation is that children with autism may fail to enter into the notion of 'properness' itself. Loveland (1991) has argued that autism involves a specific impairment not only in the child's ability to detect the significance of other people's activity (e.g. the direction of gaze, facial gesture, non-verbal gesture, speech), for their own action, but also a failure to appreciate that most of the objects they encounter have a single, definite, culturally-selected or preferred function In other words, they fail not only to discover the preferred meanings of particular object, but also do not develop a sense that objects *in general* normally have a definite function.

6 Whilst parents who had children with Down syndrome also described a heavy use of physical methods, this was reported to occur as a result of motor difficulties or 'laziness' on the part of the their child. They also reported using a wider range of strategies than did parents of children with autism.

## Cultural Canalisation Through Everyday Objects

The results also suggested that the tendency of children with autism to relate idiosyncratically to objects might add an additional obstacle to the difficulties they already have in entering into meaningful relations with other people. When questioned about their child's use of everyday objects, only parents of children with autism reported that their child's odd use of certain objects, or interest in isolated aspects of an object, interfered with attempts to get the child to use the object in an appropriate way. In other words, rather than the physical form of the object providing an additional source of cultural influence by helping to shape the child's action in conventional ways, the child's atypical reaction to the object actually becomes a barrier to the introduction and maintenance of appropriate object use by the caregiver.

All parents who had children with autism mentioned a problem relating to the object itself compared to only four parents of children with Down syndrome (when inexpert use and motor problems are excluded), and one parent of a typically developing child. Seven out of the ten parents in the autism group remarked that their child's own particular interests/ obsessions actually interfered with the parent's attempts to get the child to use an object, such as a cup, in the appropriate way. For example in the following statements the child's interest in pouring or in whatever was depicted on the cup, led the child to use the object inappropriately:

> He was easy to change from a teat to a spout. Not quite so hot going from a cup with a lid to a cup with a lid off because he had this thing in those days about pouring…so it was always very tempting for him to want to pour (child 8, autism).

> A cup is not like a vessel for drinking out of, a cup is a toy. Whatever is on the cup is the thing that he will play with. So if it's Thomas [the tank engine] on the cup it will just go straight over…drink comes out and he will just look at it whilst lying down (child 9, autism).

Another parent in this group compared their child's co-option of a set of coloured pencils or crayons for their own particular interest in lining things up in coloured sequences, with the conventional use of the same set of objects by the child's sister who did not have autistim:

> K. (sibling) wanted to scribble or draw with crayons or pencils because we introduced them to her … she would copy. With L. (child with autism) we showed her what to do. No, no, she did not want to. In fact, drawing and painting was something she did not want to do at all. She wanted to line them all up, all the pencils we had. She wanted to line them all up, … she had a different interest. They were colourful, so she was motivated by colour and the fact that they were similar objects, so she wanted to line them all up (child 10, autism).

A further problem identified from the interview statements of those parents who had children with autism was an unusual use of certain objects, particularly items of cutlery:

> When he first used his spoon he always used it upside down for some strange reason. He would always put the stuff on upside down and he would, somehow when he got to his mouth he would quickly ... he would scoop it up the right way, then when he got to his mouth he would turn it, so that he would always be using it upside down (child 3, autism).

> It's [the spoon] in his hand and it's used to scoop, but he doesn't actually put it in his mouth, it's used to pour the yoghurt into his hand, rather than put in his mouth (child 5, autism).

It is important to note, though, that these findings do not address whether it is unusual relations to objects or disturbances in joint attention that come first in development. To investigate the direction of causality, as well as the extent to which earlier forms of play underpin later ones, longitudinal studies would need to be undertaken. Ideally, these should be prospective, following children identified at a very young age as being at risk from autism.[7] However, whether or not idiosyncratic relations to objects precede deficits in joint attention, it is argued that they are likely to have a cascading, disruptive, effect on other aspects of development, given the evidence suggesting that play with, and exploration of, objects are primary modes of interpersonal interaction and learning (Bakeman & Adamson, 1984; McArthur & Adamson, 1996).

## Conclusion

In stressing the problems young children with autism have in using objects in a conventional manner, it has not been the purpose of this chapter to play down the social dimension of autism in favour of a material one. Rather, the aim has been to challenge the rigid dualism between the social and the material, which underlies most current theories of autism. It is suggested that those theories of autism deriving from the 'theory of mind' approach fail to make the link between difficulties in understanding others and relations to things, as a result of a failure to appreciate fully the importance of social mediation, including various aspects of joint attention, in the education of the child's attention towards the function of things. Challenging this rigid social-material divide necessarily involves questioning the restricted use of the term 'social' as referring only to relations to other people. In highlighting the reciprocal nature of the interactions between the child, other people, *and* objects,

---

7 The recent development of screening instruments for autism, such as the CHAT and M-CHAT, make this an increasing possibility, although considerable work still needs to be done to increase their sensitivity and positive predictive power (Baron-Cohen *et al.*, 1992; Baird *et al*, 2000; Filipek *et al.*, 2000; Robins, Fein, Barton & Green, 2001).

the findings from the studies presented here indicate that relations to objects cannot, in fact, be considered outside of the social context in which they are introduced and used. Nor can they be examined apart from the human activities they shape in common ways. Furthermore, this is not simply a theoretical problem, but also a practical one. If we are to devise successful interventions for individuals with autism it is essential that we fully appreciate the inter-penetration between different areas of development, including the child's dealings with objects and other people.

## References


American Psychiatric Association. (1994). *Diagnostic and statistical manual of mental disorders* (4th ed., rev.). Washington, DC: American Psychiatric Association.

Asperger, H. (1991). Autistic psychopathology in childhood. In U. Frith (Ed.), *Autism and Asperger syndrome* (pp. 37–92). Cambridge, UK: Cambridge University Press.

Asperger, H. (1944). Die 'Autistischen psychopathen' im kindesalter. *Archiv für Psychiatrie und Nervenkrankheiten, 117,* 76–136.

Astington, J.W. (1994). *The child's discovery of the mind.* London: Fontana Press.

Bakeman, R. & Adamson, L.B. (1984). Co-ordinating attention to people and object in mother-infant and peer-infant interaction. *Child Development, 55,* 1278–1289.

Bakeman, R., Adamson, L.B., Konner, M. & Barr, R.G. (1990). Kung infancy: The social context of object exploration. *Child Development, 61,* 794–809.

Baird, G., Charman, T., Baron-Cohen, S. Cox, A. Swettenham, J., Wheelwright, S. & Drew, A. (2000). A screening instrument for autism at 18 month age: A six-year follow-up study. *Journal of the Academy of Child Adolescent Psychiatry, 39*, 694–702.

Baron-Cohen, S. (1987). Autism and symbolic play. *British Journal of Developmental Psychology*, *5*, 139–148.

Baron-Cohen, S. (1995). *Mindblindness: An essay on autism and theory of mind.* Cambridge, MA: The MIT Press.

Baron-Cohen, S., Allen, J. & Gillberg, C. (1992). Can autism be detected at 18 months? The needle, the haystack and the CHAT. *British Journal of Psychiatry, 161*, 839–843.

Baron-Cohen, S., Leslie, A.M. & Frith, U. (1985). Does the autistic child have a 'Theory of Mind'? *Cognition, 21,* 37–46.

Baron-Cohen, S., Tager-Flusberg, H., Cohen, D. & Volkmar, F. (Eds.). (1993). *Understanding other minds: Perspectives from autism.* Oxford, UK: Oxford University Press.

Bayley, N. (1993). *Bayley Scales of Infant Development, Second Edition.* San Antonio, Harcourt Brace.

Bemporad, J.R. (1984). Recollections of a formerly autistic child. *Journal of Autism and Developmental Disorders*, *14*, 85–104.

Bosch, G. (1970). *Infantile autism: A clinical and phenomenological-anthropological investigation taking language as the guide*. New York: Springer.

Bugrimenko, E.A. & Smirnova, E.O. (1992). Paradoxes of children's play in Vygotsky's theory. In G.C. Cupchik & J. Laszlo (Eds.), *Emerging visions of the aesthetic process* (pp. 286–299). New York: Cambridge University Press.

Burack, J.A. (1997). The study of atypical and typical populations in developmental psychopathology: the quest for a common science, in S.S. Luthar, J.A. Burack, D. Cicchetti, J.R. Weisz, & D.J. Cohen (Eds.), *Developmental Psychopathology: Perspectives on Adjustment, Risk and Disorder* (pp. 139–165). Cambridge University Press.

Costall, A.P. (1995). Socialising affordances. *Theory and Psychology*, *5*, 467–482.

Darr, G.C. & Worden, F.G. (1951). Case report twenty-eight years after an infantile autistic disorder. *American Journal of Orthopsychiatry*, *21,* 559–570.

Dawson, G. (1991). A psychobiological perspective on the early socioemotional development of children with autism. In S. Toth & D. Cicchetti (Eds.), *Rochester symposium on developmental psychopathology* (Vol. 3, pp. 207–234). Hillsdale, NJ: Lawrence Erlbaum.

Filipek, P.A., Accardo, P.J., Ashwal, S., Baranek, G.T., Cook, E.H., Dawson, G., Gordon, B., Gravel, J.S., Johnson, C.P., Kallen, R.J., Levy, S.E. Minshew, N.J., Ozonoff, S., Prizant, B.M., Rapin, I., Rogers, S.J., Stone, W.L., Teplin, S.W., Tuchman, R.F. & Volkmar, F.R. (2000). Practice parameter: Screening and diagnosis of autism. Report of the Quality Standards Subcommittee of the American Academy of Neurology and the Child Neurology Society. *Neurology*, *55*, 468–479.

Frith, U. (1989). *Autism: explaining the enigma*. Oxford, UK: Basil Blackwell.

Giorgi, A. (1985). Sketch of a psychological phenomenological method. In A.Giorgi (Ed.), *Phenomenological and psychological research* (pp. 8–22). Pittsburgh, PA: Duquesne University Press.

Grandin, T. & Scariano, M. M. (1986). *Emergence labelled autistic*. Tunbridge Wells, U.K.: Costello.

Hétu, R., Riverin, L., Lalande, N., Getty, L. & St-Cyr, C. (1988). Qualitative analysis of the handicap associated with hearing loss. *British Journal of Audiology*, *22*, 251–264.

Hobson, R.P. (1993). *Autism and the development of mind*. Hillsdale, NJ: Lawrence Erlbaum.

Hutchins, E. (1995). *Cognition in the wild*. Cambridge, MA: MIT Press.

Joerges, B. (1988). Technology in everyday life: Conceptual queries. *Journal for the Theory of Social Behaviour*, *18*, 221–237.

Leontiev, A.N. (1981). *Problems of the development of mind*. Moscow: Progress Publishers.

Leslie, A. (1987). Pretence and representation in infancy: Origins of 'theory of mind'. *Psychological Review*, *94*, 84–106.

McArthur, D. & Adamson, L.B. (1996). Joint attention in preverbal children: Autism and developmental language disorder. *Journal of Autism and Developmental*

*Disorders*, *26*, 481–496.
Mundy, P. (1995). Joint attention and socio-emotional approach behaviour in children with autism. *Development and Psychopathology*, *7*, 63–2.
Park, C.C. (1983). *The Siege: The first years of an autistic child with an epilogue, fifteen years after.* London: Hutchinson.
Preston, B. (2000). The functions of things: a philosophical perspective on material culture. In P.M. Graves-Brown (Ed.), *Matter, materiality and modern culture.* (pp. 22–49). London: Routledge.
Robins, D., Fein, D., Barton, M.L. & Green, J.A. (2001). The modified checklist for autism in toddlers: An initial study investigating the early detection of autism and pervasive developmental disorders. *Journal of Autism and Developmental Disorders*, *14*, 131–44.
Schiffer, M.B. (1999). *The material life of human beings: Artifacts, behaviour, and communication.* London: Routledge.
Szokolszky, A. (2001). Using an object as if it were another. The perception and use of affordances in pretend object play. In A. Szokolszky & E. Williams (Chair), Taking 'things' more seriously: The role of objects in constraining developing action structures in typical children and children with autism. Symposium, The Tenth European Conference on Developmental Psychology, University of Uppsala, Sweden.
Tomasello, M. (1999). The cultural ecology of young children's interactions with objects and artefacts. In E. Winograd, R. Fivush & W. Hirst (Eds.), *Ecological approaches to cognition: Essays in honour of Ulric Neisser* (pp. 153–170). Mahweh, NJ: Lawrence Erlbaum.
Ungerer, J.A. & Sigman, M. (1981). Symbolic play and language comprehension in autistic children. *Journal of the American Academy of Child Psychiatry*, *20,* 318–337.
Valsiner, J. (1987). *Culture and the development of children's action: a cultural-historical theory of developmental psychology.* New York: John Wiley.
Volkmar, F.R. & Cohen, D.J. (1985). Infantile autism: A first-person account by Tony W. *Journal of Autism and Developmental Disorders*, *15*, 47–54.
Volpert, W. (1985). Epilogue. In M. Frese and J. Sabini (Eds.), *Goal-directed behaviour: the concept of action in psychology* (pp. 357–365). Hillsdale, NJ: Lawrence Erlbaum.
Williams, E. & Costall, A. (2000). The functions of things: a philosophical perspective on material culture. In P.M. Graves-Brown (Ed.), *Matter, materiality and modern culture* (pp. 97–111). London: Routledge.
Williams, E., Costall, A. & Reddy, V. (1999). Children with autism experience problems with both objects and people. *Journal of Autism and Developmental Disorders*, *29*, 367–378.
World Health Organisation. (1990). *International Classification of Diseases*, 10th edn. Diagnostic Criteria for Research (draft). Geneva: WHO.
Yardley, L., Todd, A.M., Lacoudraye-Harter, M.M. & Ingham, R. (1992). Psychological consequences of recurrent vertigo. *Psychology and Health*, *6*, 85–96.

Chapter 4

# Object Use in Pretend Play: Symbolic or Functional?

Ágnes Szokolsky

One evening I was playing with my two-and-a-half-year old son in the bedroom. Suddenly he suggested playing cooking; he grabbed a pillow from the bed, put it on the floor and said to me: '*This is the stove and I am making a soup*'. He paused as if looking for something to serve as a pot, then said: '*I am making bread*' and he started to knead the pillow. Soon he claimed that the bread was done and he was going to cut it. He picked up another pillow right away and holding it vertically, imitated cutting. This kind of pretend play, in which the child knows the object for what it is but chooses to treat it as if it were a different kind of object, is a universal dimension in play from the age of two, across various cultures (Haight, Wang, Fung, Williams, Mintz, 1999).

Psychologists have been traditionally interested in pretend play because it appears to involve the increasing symbolic capacity to treat objects representationally. Pretend object play seems to be a sophisticated cognitive activity that implies the ability (a) to think of one object as two things at once, (b) to think of one object as representing another, and (c) to represent mental representations. That the manipulation of mental representations is the primary driving force and explanatory principle behind pretense is, in fact, generally not argued but taken as axiomatic. The pretend act of using a block as a horse is self-evidently described as a process in which 'one employs one's own mental representation of the block and applies that representation to the horse' (Lillard, 1993a, p.373). Neo-Piagetian research focused on how children choose pretend objects and found evidence for symbolicity increasing with age. More recent research found new theoretical significance in pretense because it seems to open a window on the child's developing theory of mind inasmuch as it involves the understanding that the mind has internal symbolic contents that represent the world and the ability to represent the mental state of another person. For this reason, Alan Leslie (1987, p. 416) has suggested that 'the emergence of pretense is not seen as a development in the understanding of objects and events as such, but rather as the beginnings of a capacity to understand cognition itself'.

In this chapter I argue for an alternative functionalist-ecological view on pretend object play. Pretense involves culturally mediated, structured and sequenced actions that are recreated in a highly 'compressed' way. Objects play a central role in such activities. I suggest that in pretend object play the child's intention to realize a play theme leads her/him to use an available object functionally in place of the real object. Functional properties of interest are defined by the demand of the pretend action. However, perceiving a functional property can also make the child modify his original intention. In the above example, when launching the play theme the child used the pillow as a stove and had the idea of making soup. Then he changed his idea from making soup to making bread, probably because baking bread was an activity in which he had previously participated and also because he realized that the pillow was perfectly knead-able. As the play theme unfolded, the action of cutting the bread came into focus – the child needed an object that could be used as a knife. Without hesitation he grabbed another pillow and used it as if it were a knife.

From an external point of view, a pillow is very good for a dough but not so good for a knife. However, pretend objects need to support pretend acts, not real acts; a pretend knife does not need to afford cutting, it only needs to afford *pretend cutting* which is a much less definite act than real cutting. The task of the child is to select an object that is *good enough* to support the enactment. As long as the object functionally fits the pretend act well, the action looks very much as it would with the real object. When the the object is functionally less fit for the pretend act, the child compensates for the deficiency by making the best possible use of the object (such as when holding the pillow vertically so that it has an edge and moving it to and fro over the 'bread'). In neither case is the pretend object 'standing for' the target object as a detached representation. Rather, the pretend object is integrated into the action as a partial embodiment of the target object, supporting the pretend act.

The approach taken here suggests that pretend object play is a perceptually grounded activity that involves perceiving and using functionally relevant properties of objects. Such functional properties are best defined as *affordances*. In the ecological psychology of James and Eleanor Gibson, affordances are directly meaningful functional object properties that specify potential actions for a given actor, with a given intention (J. J. Gibson, 1979, E. J. Gibson, 1982). For an actor intending to grasp an object or walk on a surface, the object must be graspable and the surface must be walk-on-able. Graspability or walk-on-ability are not functional properties in the traditional sense. Traditionally, functional properties are taken to be predetermined properties of objects that define what the object is good for – pillows are for sleeping, and knives are for cutting. Affordances, on the other hand, are defined as action potentials in relation to the particular actor at a more basic level of on-line coordination with the object world. When climbing a stair, reaching for an object or walking through an aperture, we perceive and use affordances (Mark, 1987; Warren, and Wang, 1987; Carello et al., 1989). Infants detect affordances (e.g. Walker, 1982, Gibson and Walker, 1984, Adolph, Eppler and Gibson, 1993) and affordances provide a basis for object categorization and tool use (Smitsman and Pick, 1982; Smitsman, Loosbroek and Pick, 1987; Pick and Heinrichs, 1989; Leeuwen et al., 1994).

Any object has an immense number of action possibilities, but these cannot be known in advance, in separation from the actor and the action (Costall, 1995). In the course of everyday actions we routinely use objects differently from what they are meant for; we may rest our legs on the table, use a heavy book to press a wrinkled piece of paper, and so on. Unconventional object use deviates from culturally prescribed object use, even though it still involves the use of affordances. Tomasello suggested that in using artifacts children use the 'intentional affordance' of the object – what the object is culturally made for. In pretense the child directly perceives the intentional affordance of the pretend object and then, in a second step, 'decouples' it from the object so that the 'inappropriate' object can be used playfully, as a symbol. He also notes, however, that this process is 'very poorly understood at this point' (Tomasello, 1999, p. 158, p.160). I agree but I suggest that better understanding will stem from viewing pretend object play as the proper use of available affordances. Certainly, the available affordances of objects differ in their appropriateness to be used as the target object. But children are satisfied with using a good-enough affordance and fine-tune the action accordingly. Mentally 'decoupling' the culturally preferred affordance does not present a profound problem because knowing what the object is made for is not essential for the actual use of affordances.

## The Symbolic Framework and its Underlying Assumptions

Piaget and Vygotsky presented the background from which modern cognitive views about pretend play have derived. Piaget's widely accepted account of pretend play was an extension of his general theory of play (1962). According to Piaget, play 'manifests the peculiarity of a primacy of assimilation over accommodation which permits it to transform reality in its own manner without submitting that transformation to the criterion of objective fact' (1971, p. 338). Viewed as a subordination of reality to the desires of the self, play could not be a significant factor of cognitive growth. Play is some sort of compensation for the inadequacy of cognitive development; it exists because thought is not yet adequate to its task. Pretense, however, plays a significant role in cognitive development, because it is the beginning of the differentiation between the signified and the signifier. The differentiation rests initially on an iconic relationship in which signified and signifier are closely linked and perceptually similar, as when reenacting one's own activities (pretend sleeping), or when a toy car is used as a car. With development the differentiation grows into a more developed form of symbolism, when signified and signifier are related more arbitrarily, although this relationship never reaches the fully-fledged arbitrariness of linguistic signs.

Vygtosky's account of play (1976) contained two somewhat contradictory lines of argument. On the one hand, he presented an anti-intellectualistic position, implicitly criticizing Piaget. He warned that theories of play tend to view the child as a theoretical being: 'If play is to be understood as symbolic, there is the danger that it might turn into a kind of activity akin to algebra in action. ... Here we look upon the child as an unsuccessful algebraist who cannot yet write the symbols on paper, but depicts them in action' (p. 540). Purely cognitive accounts neglect the affective side of play and also the actual circumstances of the child's activity, he claimed. At the heart of pretend play is not the beginnings of symbols but imaginative situations and the practicing of social rules. Vygotsky and his followers concentrated on the function of activity in establishing pretend relationships between object and word. Based on the experimental work of Bugrimenko and Smirnova (1992), they concluded among other things that for object substitution the important condition was that the child was able to act with the object in certain ways. On the other hand, Vygotsky (1976) argued that in play the child is liberated from situational constraints. With development in imaginary play 'thought is separated from the object and action arises from ideas (rules) rather than from things' (p.546). Separation of meaning and object is a gradual process, which needs, in the beginning, a 'material pivot to keep the meaning from evaporating' (p.548). Thus, pretend play is a transitional stage at which the child cannot yet separate the thought from the object, and so must have a substitute object. The substitute object is not a symbol, only a reflection of the process in which the semantic aspect moves from a subordinate to a dominating position. At the same time, the specific properties of the pivot are still relevant; thus, for a child a postcard, for example, can never serve as a pretend horse.

Based on Piaget's legacy, a distinctively cognitive research program took shape in the 1970's and 1980's (Fein, 1975, Lowe, 1975, Nicolich, 1977, Watson and Fisher, 1977, Jakowitz and Watson, 1980, Kagan, 1981, Pederson, Rook-Green and Elder, 1981, Ungerer, Zelazo, Kearsley, and O'Leary, 1981, Crum, Thornburg, Benninga, and Bridge, 1983, Winner, 1988). Experimental studies on solitary pretend object play provided children with a range of possible substitute objects to determine children's capacity and willingness to use one object as if it were another. In a typical study, such as Elder and Pederson (1978), substitute objects differed from the target object in similarity of size and shape and also in having a definite conventional identity or not. Children between 2.5, and 3.5 years of age were asked to perform pretend actions (1) with similar objects that had no definite identity (a tinkertoy stick as a hammer); (2) with dissimilar objects that had definite identity (e.g. a toy apple as a hammer); and, (3) with no objects present (hammering without an object). The youngest children performed best with similar objects, the three-year-olds performed equally well with similar and dissimilar objects but less so with no object present, while the oldest children performed equally well in all conditions. The authors suggested that in fully developed pretense, therefore, children are able to use signifiers arbitrarily, as true symbols. Once this is achieved, 'similarity between the substitute and the referent does not appear to be important' (p.503).

Another study with children between 18 and 34 months of age (Ungerer, Zelazo, Kearsley, and O'Leary, 1981) also defined perceptual support as 'high physical similarity between the object used and the object represented' (p.189). Object substitutions were categorized as: (1) high physical support with action (e.g. the child lifts a rectangular block to his ear and says 'hi'), (2) high physical support without action (the child picks up a cylindrical yellow block and says 'carrot'), (3) low physical support with action (the child pretends combing with a baby bottle), and (4) low physical support without action (the child hands a table to his mother and says 'this house'). Younger children chose as signifiers objects whose perceptual and functional properties presented 'the least conflict with those of the signified objects and, therefore, were the easiest symbolically to transform.' Older children were 'capable of violating an object's perceptual and functional features and using as signifiers objects with clear and conflicting functions which were perceptually different from the signified objects' (p.194).

In general, these early experimental studies identified three main factors that made pretense difficult for young children: 1. No substitute object present, because this condition requires the child to generate symbols internally; 2. Dissimilar substitute object, because this requires the child mentally to override conflicting perceptual cues; and 3. Substitute objects with definite conventional identity, because this requires the child to prohibit established object-associated motor responses and violate firm semantic boundaries. Design of the studies as well as their interpretation manifested the following core assumptions: 1. Perceptual (physical) support consists of simple structural features such as size, shape and color. Reliance on these perceptual cues is a limitation that needs to be overcome; development means less and less dependence on such cues. 2. Objects with definite identity (artifacts) are represented as concepts with firm semantic boundaries. To use a concept differently goes against the established order of the mental machinery and this 'violation' requires substantial mental effort. 3. Actions are guided by representations and are unproblematic: once the representation is symbolically redefined, the associated motor response is in place, too. These assumptions have been basically supported by more recent research that has revealed hitherto underestimated capacities of young children for interpersonal communication and coordination in collective pretend play (Stambak and Sinclair, 1993). Research on children's coordination with objects has, however, not been pursued any further because the assumption has persisted that the 'separation between action and object' is integral to mental development (Stambak and Sinclair, 1993, p.ix).

The assumptions underlying the symbolic approach to pretense leads to paradoxes. If the ability to violate mental order is a criterion for advanced cognition, then development manifesting itself in pretense is not the development of a normal function. The paradoxical situation was noted by Leslie (1987, p. 412): 'The perceiving, thinking organism ought, as far as possible, to get things right. Yet pretense flies in the face of this fundamental principle. In pretense we deliberately distort reality'. Assuming that significant human behaviors have biological proper functions (Millikan, 1993), we can assume that, whatever proper function cognition has, it is not the deliberate distortion/violation of reality. The theme of violation is familiar from research on metaphor. A deep puzzle presented by metaphors to traditional cognitivist thinking is that they seem to violate semantic order (Ortony, 1993). A solution to the puzzle is that there is no violation. The idea of violation, is relevant only if a rigid order of mental representations is assumed. Given the epistemic assumption that organisms are in a constant dynamic flow of coordination with their surroundings through action, perception and cognition, reasons to assume rigid representations, along with perplexing forces that violate them, evaporate. Metaphor can be defined as the perceptually grounded detection of dynamic properties that remain invariant across different objects and events (Dent-Read and Szokolszky, 1993) and pretend play can be similarly considered as perceptually grounded action.

The symbolic approach to pretense is paradoxical, on a second ground, because it cannot present conceptual limitations on 'violation'. Once pretense has acquired its mature, truly symbolic form, practically anything can stand for anything else. In principle, the stronger the violation, the more highly developed it is. The assumption that pretense is symbolic transformation does not set constraints on arbitrariness, even if it is assumed that pretense would not reach the fully-fledged arbitrariness of true symbols. Empirical evidence shows that such limits exist and that younger and older children as well are sensitive to object appropriateness (e.g. Golomb, 1977, Copple, Cocking and Matthews, 1984). Vygotsky argued for the role of functional object properties, but functionality and arbitrariness do not go together, if arbitrariness is understood as complete freedom from situational constraints, a sort of 'stepping out of reality'. Assuming, however, that functional coordination with the object world is maintained in pretense, pretend play is a matter of 'staying in' as well as 'stepping out'.

The symbolic approach to pretense is paradoxical, on a third ground, because the essence of pretense is regarded as essentially mental in nature, whereas pretense is, in the first place, a matter of *doing*. One only has to observe children when they are pretending: they move, they pick up objects and use them certain ways – they *act* and it is the action that is focal. Talk also serves the action; an utterance like 'I am making soup' confirms but does not establish what is going on. In the experimental studies described above, pretend acts were of interest only to the extent they provided evidence for symbolic use. For example, when a child used a baby bottle to comb the doll's hair, the act was taken as evidence for the symbolic use of the bottle; the action itself – *how* the child used the bottle – was ignored as an issue for investigation. As Reed (1996, p.13) has observed, theories that try to account for complex behaviors by a set of cognitively stored representations and commands 'have a tendency to make psychologists skip over the arduous task of describing behaviors accurately'. For the perspective taken here, actions are interesting in their own right and the detailed observation and description of pretend actions is a central task.

The previous research on pretense has neglected the possibility that children perceive and use available affordances of pretend objects. Perceptual support was defined as limited to the similarity of simple features. Experimental design based on the similarity notion has, generally, obscured the role of functional fitness in pretense. The results, as a consequence, may have been methodological artifacts: children's dependence on similarity may have reflected nothing more than reliance on context-free likeness when only such likeness was offered. However, if we consider task-specific affordances as perceptual support, it turns out that a similar object is not necessarily more fit to be the substitute than a dissimilar object. For example, an iron rod can be very similar to a sword but it can be very heavy for the child; but he can be perfectly happy to use a pencil, or his finger as a sword. A flat piece of wood is unquestionably more similar to a comb than is a rubber ball (example from Elder and

Pederson, 1978), but if we consider that pretend combing is nothing but repeatedly moving the object along the head, both the flat piece of wood and the rubber ball are appropriate because both of them afford this schematic action. Of course, form and function go together. Yet it does not mean that surface similarity *per se* is the perceptual basis for pretense, or when using a dissimilar object there is no perceptual support to the pretend act. The task-specific functional fitness of a pretend object depends on the the structure of the intended action, the action capabilities of the child, and the affordances of the object, and not on simple resemblances.

## The Functional Study of Pretense

Functional fitness of a pretend object is a matter of degree; an appropriately sized broom supports pretend horse riding better than a fishing rod, although it is not entirely impossible that the latter also could be used as a pretend horse. A few early studies produced evidence that object suitability is an important factor in pretense for children. In a study by Golomb (1977) children between 2.8 and 5.8 years of age faced a variety of substitute objects ranging from suitable to highly unsuitable objects. As first choices children selected suitable objects. When all suitable objects were exhausted, children could be induced to make further selections, but when only incongruous objects were available, selection sharply declined at all age levels. Other studies have also shown sensitivity to the functional demands of pretense situations. For instance, children, as young as 12 to 20 months old, selectively matched appropriate feeding tools to recipients in pretend feeding acts (Fein and Apfel, 1979). In another study children between 3 and 5 years of age proved to be sensitive to critical affordances of substitute objects; when they had to choose a pretend spoon for scooping they chose an eggshell, but when they were to find a pretend spoon for stirring they chose a stick (Copple, Cocking and Matthews, 1984). Criticisms of the cognitivist position have noted the tendency to overintellectualize interpretations of pretend play. Culturally recognizable pretend activities (such as feeding a doll) are more parsimoniously interpreted as affordance use; when a child performs the pretend act s/he can be mimicking routines modeled by adults, or, can be 'following affordances revealed by objects'. The child's understanding about 'how things are related is not arbitrary but emerges as the co-participants continuously interact with the perceptually available particulars in the situation' (Zukow, 1984, p.166, 168).

Based on these theoretical and empirical preliminaries an experimental study was designed to investigate how children use the affordances of substitute objects in solitary pretend play. Sixty-four children, half of them between 3 and 4 and the other half between 4 and 5 years of age, were asked to play with pretend objects and rank them according to their appropriateness. The pretend objects differed in their degree of affordance–based functional fitness and in conventional identity. Degree of object fitness was judged by groups of undergraduate students who saw demonstrations of the pretend use of candidate objects and rated them. Objects were repeatedly changed and rated by new observers, until the final selection was made. Three sets of objects were selected, each set containing one realistic target object and three pretend objects. In each set the three pretend objects were clearly different in their appropriateness for the pretend task, one being *highly fit,* one *less fit* and one *least fit*. In each set the highly fit and the least fit objects had definite identities while the moderately fit object did not ('blank' object). Evidence was gained that children indeed knew the conventional identities of the definite objects and could not tell what kind of objects the blank objects were.

This procedure differs from natural pretend play in two basic respects: the intention is not the child's own – the play theme is suggested and presented as a sort of task; neither is explicit verbal judgement of how good a substitute object a part of natural pretend play. The reason for the design was the goal of comparability to previous experimental studies that have been briefly sketched in the section on the symbolic framework. As the main purpose of the present study was to challenge the work motivated by the symbolic approach to pretense, following the methodology of previous studies appeared to be necessary. Externally pre-establishing the group of objects that were highly fit, moderately fit and least fit was also a methodological aspect of previous experimental studies. In fact, in previous studies the degree of the object's appropriateness was simply assumed. The present study established object appropriateness empirically and in a perceptually grounded procedure: judgements were based on actually watching the pretend objects being used as the target object (for example, watching 'the doll taking a nap' with a soft lamb-as-a-pillow, a car-as-a-pillow, and other objects).

Children were individually tested and videotaped in 20 minute long sessions. The first play episode was about a doll taking a nap. The target object was a *pillow* and the pretend objects were a stuffed lamb (fit, definite object), a wedge made of cardboard (less fit, blank object), and a plastic car (least fit, definite object). The second episode was about 'cleaning up mess from the kitchen floor'. The target object was a small *broom* and the pretend objects were a bunch of plastic flowers (fit, definite object), a so called tassel (less fit, blank object), and a fork (least fit, definite object). The third episode was about a doll wanting to take a boat ride. The target object was a small toy *boat* and the pretend objects were a wooden shoe (fit, definite object), a basket-like object (less fit, blank object), and a toy skate board (least fit definite object; see Table 4.1 and Figure 4.1).

After some warm-up play, the experimenter modeled the play act with the realistic target object and asked the child to repeat the act with the same object. Then she put the target object away and said: '*Now we don't have the (target object) but we have these'* (pointing at the substitute objects). *'Play with all of these things for a while.'* After 2 minutes of free play the experimenter put the substitute objects in front of the child and asked her 'to pick the object that would be the best (target object), then the second best and, finally, the least good object. The children were also asked to show how these objects could be used as the target object.

The experimental hypotheses were as follows: In picking the best, second best and least good objects, the children were basically expected to agree with the pre-

**Table 4.1 Target and substitute objects**

| | Target Objects | Substitute Objects | Object Identity | Fitness to the Task* |
|---|---|---|---|---|
| **First Set** | PILLOW | – LAMB<br>– 'WEDGE'<br>– CAR | – Definite<br>– Blank<br>– Definite | – High<br>– Moderate<br>– Low |
| **Second Set** | BROOM | – FLOWERS<br>– 'TASSEL'<br>– FORK | – Definite<br>– Blank<br>– Definite | – High<br>– Moderate<br>– Low |
| **Third Set** | BOAT | – WOODEN SHOE<br>– 'BASKET'<br>– SKATEBOARD | – Definite<br>– Blank<br>– Definite | – High<br>– Moderate<br>– Low |

* As judged by groups of undergraduate students.

established judgements. Specifically, both younger and older children were expected to pick highly 'fit/definite' objects as first, and least 'fit/definite' objects as last choices, since in these cases fitness, or the lack of it, was easy to perceive. This was in contrast to expectations that would have been generated by the symbolic approach. Namely, on the symbolic approach one would expect that definite object identity will cause difficulty for younger children in perceiving object fitness. In addition, one would expect that older children would show a tendency to disregard lack of object fitness. The main interest was, however, related to pretend actions since previous studies tended not to look at qualitative aspects of pretend acts. Pretend acts with functionally fit objects were expected to be qualitatively different from pretend acts with functionally less fit objects. This was based on the idea that when no ideal fit is possible, the child would opportunistically exploit the available affordances and this 'compromise' would show up in the qualitative character of the act.

As a first approach to the qualitative analysis of pretend actions, three main types were differentiated. *Integrated actions* were smooth and adequate, similar to what those actions would have been with the proper use of the realistic target object. For example, the child puts the lamb on its side to make it a good pillow. *Discrepant actions* were jerky and fragmentary, different from what they would be with the proper use of the realistic target object. For example, the child puts the doll's head on the point of the wedge, the dolls head is hanging down. *Bridging* actions involved special effort to make the object fit for the task. For example, the child wraps the blanket (on which the objects were presented) around the car to make it an acceptable pillow. Two trained observers segmented the flow of videotaped actions into basic level units; agreement was 86% on thirty percent of the data. A basic level unit was defined by accomplishing a meaningful action with one object in focus (cf. Reed et.

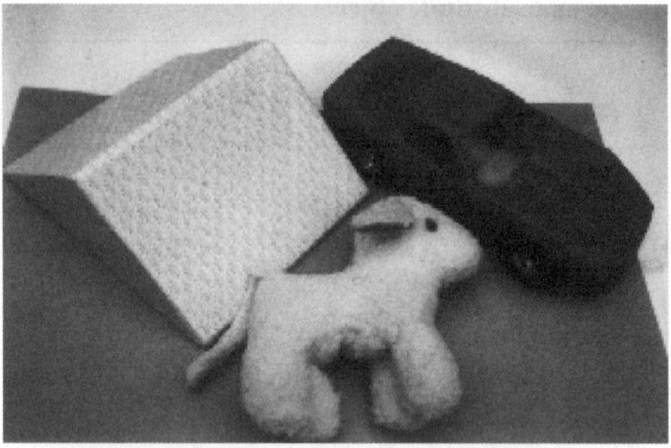

**Set 1. The Lamb, the Wedge and the Car**

**Set 2. The Flowers, the Tassel and the Fork**

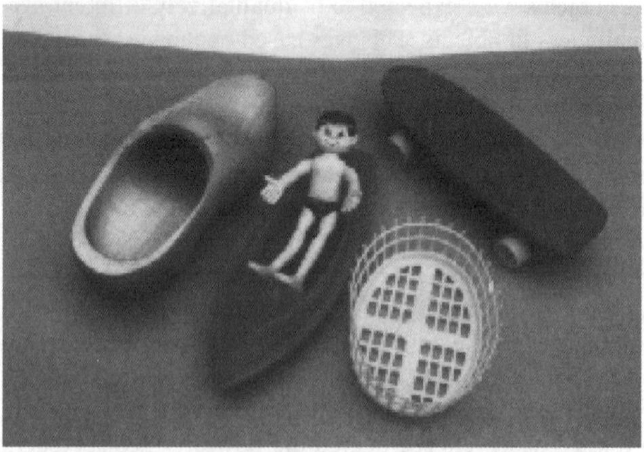

**Set 3. The Shoe, the Basket and the Skateboard**

**Figure 4.1 Photographs of the experimental objects**

al., 1992). Action units were then categorized as integrated, discrepant, or bridging actions by two scorers different from those who scored for action units; agreement was 89% on 30% of the data.

Results regarding the ranking of the objects basically followed fitness as previously judged, but not as tightly as expected. Results were analyzed by an Age x Object ANOVA. (See Figure 4.2 for the ranking of the substitute objects.) In

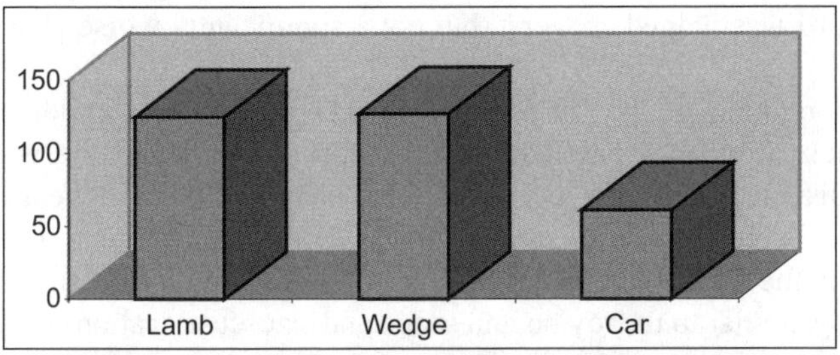


**First Set. Judged Fitness of the Lamb, the Wedge and the Car as a Pillow**

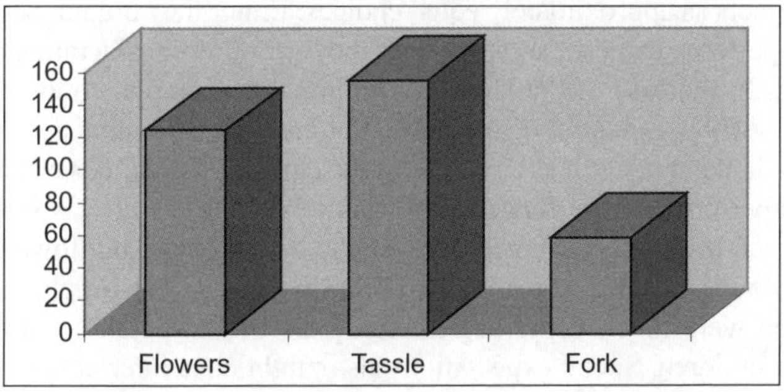


**Second Set. Judged Fitness of the Tassel and the Fork as a Broom**

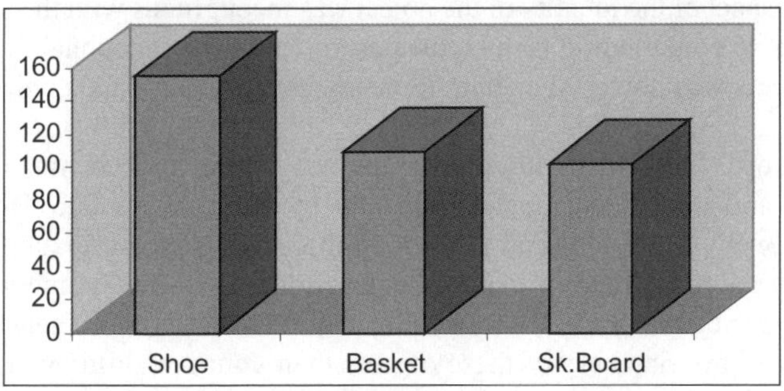


**Third Set. Judged Fitness of the Shoe, the Basket and the Skateboard as a Boat**

**Figure 4.2 Ranking of the fitness of the substitute objects**

the *first set* children judged the lamb and the wedge as equally fit to be the pillow (F[2,120]=14.04, p< .01) and the car was ranked last. In the *second set* children judged the tassel as somewhat better to be the broom than the flowers (F[2,120]= 21,61, p< .01); the fork was judged as the worst. Older children appreciated the fitness of the flowers for a broom significantly more than younger children (F[1,60]= 8,405, p< .01). In the *third set* children in both age groups judged the wooden shoe as significantly better to be a boat than the other two objects (F[2,120]=11.84, p<.01). The skateboard was judged as worst, but not a significantly worse choice than the basket.

The high ranking of the 'fit/definite' objects showed that children generally perceived their affordance-based fitness. The boat-potential of the wooden shoe was readily detected. Knowing its conventional identity did not prevent even young children from perceiving its functional fitness in the new context. The choice of the shoe over the basket could not be due to simple similarity, since both were approximately similar to the toy boat in shape and size. Justifications confirmed that children paid attention to those affordances of the shoe that made it a good boat and not to simple similarity of shape.

In the first and the second sets children ranked 'fit/definite' and the moderately 'fit/blank' objects as approximately equal choices. Either they did not perceive clear functional superiority in these cases, or else, if they did, other considerations influenced their ranking. In the case of the lamb-as-a-pillow, for example, children may have perceived the pillow-potential of the lamb, but concern for lambs as living beings may have made them reject it as a pillow (as the children sometimes explained). The functional superiority of the flower-as-a-broom over the tassel was more difficult to perceive than originally assumed because the bunch of plastic flowers had to be held upside down in order to realize its broom-potential. This might explain why older children were much better at perceiving the broom-potential of the flowers than younger children. Social expectations also might have interfered with ranking: flowers are not supposed to be used as a broom. In summary, 'fit/definite' objects received a lower than expected ranking when the the affordance was not obvious when some aspect of the identity of the object was incongruous with the pretend use. In spite of these confounding factors, the perception of the functional fitness of 'fit/definite' objects was powerful enough to make them at least equal choices to blank objects.

Furthermore, the least 'fit/definite' objects were ranked far behind the 'fit/definite' and the 'blank' objects not only by the younger but also the older children, as well. Older children did not tend to disregard the inappropriateness of these objects more readily than younger children, as the symbolic approach would have predicted. In fact, older children proved to be more sensitive to the functional inappropriateness of these objects than younger children. This finding is in accordance with other results (Golomb, 1977) showing that younger children were more willing to make incongruous object selections than older children. The third set was an exception in that the skateboard-as-a-boat was rated as a not significantly worse substitute than the blank object. This may have been because children generally found the skateboard to be an attractive object.

The ranking task required children consciously to judge object appriopriateness. Experimental procedures that require conscious judgment are known to less accurately reflect the perception of affordances than actions themselves (Heft, 1993, Runeson and Frykholm, 1986). Under natural conditions children do not stop to make judgements of potential pretend objects. Therefore, a more ecologically valid approach to the analysis of pretend object play is to look at what children actually do when they use pretend objects. Action measures came from free play and from the ranking task, where children were instructed to show how the given object would be used as the target object. Results are summarized by object types in order to reveal tendencies that overarch individual sets (see Figure 4.3).

Regarding pretend actions the main finding was that distinct patterns have emerged depending on degree of object fitness. Although during free play there was less pretend object use than in the ranking task, the overall pattern of results was basically in agreement in both situations. The use of the *'fit/definite' objects* (the lamb, the flowers, and the shoe) was characterized by a tendency for a high number of integrated actions, a low number of discrepant actions, and virtually no bridging. The use of the *'least fit/definite' objects* (the car, the fork and the skateboard) was characterized by an insignificant number of integrated actions (with the exception of the car in the ranking task; in free play the car was ignored altogether), a high number of discrepant actions, and a relatively high number of bridging. The use of the *'moderately fit/blank' objects* (the wedge, the tassel, and the basket) was generally characterized by a relatively high number of integrated actions, as well as a relatively high number of discrepant actions, and an increased amount of bridging. In conclusion, the three object types were associated with recognizably different action patterns, along with some variation and exception. Action patterns associated with clearly fit and unfit objects were dominated by one particular action type in a relatively stable manner, whereas action patterns associated with blank objects had a more varied character.

Besides object fitness, the actions also depended on children's ability to perceive and willingness to realize the goal-specific affordances. An object could be ideally suited to the pretend task, yet used discrepantly for the pretend action, and vice versa, depending on the skills, intentions and motivational state of the child. Clearly, children were not 'passive users' of affordances. Occasionally they changed the available affordance in order to create better support for the action. Functional fitness constrained actions but intentional actions could, and sometimes did, change functional fitness in order to optimize performance.

The explanatory framework of the symbolic approach falls short of an adequate account of the above results. The symbolic approach proposes that children need to inhibit established motor responses when using definite objects (e.g. Elder and Pederson, 1978). This means that when children use, for example, a hair dryer as a car, they would inhibit motor responses associated with the hair dryer and would apply

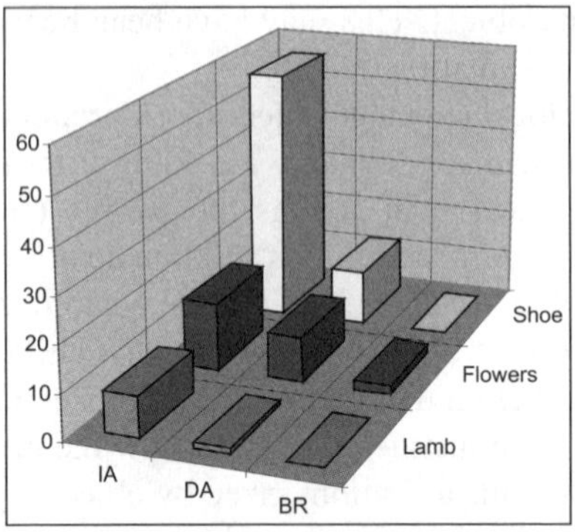


**Action Types with 'fit/definite' objects in Free Play**

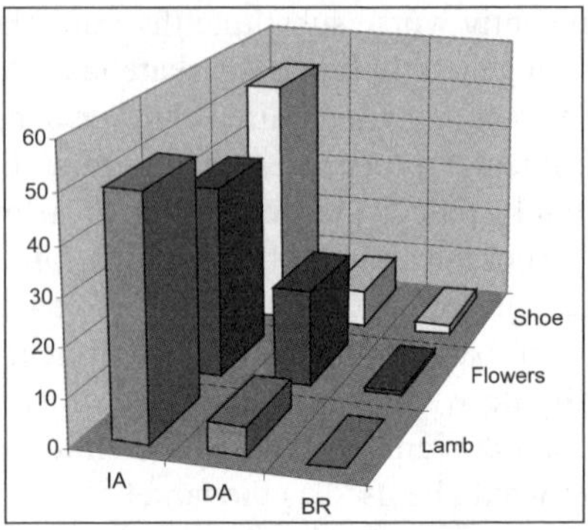


**Action Types with 'fit/definite' objects in the Ranking Task**

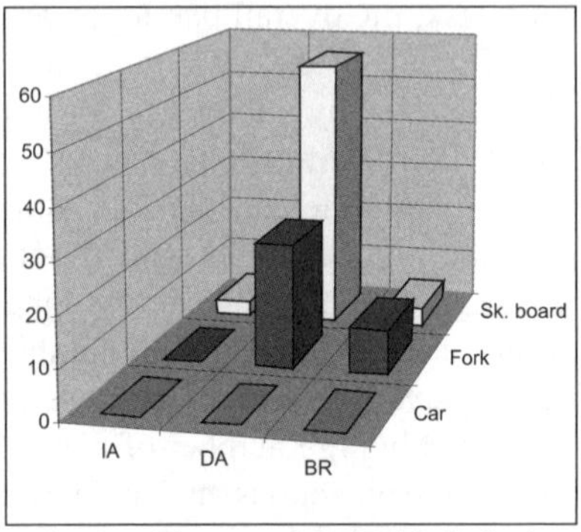


**Action Types with 'fit/definite' objects in Free Play**

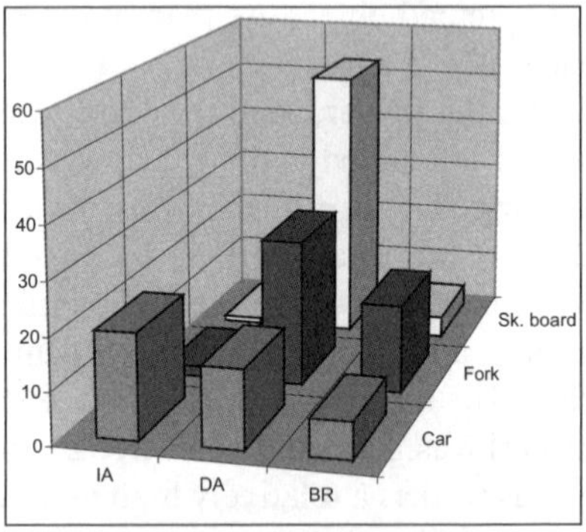


**Action Types with 'fit/definite' objects in the Ranking Task**

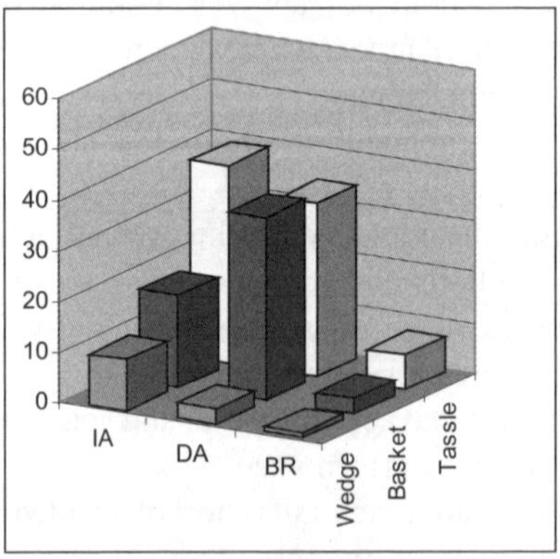


**Action with Blank Objects in Free Play**

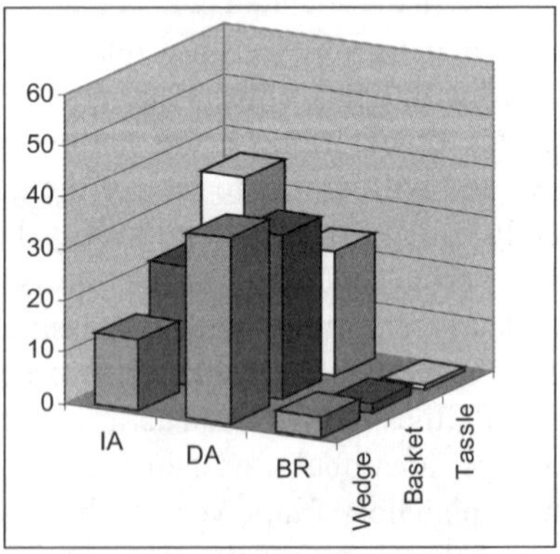


**Action with Blank Objects in the Ranking Task**

**Figure 4.3 Frequency of action types**
IA = integrated action; DA = discrepant action; BR = bridging.

motor responses associated with toy cars. However, the fact that children's actions were influenced by affordance-based fitness suggests that they did not simply replace one fixed set of motor responses with another fixed set, but rather, they adapted their actions to the properties of the substitute objects. In symbolic accounts the focus on decontextualized mental representations obscures the possibility that in some basic ways pretend object play involves functional coordination with objects. The above results suggest that pretend object use involves a flexible and subtle reliance on perceptual support and not an increasing disregard of it. Pretend object play has been traditionally framed as an analytical task, but it is more likely, especially under natural circumstances, that it is essentially a perception-action task that involves goal-driven, but not necessarily intellectually driven actions.

## Pretend Object Play as Pragmatic Tool Use

Pretense can be viewed as the unconventional use of an object in place of another object in order to achieve a goal. In this regard pretend object use is, in some ways, analogous to unconventional tool use when, for example, a screwdriver is used to hammer in a nail. Conventional tools are specific objects that aid us in achieving goals that would be otherwise difficult to achieve. When, however, in the course of everyday activity proper tools are not available, we often use another object that will do the job. We are perfectly aware that an artifact has a proper function but we do not hesitate to use it quite differently if this is advantageous. This use is 'improper' only when extrinsically viewed, according to its socially assigned proper function. From the intrisic viewpoint of the action, however, the unconventional use of the object is proper to the task at hand. In addition, it can be argued that the unconventional use of an artifact is more parsimoniously explained by assuming affordance selection than a process involving representational 'decoupling'. Objects have a multitude of affordances and intentional actions flexibly select the required affordance (Reed, 1993, Heft, 2001). Decoupling assumes that socially assigned proper functions are rigidly associated with objects. However, in our everyday actions we routinely use objects 'differently'; we tap on desks with pencils, use a chair to prop open the door, climb up on the table to reach the curtain-rod, and so on. Whereas the symbolic approach suggests that such acts involve the cognitive act of *de*contextualization and mental redefiniton of pencils, chairs and tables, the framework presented here suggests that they involve the ever present pragmatic *re*contextualization of object use.

Pretend object use is also the dynamic recontextualization of reality aimed at the playful re-enactment of culturally learned actions. To view pretend objects as unconventional tools may illuminate an important aspect of the developmental significance of pretend object use. Tools create new opportunities for action by enhancing, extending, or restoring the action capabilities of the actor. Tools focus behaviors and promote the fit of actors to their task environments in more visible ways than actions that do not depend on tools (Shaw, Flascher, and Kadar, 1993).

Pretend objects, as unconventional tools, may help *focus behavior* and this may explain why pretense without objects is more difficult than pretense with objects: the difficulty lies not in the lack of external cues that would activate *representation*, but in that there is no material basis that would guide and focus the activity.

Unconventional tool use by adults is, of course, not playful. The adult is not pretending that the screwdriver is a hammer, but simply uses it, for that purpose. For an activity to be playful it means that it has no goal beyond the realization of the activity. Compare real cutting to pretend cutting: in the former the goal is that something gets cut. In pretend cutting the goal is to do the cutting *except* that nothing gets cut. The material constraints for real cutting are tight: there has to be a fit between the hand, the tool and the thing; if the thing is hard, the hand is weak or the knife is dull the act will not succeed. In pretense, however, the joy and satisfaction comes from 'as if' cutting, where such tight constraints do not exist. As argued above, this does not mean that no constraints are present, but only that the constraints are much looser than in real acts. The looseness of constraints contributes to the basic character of pretense, which is its dynamic, fluid nature.

## Pretend Object Play as Fluid Action

The dynamic and fluid nature of cognition is well demonstrated by metaphors, analogies, jokes and the like. What is more, these forms of cognition are not a separate 'fluid realm' added to the 'solid realm' of literal thought; cognition is inherently fluid. From an ecological standpoint, it is important to emphasize that the fluidity of thought basically comes from the fluidity of perception and action. Fluidity means flexibility, adaptability, pliancy, continuousness (Hofstadter, 1996, p.2). Pretend play is an especially good example of the fluid and dynamically intertwined presence of perception, action and cognition. Recontextualization in pretense is a dynamic process of relating the affordances of the object to the demands of the pretend intention. The interplay between the pretend intention and the affordances of the object involves the use of affordances that may support the pretend action to various degrees; it may also involve the changing of the affordances in case they are not ideally supporting the pretend action. It may also be that, upon perceiving or conceiving a new possibility for action, the original intention is quickly dropped and replaced by a new intention. Pretend intention is volatile, prone to flickering change in the context of ongoing action and perception in play. Pretend actions typically involve rapid decisions without reflection on the appropriateness of the pretend object. The temporary new role of the object is *constituted in the action*, which only shows, in an exceptionally clear way, that our dealings with the world is not pre-given, they require a versatile fit.

The methodology used in the study described in this chapter basically replicated the experimental procedure established within the traditional symbolic framework.

This was necessary precisely to challenge that body of experimental work. However, to get a better understanding of pretend object play, a methodology better suited to the assumptions of the ecological-functional framework is needed in the future. In-depth, qualitative observation of object pretend play under natural circumstances has to play an important role in exploring how children actually use objects in pretend play. Pretense is indeed magic, in a way, with lots of room for imaginative, unusual use of objects. But this, however, is no ground for regarding it as a distortion of reality. Earlier I cited Leslie in saying that pretense is paradoxical because it flies in the face of the fundamental principle of 'getting things right'. I suggest that there is no paradox, as claimed by Leslie. Children do get things *right* in pretense. Pretend play is imaginative, but not by turning away from the real world. Children perceive and use affordances while they play and this is surely part of the developmental significance of pretend play.

**References**


Adolph, K.E., Eppler, M.A. & Gibson, E.J. (1993). Development of perception of affordances. In C. Rovee-Collier and Lipsitt, L.P. (Eds.), *Advances in infancy research*. Vol.8. (pp.51–98). NJ: Ablex Publishing Corp.

Balzano, G.J. & McCabe, V. (1986). An ecological perspective on concepts and cognition. In G.J. Balzano & V. McCabe (Eds.), *Event cognition: An ecological perspective*. Hillsdale, New Jersey: Lawrence Erlbaum.

Bugrimenko, E.A. and Smirnova, E.O. (1992). Paradoxes of children's play in Vygotsky's theory. In G.C. Cupchik and J. Laszlo (Eds.) *Emerging views of an aesthetic process*. Cambridge: Cambridge University Press.

Carello, C., Grosofsky, A., Reichel, F.D., Solomon, H.Y. & Turvey, M.T. (1989). Visually perceiving what is reachable. *Ecological Psychology*, *1*, 27–54.

Copple, C.E., Cocking, R.R. & Matthews, W. (1984). Objects, symbols, and substitutes: The nature of the cognitive activity during symbolic play. In T.D. Yawkey & A.D. Pellegrini (Eds.), *Child's play: Developmental and applied*. Hillsdale, New Jersey: Lawrence Erlbaum Associates.

Costall, A. (1995). Socializing affordances. *Theory & Psychology*, 5, 467–481.

Crum, R.A., Thornburg, K., Benninga, J. & Bridge, C. (1983). Preschool children's object substitutions during symbolic play. *Perceptual and Motor Skills*, *56*, 947–955.

Dent-Read, C. & Szokolszky, A. (1993). Where do metaphors come from? *Metaphor and Symbolic Activity*, *8*, 227–242.

Elder, J.L. & Pederson, D.R. (1978). Preschool children's use of objects in symbolic play. *Child Development*, *49*, 500–508.

Fein, G.G. (1975). A transformational analysis of pretending. *Developmental Psychology*, *11*, 291–296.

Fein, G.G. & Apfel, N. (1979). Some preliminary observations on knowing and pretending. In N. Smith & M. Franklin (Eds.), *Symbolic functioning in childhood*. Hillsdale, NJ: Lawrence Erlbaum Associates.

Gibson, E.J. & Walker, A.S. (1984). Development of knowledge of visual-tactual affordances of substance. *Child Development*, *55*, 453–460.

Gibson, E.J. (1982). The concept of affordances in development: The renascence of functionalism. In W.A. Collins (Ed.), *Minnesota Symposia on Child Psychology*, *The concept of development*, *15*. Hillsdale, N.J: Lawrence Erlbaum Associates.

Gibson, J. (1979). *The ecological approach to visual perception*. Boston: Houghton Mifflin Company.

Golomb, C. (1977). The role of substitutions in pretense and puzzle games. *British Journal of Educational Psychology*, *47*, 175–186.

Haight, W.L., Wang, X., Fung, H., Williams, K. & Mintz, J. (1999). Universal, developmental and variable aspects of young children's play: A cross-cultural comparison of pretending at home. *Child Development*, *70*, 1477–1488.

Heft, H. (1993). A methodological note on overestimates of reaching distance: Distinguishing between perceptual and analytical judgments. *Ecological Psychology*, *5*, 255–271.

Hofstadter, D. (1996) Fluid concepts and creative analogies. New York: Basic Books.

Jakowitz, E.R. & Watson, M.W. (1980). Development of object transformations in early pretend play. *Developmental Psychology*, *16*, 543–549.

Kagan, J. (1981). *The second year: The emergence of self awareness*. Cambridge, MA: Harvard University Press.

Leeuwen, L. van Smitsman & Leeuwen, C. van (1994). Affordances, perceptual complexity, and the development of tool use. *Journal of Experimental Psychology*, *20*, 174–191.

Leslie, A.M. (1987). Pretense and representation: The origins of 'theory of mind'. *Psychological Review*, *94*, 412–426.

Lillard, A.S. (1993). Young children's conceptualization of pretense: Action or mental representational state? *Child Development*, *64*, 372–386.

Lowe, M. (1975). Trends in the development of representational play in infants from one to three years. An observational study. *Journal of Child Psychology and Psychiatry*, *16*, 33–47.

Mark, L.S. (1987). Eyeheight – scaled information about affordances: A study of sitting and stair climbing. *Journal of Experimental Psychology: Human Perception and Performance*, 13 (3), 361–370.

Nicolich, L. (1977). Beyond Sensorimotor intelligence: Assessment of symbolic maturity through analysis of pretend play. *Merrill-Palmer Quarterly*, *23*, 89–99.

Millikan, R.G. (1993) White queen psychology and other essays for Alice, Cambridge, MA: MIT Press.

Pederson, D.R., Rook-Green, A. & Elder, J.L. (1981). The role of action in the development of pretend play in young children. *Developmental Psychology*, *17*, 756–759.

Piaget, J. (1962). *Play, dreams and imitation in childhood*. New York: Norton.

Piaget, J. (1971). Response to Brian Sutton-Smith. In R.E. Herron and Sutton-Smith (Eds.), *Child's play*. (pp. 337–339). New York: Wiley.

Reed, E.S. (1993). The intention to use a specific affordance: A conceptual framework for psychology In R.H. Wozniak and K. W. Fisher (Eds.) *Development in context. Acting and thinking in specific environments*, Hillsdale, N.J.: Lawrence Erlbaum, 45–76.

Reed, E.S. (1996). *Encountering the world. Toward an ecological psychology*. New York, Oxford University Press.

Reed, E.S., Montgomery, M., Schwartz, M., Palmer, C. & Pittinger, J.B. (1992). Visually based descriptions of an everyday action. *Ecological Psychology, 4,* 129–152.

Runeson, S. & Frykholm, G. (1986). Kinematic specification of gender and gender expression. In V. McCabe & G.J. Balzano (Eds.), *Event Cognition: An ecological perspective*. Hillsdale, NJ: Lawrence Erlbaum Associates.

Shaw, R.E., Flasher, O.M. & Kadar, E.E. (1993). Dimensionless invariants for intentional systems: Measuring the fit of vehicular activities to environmental layout. In J.M. Flach, P.A. Hancock, J.K. Caird & K.J. Vicente (Eds.), *An ecological approach to human-machine systems I: A global perspective*. Hillsdale, NJ: Lawrence Erlbaum Associates.

Smitsman, A.W. & Pick, A.D. (1982). Perception of inclusion in collection of objects. In D. Rogers & J.A. Sloboda (Eds.), *The acquisition of symbolic skills*. (pp. 335–342). New York: Plenum Press.

Smitsman, A.W., Loosebroek, E. van & Pick, A.D. (1987). The primacy of affordances in categorization by children. *British Journal of Developmental Psychology*, *5*, 265–273.

Stambak, M. & Sinclair, H. (1993). Pretend play among 3 year olds. Hillsdale, NJ: Erlbaum.

Ungerer, J.A., Zelazo, P.R., Kearsley, R.B. & O'Leary, K. (1981). Developmental changes in the representation of objects in symbolic play from 18 to 34 months of age. *Child Development*, *52*, 186–195.

Vygotsky, L.S. (1976). Play and its role in the mental development of the child. In J.S. Bruner, A. Jolly & K. Sylva (Eds.) *Play – Its role in development and evolution* (pp. 538–554). New York: Basic Books, Inc.

Walker, A.S. (1982). Intermodal perception of expressive behaviors by human infants. *Journal of Experimental Psychology*, *33*, 514–535.

Warren, W.H. & Wang, S. (1987). Visual guidance of walking through apertures: Body-scaled information for affordances. *Journal of Experimenal Psychology: Human Perception and Performance*, *13*, 371–383.

Watson, M.W. & Fisher, K.W. (1977). A developmental sequence of agent use in late infancy. *Child Development*, *48*, 828–836.

Winner, E. (1988). *The Point of words*. Cambridge, MA: Harvard University Press.

Zukow, P.G. (1984). Criteria for the emergence of symbolic conduct: When words refer and play is symbolic. In L. Feagans, C. Garvey and R. Golinkoff (Eds.), *The origins and growth of communication*. New York: Ablex.

# Chapter 5

# Culture, Language and Canonicality: Differences in the use of Containers between Zapotec (Mexican Indigenous), and Danish Children*

Kristine Jensen de López

> W.J. McGee, having observed that the Seri Indians of California had no notion of knives, believed them to be the most primitive human beings (McGee, 1889, cited in Mauss, 1979).

Compared to the Piagetian infant, contemporary psychology credits infants with the possession of a surprising amount of basic knowledge or what Spelke (1991) calls 'core' knowledge and Mandler (1996) refers to as 'image-schemata', concerning the spatio-temporal properties of material objects.[1] Tomasello (1999) has critically defined this new theoretical and methodological perspective within developmental psychology as philosophical nativism.[2] Here are some of the abilities now attributed to very young children. For example, at the age of 3 or 4 months, infants express surprise (as measured in terms of how long they look at a scene presenting a violation of what would be expected in the possible physical world) when presented with objects that violate the constraint of continuity. Infants know that objects cannot be in two places at one time. They also express surprise when presented with the violation of the notion of solidity. So infants also know that solid objects cannot pass through one another. Furthermore, at the age of 6 months infants appreciate the constraints of gravity and inertia (Spelke, 1991). One important insight from this neo-nativist paradigm is that Piaget's emphasis on the active exploratory manipulation of objects, as the crucial

* The study was supported by Aarhus University, Denmark, the Danish Research Council for the Humanities and by Inge Lehmann's Scholarship of 1983.

1 This revisited view concerning infant's abilities to predict the actions of objects in the physical world has emerged over the last two decades from the results gained within the preferential looking paradigm (Spelke et. al. 1992; Mandler, 1996).

2 Tomasello's motivation for classifying this perspective in terms of a philosophical nativism is grounded in the fact that similar to other first generation cognitive scientists, such as Chomsky (1980) and Fodor (1983), the conclusions drawn by Spelke concerning infants' innate core-knowledge are drawn from logical considerations only.

aspect of the sensory-motoric child's development of spatial conceptualizations, now seems a less crucial developmental activity. However, core knowledge or spatial image-schemata in themselves do not embrace notions concerning the intentional, relational and socio-cultural meanings of objects, nor the canonical way of relating two objects to each other in a spatial relationship. Hence, in themselves, these innate abilities do not account for how the developing child becomes a situated participant of a specific culture. To develop this ability, infants need to be enmeshed in at least three correlated scenarios; a) they need to understand others as intentional agents with an interrelated functioning goal, attention, and behavioral strategy, as expressed in infants' ability to engage in joint attentional activities emerging at the age of nine months (Carpenter, Nagell and Tomasello, 1998), b) they need to become an active part of a cognitive 'habitus' (Bourdieu, 1977) in order to be presented to the intentional and canonical functions of objects and artifacts, and finally c) they need some basic source of active instruction from adults, for example, scaffolding (Wood, Bruner and Ross, 1976) or engagements within a zone of proximal development (Vygotsky, 1986/1994; Tomasello, 1999; Sinha, 1999).

To illustrate the notion of a culturally situated participant, imagine the ongoing imitative play of a two-year-old Zapotec indigenous girl, named Mita.[3] While squatting in front of a small container filled with water, Mita suddenly picks up a 20 cm long round wooden artifact, carved in such way that it gradually becomes thicker at one end. One might perhaps anticipate Mita's following action to consist of her inserting the artifact into the container, in order to imitate the well-known stirring activity of her mother preparing dinner in a large clay pot. Despite the fact that Mita does insert the artifact into the container, she does not engage in a stirring action, but instead performs the motoric task of balancing the artifact between the palms of her hands, while quickly rubbing them against the artifact to create a rapid circular movement. The above anecdote is based on a video observation I made during an extended period of fieldwork in the Zapotec village where Mita lives. The particular artifact employed by Mita consisted of a miniature version of what she, many times prior to her engagement in the described event, had observed women using with the purpose of whisking up a foaming topping on the hot chocolate, which is daily served for breakfast in this Zapotec village. Having now added this important piece of information, it may immediately seem obvious to the reader why Mita was so eagerly encouraged to activate the whisking affordance rather than the stirring affordance equally offered by this particular artifact. When following a strict Gibsonian interpretation of Mita's object manipulation, contrary to what might be predicted, there is nothing inherent in the immediate properties of the object which should license or motivate Mita to prefer this particular action. The whisking action is in fact motorically[4] more demanding than the more simple action of stirring. In

3 This particular activity involved delayed imitation.

4 Note that this motoric action goes against the human reflex of grasping the object, because it requires that one's hands are slightly arched outwards in order to fit the round form of the object.

fact, when I presented this particular Zapotec artifact to my Danish undergraduate psychology students, their best guess concerning its specific functionality was in fact to categorize it as a type of rolling pin. Two-year-old Mita's cognitive advance, when compared to Danish undergraduate students, illustrates the fact that what objects afford is not strictly objective and immediately equally perceptual to all humans in an identical way. Affordances are culturally and interpersonally mediated (Costall, 1995) and children become aware of them through their interpersonal experiences, which form part of their early expectation that others are intentional agents (Carpenter, Nagell & Tomasello, 1998; Sinha & Jensen de López, 2000).

The above argument is not new. It is the cornerstone of the socio-cultural approach established by Vygotsky (1978) and Luria (1979/1984). In their approach the given function of an object cannot be accounted for as an inherent property of the artifact, but rather as mediating, cultural-historically constructed, meanings (Jensen de López, 2001). A similar attempt in the same direction was launched by von Uexküll (1949, in Ingold, 1992) in employing the concept of *Umwelt* to describe those qualities of objects which are subjectively added on to the neutral object (e.g. Mita's choice to use the wooden stick for whisking rather than stirring). However, there is an important contrast to be drawn between the concept of Umwelt and the essences of Vygotsky's approach. For von Uexküll, qualities are (according to Ingold) subjectively encountered by each individual and enclosed within his own 'reality bubble'. However when following Vygtosky's socio-cultural approach – recently extended by Tomasello (1999) – the notions of intersubjectivity and intentionality should equally be viewed as playing crucial roles for children in understanding how to manipulate objects in a meaningful way.

Returning to the example of the wooden stick used as a whisk, although certain socio-cultural potentials of the object were already there prior to Mita's attempt to manipulate the object, these potentials were not merely part of Mita's subjective Umwelt. They are potentials which have been constructed socially as a particular habitus into which Mita was born and thus passed on to her through the process of what Tomasello *et al.* (1993) call *imitative learning*. This view is in contrast to Gibson's notion of human interaction with objects as a solipsistic learning processing, which does not rely on the individual being able to imitate the way others use objects. The functions or *affordances* of an object are, according to Gibson, directly available to the user (1979). Imitative learning, in contrast, used for learning how to manipulate tools and artifacts demands that the child place itself in the intentional space of the user, for, thus discovering what Tomasello (1999) calls 'intentional affordances', i.e. how 'we' as a cultural group use this object. The notion of this specific type of affordances – and which is in accordance with what Cole (1996) calls the 'ideal dimension' of objects – makes it possible to capture and emphasize the important distinct between an object's natural affordances (as expressed by Gibson) and its intentional or canonical affordances , which – at least in part – are social constructions. The distinction between natural affordances and canonical affordances may also be seen as parallel to Vygotsky's distinction between the natural and the cultural lines in ontogenesis (Vygotsky, 1978; 1986). However, as pointed out by Emma Williams (personal communication) there also exists a problem within Vygotsky's distinction between the natural and cultural line, in that it leaves unresolved the dichotomy between the individual and the environment or the individual and the culture.

## Meanings and Actions

According to the developmental psychologist Bremner, and in opposition to the philosophical nativism view addressed earlier, infants' engagement in the world is best described in terms of: *'infants being busily engaged in working out what the world offers for action rather than what the world is in physical terms'* (Bremner, 2001: 176, emphasis in the original). With this quote Bremner stresses the importance of conceiving children as active explorers of their Umwelt rather than passive observers of the physical properties inherent to objects. Hence, Bremner's alternative view emphasizes the notion of action rather than percept, as mentioned in his formulation of *what the world offers*. Despite the advance gained in Bremner's reformulation concerning infants' interest in *actions* rather than in *objects*, it may seem to face similar limits to those seen in Gibson's notion of affordance. The limitation is seen in the fact that not just anything offered in the world will actively be attended to by the child. The child needs to rely on some kind of constraint in order to know which actions and affordances are important to pay attention to and which not. In order for the child to become culturally enmeshed, her task consists of going beyond simply working out any, or perhaps all, the functional properties of an object and instead working out what the world *means* in terms of acting on specific socio-historical constructed objects with purposeful and intentional functions. The case of the autistic child, as presented in the work of Williams and Kendell-Scott (this volume), demonstrates that the lack of such 'natural' constraint may delay the child in acquiring knowledge about how to use everyday objects. I therefore suggest that Bremner's description concerning the main interest of infants' becomes more appropriate, if the notion of *what the world offers for action* is substituted for the notion of *what the world means for action*. A similar view is suggested by Costall, who argues in favour of an ecological realism, in which the social and the cultural should be viewed as the primary qualities *'learning affordances does not simply concern the uses an object happens to afford, but what it is meant to afford'* (Costall, 1995, p. 472). For developmental psychology, this new approach means that children's appropriation of symbolic usage emerges within and as a result of specific situated, culturally embodied desires and needs (Sinha & Jensen de López, 2000). Having stressed the importance of a situated embodied approach to children's learning of object usage, I will later extend this same view to children's acquisition of other cultural practices, such as linguistic practices. In this sense objects are not viewed as culturally neutral, but as mediating cultural schemas or habitus, and hence the notion of embodiment also becomes constituted and exemplified by participating with objects in an entire matrix of cultural practices, some which are nonlinguistic and some which are linguistic (Sinha & Jensen de López, 2000, p. 36). First, I briefly review some of the relevant literature concerning children's early concept formation for understanding the spatial properties of objects.

## Infants' knowledge about what containers are for

Consistent with Spelke's notion of infants' core knowledge, researchers assessing children's early concept formation have argued that infants possess a conceptualization of the notion of containment prior to acquiring the concept in language (Pieraut-Le Bonniec, 1985; Freeman et al. 1980; Caron, Caron and Antell 1988; MacLean and Schuler, 1989; Aguiar &Baillargeon, 1998). The results from these studies suggest that the conceptualization of containment is either an innate, or at least a very early acquired concept, universally present in all infants. However, three major limitations can be identified concerning these previous empirical studies; a) they all test the physical properties of objects only, b) most of them do not integrate the role of meaningful socio-cultural functions of objects, and, c) they were all carried out in Western cultures, primarily with American middle-class children.

The first and second problems were addressed by Freeman et. al. (1980) and Sinha (1982). They suggested that infants' understanding of the function of an object does not only rest on the infant's ability to analyze the physical properties of that object, but requires the ability to know about the canonical functions of objects. Take for example the notion of containment as presented by container-shaped objects in an upright orientation, such as cups or open-topped hollow cubes. How does the infant learn to use a cup or a cube properly. Freeman et. al. (1980) and Sinha (1982) suggest that due to children's experiences with cups used as containers for constraining liquids from falling onto the floor, they become able to conceptualize cups as canonical container objects. In an imitation task Sinha illustrated that infants rely heavily on how object manipulation is modeled to them by adults in constructing their own conceptualizations with respect to finding out what the 'natural' or proper relationships between objects consist of (Sinha, 1982). For example, if an object with an ambivalent canonical function – such as an open-topped cube which can equally be used to contain as support another object – is previously modeled by an adult to offer the functionality of a container, infants will treat this 'neutral' object in terms of affording a containment function, although the physical properties of the cube could equally afford that of support. This specific phenomenon or preference, referred to as the 'canonicality effect', is described in terms of '*...a specific, and privileged instance of a much more general phenomenon whereby the significance of objects and events is evaluated by children according to criteria derived from joint praxis*' (Sinha, 1982, p. 151). Children's reliance on the canonical function of an object has been tested with 18 to 36 month old infants, who were required to evaluate an object in a canonical or a non-canonical orientation against a relational conceptual schema. The tasks were presented as an imitation task and as a linguistic task, where the children were tested on the acquisition of the spatial relational terms IN, ON or UNDER. English-acquiring children were requested to 'put a toy/block IN, ON or UNDER a box/cup' (Clark 1973; Wilcox and Palermo, 1975; Freeman, Lloyd & Sinha, 1980; Sinha 1982). The youngest infants almost exclusively produced IN responses to these containment-affording objects, independent of whether the objects were oriented up-right or inverted. This behavior was interpreted as a canonicality effect. Consistent with this, the errors produced by the children consisted of responding with IN configurations to ON instructions, and of responding with IN and ON responses to UNDER instructions. Explanations as to what caused this specific pattern of non-linguistic strategies expressed in children's errors indicated that the children were relying on one of the following non-exclusive strategies:

a) on the perceptually most salient affordance – and hence they were constrained by the hypothesis, that *if the object looks like a container place the second object IN it, but if it looks like a support, then place the second object ON it* (Clark, 1993; Clark, 2003).
b) on the easier motoric execution – an upright oriented container, thus offers an IN configuration, as well as the same object in an inverted orientation offers an ON configuration (Wilcox and Palmero, 1975).
c) on contextual cues, with the contextual sensitivity being based on a highly functional and adaptive cognitive mode (Sinha, 1982).

Sinha's suggestion (strategy c) concerning children's flexibility and sensitivity in applying contextual cues was in part supported by the fact that only children's errors to UNDER instructions were not so strongly influenced by whether the cup was first presented in an upright or inverted orientation. He argues that IN and ON configurations share similar properties, in that when the cup is first placed or topicalized in its correct orientation, placing the second object is straightforward, while for an UNDER configuration, the block first needs to be in place or topicalized followed by the cup. Several studies have, in fact, shown that UNDER spatial relationships are more difficult for children to acquire in cognition and in language than are the spatial relationships IN and ON. Rohlfing (2002) suggests that children's relatively late acquisition of POD (UNDER in Polish) is in part due to the perceptual relations referred to by the notion of UNDER (e.g. the *underside* of an object) being less salient than is the case of IN or ON, which on the other hand rely on the *inside* or the *surface* of an object. The inside and the surface region of an upright container object are both perceptually salient, whereas the inner region of an inverted container is not perceptually salient.

Since these studies were all carried out with Western children acquiring prepositional languages it is not clear whether this preference for perceiving objects as containers rather than supports and the later acquisition of the notion of UNDER is a universal developmental sequence. If this claim is viewed in parallel with the notion of canonicality effects derived from joint praxis and actions with members of the adult speech and conceptual community, it seems plausible that the container-bias might be relative to the specific praxis and speech community of the child. I have tested this hypothesis in a comparative study of Danish and Zapotec children's action imitation and language comprehension of the spatial configurations IN, ON and UNDER. The results indicate that the degree to which infants' responses are the result of an IN-biased canonicality effect is dependent on the child's cultural and linguistic experiences and practices concerning the social-historical and meaningful functions of physical and symbolic objects. In order to appreciate the results from the study, it is first necessary to introduce briefly the main differences between canonical object manipulation within the two cultures and in parallelism to the different semantic structures employed by each of the two languages in referring to spatial relationships between objects.

## Culturally Specific Usage of Objects

Due to the restricted diversity of objects available within this particular Zapotec[5] culture, many objects are used with multi-functional purposes. A stool which to the Western mind may primarily be viewed as affording sitting on, will to the Zapotec mind be equally defined with the purpose of supporting a dish while eating one's meal (similar to a table), or when inverted, as a pot-holder for constraining a large clay cooking pot just removed from the fire. Thus, the function of a seat is not taken to be the essence of the chair, and despite its cultural-historical identity being that of a seat, it affords a large amount of other functions as well. These kinds of 'intentional affordances' of objects (Tomasello, 1999), 'ideal dimensions' of objects (Cole, 1996) or 'canonical functions' of objects (Sinha, 1982) are naturally explored for their multi-functional uses by the villagers. Hence, many traditional artifacts are purposefully constructed to possess a variety of diverse functions. I will exemplify this through the description of a second object, namely the traditional one-and-a half to two meters long woven shawl, owned by all Zapotec women and young girls, and which conventionally affords several purposes. When worn across the shoulders, the shawl protects the women from cold and breezes or is used as a handy cloth. However, when the shawl is placed over one's head it serves as a protection from the strong mountain sun. A rolled-up shawl placed in a circle position on one's head serves as a 'cushion' and support for baskets or other artifacts, which are transported on the head. Yet, a fourth conventional function of the shawl consists of using it to strap infants onto their mother's back, or to transport firewood and other types of large materials. Finally, the shawl also conventionally serves to cover-up and protect infants from insects, while taking a nap on a mat spread out over the ground.

Gourds are one of the main container objects used by the villagers for drinking liquids, for serving food, for measuring and scooping up liquids or dry substances. However, when inverted, gourds can equally be used to protect items of food from

5 All information concerning the particular Zapotec culture and language were collected by the author during a field work period of 20 months in total, running from 1995 to 2001. The community is rural, basically very poor, and villagers are semi-self-sufficient farmers. Zapotec is the language spoken in the village.

dust and insects. A second main container object used in this Zapotec community consists of woven baskets, which come in various sizes with various names. Rigid baskets without handles serve both the purpose of transportation (e.g. the harvest is transported in this type of basket, which is carried on people's backs with a strap across their foreheads) and that of the storage of crops, the daily baked tortillas, and even brooding hens. The lack of a handle is in fact an important aspect of this type of basket, since it permits the basket – when placed in an inverted orientation – to serve the purpose of a constrainer rather than a container object. The basket is therefore conventionally used to capture brooding hens or other kinds of small animals, which would otherwise normally run freely around in the compound. One more example of multi-functional tool or object use is the case of tortillas. In the village tortillas not only function as food to be eaten, but also function as eating utensils, and are the only object used for wrapping-up 'lunches' to take on day trips or to take to school. The human body is employed as an integrated vehicle of transportation and as an 'implement' during daily practices. Heads and backs have already been mentioned as the standard means of transportation. In addition hands are used as conventionalized instruments for measuring dry materials, for stirring foods during cooking or eating, and even a fully extended arm serves perfectly to stir large portions of foods, as for example in the fiestas. To my knowledge, feet are not employed for anything other than walking and sweeping fodder to the oxen. So, it seems that Zapotec villagers make use of a whole set of properties within each single object available in the community, and this is an integrated aspect of their cultural habitus.

The main purpose of the following study was to investigate whether, and if so, to what extent the non-linguistic and linguistic spatial conceptualizations of Western middle-class English and Danish infants – when compared to Indigenous 'primitive' Zapotec infants – concerning their abilities to imitate and to comprehend basic spatial relations can account for universal developmental processes. The general claim underlying the present study rests on the notion that neither object manipulation nor linguistic conceptualization develop in a socio-cultural vacuum. Therefore a brief description of the cultural and semantic differences of the two groups of children forming part of the study is in place. Since Danish is a Western culture and since the Danish language employs prepositions for referring to spatial relations, similar to the structure of English, the focus in describing the cultural and linguistic differences between the two groups of children will mainly be restricted to descriptions concerning the case of the Zapotec language.

## The Relativity of Linguistic Spatial Concepts

Similar to tools and objects language is also a symbolic system, and the proper meaning of a word is constructed within a particular social usage. Therefore the view addressed in an earlier section concerning children's appropriation of the properties or affordances of physical objects can equally serve to account for children's acquisition of linguistic concepts during the process of language acquisition. According to

Vygotsky (1986), words should be conceived as symbolic and meditated artifacts in a similar way as material objects are. A similar view of tools and meaning as related mediators is also presented by Karpatschof (2001).

Likewise in the traditional view on the function of objects, which holds that objects possess inherent properties that determine their function, researchers within formal semantics have claimed that linguistic concepts refer to well-defined objects or categories in the world. However, more recently within the discipline of Cognitive Semantics by Lakoff (1987), but also anthropological linguistics, such as Duranti (2000) and Palmer (1996) it is argued that linguistic meanings are not inherent properties of the word, but, psychologically speaking, are cognitively and culturally motivated within cultural practices.

Also of parallel importance to these rapidly emerging new paradigms is the reassessment by Lucy (1992a) of the linguistic relativity hypothesis proposed by the American linguistic anthropologist Whorf (1956) which has now been tested empirically by Lucy (1992b) and by researchers at the Max Plank for Psycholinguistics led by Levinson (1996). These studies demonstrate that languages vary profoundly concerning how the spatial environment is segmented, and that adults' performances on non-linguistic tasks correlate with these specific language differences. Hence, within the last two decades several empirical studies have been offering support for the weak version of the Whorf hypothesis, namely that language influences habitual thought (Whorf, 1956).

One main problem, however, in most contemporary studies re-examining the view addressed by Whorf is that they rarely consider the impact that the cultural habitus of the speakers may have on such cross-linguistic differences (Palmer, 1992) (but see Hanks, 1996, for an exception). A second problem is that so far only one study has approached this issue from an ontogenetic point of departure. The exception is the work of Bowerman (1996). In joint research with Choi, Bowerman compared elicited spatial relational utterances produced by English-acquiring children with those produced by Korean-acquiring children. One main reason why these specific languages are interesting for comparison is that they structure the spatial array in different ways. Some of these language-specific semantic structures were present in the very early utterances of the children. Bowerman and Choi found that by the age of two years Korean-speaking, but not English-speaking children had formed distinctive semantic categories for reference to tight-fit versus loose-fit spatial relationships. In other words, a difference between these two groups was already apparent at the outset of their language acquisition. To illustrate this difference, Korean children used different spatial verbs to express the notion of *a peg in a hole* (a tight-fit relationship) as opposed to *a pencil in a cup* (a loose-fit relationship), while the English-acquiring children simply referred to both spatial notions as IN-configuring relations, using the preposition IN. Bowerman argues that many spatial concepts are not fully formed prior to when children start learning their first language, and that while acquiring the semantic structure of one's language, children are actually acquiring language-specific spatial categories for how to refer to or how to 'profile' a spatial relationship between objects for the purpose of communicating with other people. Thus, the way languages vary in how they structure or 'partition' the spatial environment will motivate infants to conceptualize the world in accordance with these semantic categories. Presenting the case of Zapotec, the following section introduces yet another variation of how languages can choose to partition the spatial array, and predicts that children acquiring such system consequentially will conceptualize spatial relationships different from those acquiring an Indo-European language.

## Zapotec Spatial Words

The particular Zapotec[6] language forming part of this study, has not, to my knowledge, been described in detail previously, and is still far from fully comprehended in detail. The main linguistic means for referring to basic spatial relational conceptualizations in Zapotec (e.g. the configuration expressed in English, as the cup is ON the table), consist of the reliance on a core group of 7 body-part nouns used for locative reference (Jensen de López, 2002, 1998). The meanings of body-part locatives derive from the metaphorical extension of the human body in an upright position (MacLaury, 1989). Hence, the term for head, QUIA, is often used in reference to the highest region, NII (foot) to the lowest region, LÁANI (stomach.region) to the inner region of an object, LLAAN (butt.region) to the lower region, and DETS (back) to the region behind an object and so on. For the present study it is sufficient to understand the general semantics underlying only 2 locative body-part spatial nouns; namely LLAAN, which literately means butt and LÁANI, which literately means stomach, since these are the nouns investigated in the present study.

Despite what at first sight may seem a relatively simple and straightforward system, the meanings of locative body-part terms are in addition often 'intrinsic' (see Levinson, 1996) to the object in such a way that when inverting an object so that what initially was the lower region now becomes the highest region, the spatial gram employed does not change. So for example, the lower or bottom region of a basket in an upright orientation is referred to by the term LLAAN (butt.region), and even when the basket is inverted, offering a surface region, this region is still referred to with LLAAN (butt.region), and not (as might be predicted from the metaphorical extension) as QUIA (head). This notion of an intrinsic frame of reference may be seen as motivated by the canonical functional of the object. Hence, since baskets are canonically containers the bottom or butt region remains referred to using the body-part noun LLAAN (butt.region) independent or how the basket is oriented. The bodypart LÁANI (stomach.region) similarly translates into meanings, which in English are expressed using the prepositions *in*, *under* or *through* (Jensen de López, 2002) with many of these meanings derived from cultural and socially canonical practices. Figure 5.1 illustrates the salient semantic distinction concerning the containment schema configured in Danish and Zapotec.

6 Zapotec is an Otomanguean language spoken in the Southern Mexican state of Oaxaca. Zapotecan languages are primarily spoken in the central valleys near Oaxaca City.

As illustrated in figure 5.1, whereas in Danish (and in English) two linguistic concepts are applied when referring to the depicted spatial configurations, in Zapotec just one linguistic concept is employed to refer to both spatial configurations. This phenomenon, in fact, correlates with the cultural characteristic, noted earlier, of this particular Zapotec community, that objects are conventionally employed with one-to-many functions. Hence, the Zapotec linguistic terms used to refer to location, too, can be said to follow a one-to-many referential system.

## Zapotec and Danish Children's Imitative and Linguistically-Guided Object Manipulation

A total of 33 Zapotec and 71 Danish monolingual children were tested in a cross-sectional developmental study for their ability to imitate and comprehend spatial configurations in a naturalistic experiment involving the placement of a piece of corn-maize either IN, ON or UNDER a small woven basket. The children were 17 to 46 months of age. The procedure of the task consisted of the child seated facing the adult. It was explained to the child that it was going to engage in a small game with the baskets. The game involved an action imitation and a language comprehension task. In the action imitation task two identical baskets and two pieces of corn-maize were employed; one manipulated by the child and the other manipulated by the adult, while in the linguistically-guided task it was only the child that manipulated just one basket and one piece of corn-maize. In both tasks the basket was presented to the child in two different orientations. In one condition the the basket was initially presented to the child oriented in an upright and canonical orientation. In the other, condition the the basket was initially oriented in an inverted and noncanonical orientation.

As a whole the two groups of children differed in terms of the response patterns produced to each of the tasks. The response pattern of the Danish toddlers replicated

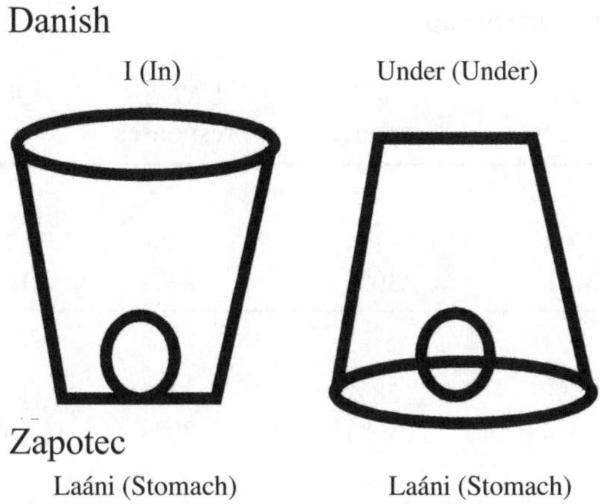


**Figure 5.1 Illustration of the semantic differences expressed in Danish and Zapotec**

the pattern of American and British toddlers, reflecting a preference for responding with IN responses (respectively 39% of their responses), followed by ON responses (respectively 31% of their responses) and finally UNDER responses (respectively 23% of their responses). However, the Zapotec children responded differently, in that their responses expressed an almost equal preference for all three spatial response types (respectively 30%, 30% and 28%) (see table 5.1).

Thus, the Danish children, like the American and British children, were highly influenced by the IN-biased canonicality effect described by Sinha, whereas the Zapotec children were equally happy to respond with any of the three target spatial response types. However, this pattern, as we shall see, was not a result of the Zapotec children simply responding in an arbitrary fashion.

**Results of the Imitation Task**

When modeled to imitate the spatial configuration of placing the corn-maize UNDER the basket, the patterns of errors and hence, the non-linguistic strategies employed by the two groups of children differed. The patterns of errors produced by the Danish children seemed, in particular, to be influenced by the initial orientation of the basket, resulting in the initial-upright and canonical orientation motivating the children to mainly produce IN-errors (see figure 5.2), while the initial-inverted and non-canonical orientation of the basket motivating them to mainly produce ON-errors (see figure 5.3). Hence, they seemed influenced by both the canonical function of the basket and the perceptually and motorically most salience response as suggested in the literature. The Zapotec children, on the other hand, when responding erroneously to the UNDER imitative instruction, produced ON errors in both orientations, but hardly any IN errors (see figures 5.2 and 5.3).

**Table 5.1 The three main response types to the imitative and the linguistically-guided task by language group**

| Task responses | *IN* responses | *ON* responses | *UNDER* responses | Other | Total |
|---|---|---|---|---|---|
| **Imitation** | | | | | |
| Danish | 39% | 31% | 23% | 7% | 100% |
| Zapotec | 30% | 30% | 28% | 12% | 100% |
| **Language** | | | | | |
| Danish | 44% | 28% | 13% | 15% | 100% |
| Zapotec | 34% | 36% | 20% | 10% | 100% |

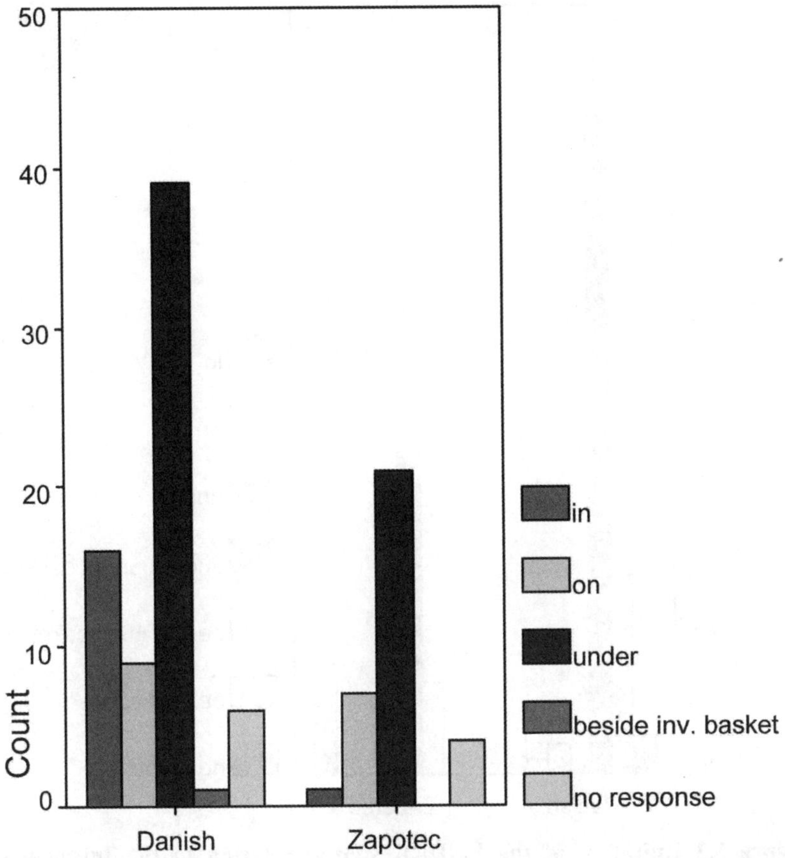


**Figure 5.2 Imitation of the UNDER spatial relation to the Initial-Canonical oriented basket**

These differences suggest that the two groups of children were relying on different strategies with the Danish children directed by the canonical orientation of the basket, thus mainly putting the corn-maize inside the basket, whereas the Zapotec children did so to a much lesser degree. In addition, for the initial-inverted and noncanonical orientation trial, only Danish children responded by turning the basket into its canonical orientation in order to place the maize-corn inside it, while the Zapotec children never did this. Overall, the Zapotec children almost never responded with IN-errors to the UNDER imitation trials, while the Danish children did – especially for the initial canonical trail.

When investigating the responses of the youngest children aged 17–24 months, the Danish children responded in a way which suggests at least two nonexclusive strategies; a) they were not 'able' motorically to invert the initial-upright oriented basket in order to place the corn-maize underneath it and thus simply executed the motoric easiest action consisting of an IN response, or b) they were not able to 'resist'

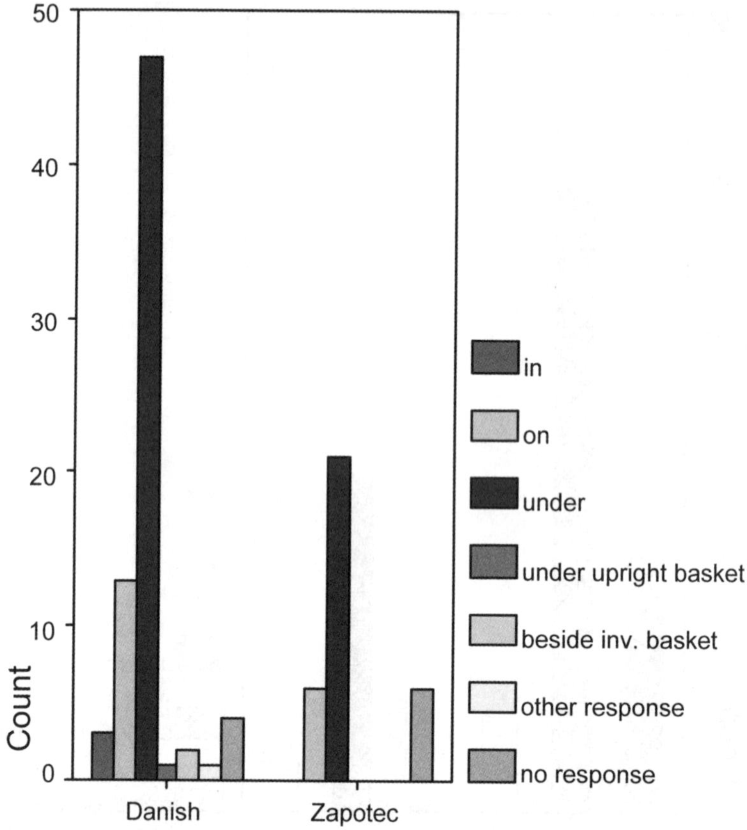


**Figure 5.3 Imitation of the UNDER spatial relation to the Initial-Inverted oriented basket**

the canonical IN-bias demonstrated by the container function of the basket leading them to place the corn-maize inside it. When these two hypotheses are viewed in the light of the level of motor abilities displayed by the Danish toddlers during the remaining parts of the task, the second explanation seems much more plausible. Thus, the explanation of why the Danish children responded in such fashion can be accounted for in terms of all three explanations suggested in the literature concerning American and English children. These are: the children were affected by the perceptual properties of the basket, by the motorically easiest response, by the canonical effect of the basket as a container object or by all three in combination. As for the youngest of the Zapotec children (age 17 to 25 months), exactly half of them responded with an IN configuration while the remaining half responded with UNDER configurations, and none responded with ON configurations, although ON-responses have been argued to be motorically easier than UNDER-responses. Thus, the results from the Zapotec children cannot fully be accounted for by the three explanations available in the literature, and hence these children were relying on different response strategies than Danish and English speaking children rely on. These cross-cultural differences demand further explanation.

First, there seem to exist two immediate and nonexclusive explanations for the Zapotec children's response strategy, when manipulating the basket. Both explanations were addressed in the above descriptions concerning the general culture and habitus of the Zapotec children and in the description of the specific semantic structure underlying the spatial grams present in the language acquired by these children. First what needs to be to recalled is the prevalence of multi-functional object usage, culturally inherent in the habitus of the Zapotec villagers, and which (from a Western point of view of objects) seems to offer a much broader range of canonical and intentional functions. In contrast, the everyday UmWelt of the Danish children consists primarily of objects with just a few specific or canonical functions. Now keeping this distinction between one-to-many versus many-to-one functions in mind, we may now appreciate that: a) the response patterns of the Zapotec children seem to reflect the children's conceptualization of one-to-many functions offered by the objects, while b) the response patterns configured by the Danish children, conversely, may be seen as reflecting the conceptualization of many-to-one functions in relation to the functions container objects offer for configuring spatial relationships between two objects.

*Results of the language task*

The second study set out to investigate whether the two groups of children also differed in their linguistic conceptualization of spatial relationships, and, in addition, whether in accordance with Vygotsky (1978), this might be accounted for by an explanation that is parallel to the one suggested for the differences in the imitation task. In the linguistic task the children were assessed for their ability to respond to linguistic instructions, conveying the same three spatial relational configurations as in the imitative manipulation of objects task. In accordance with the semantic structure of Zapotec, the Zapotec children were tested on their comprehension of the body-part terms LÁANI (inner.region) and LLAAN (butt.region), whereas the Danish children were tested on their comprehension of the Danish prepositions I (in), PÅ (on) and UNDER (under).

Similar to in the imitative object manipulation task, the two groups of children responded to the linguistically guided manipulation of the basket in different, although language- and culture-specific, ways. The pattern of responses to this task were, however, not identical to those to the imitative task. For the Danish group, the discrepancy between the children's overall responses of the type IN and UNDER were larger than in the imitative task, whereas although the Zapotec children responded with larger variation than in the imitative task, their responses were still more evenly distributed as in the imitation task (see table 5.1). In fact, when compared to the results for the imitation task, the Danish children responded with three times as many IN as UNDER responses, whereas the Zapotec children, on the other hand, responded with slightly more ON responses than IN responses.

When instructed to place the corn-maize PÅ (on) and LLAAN (butt.region region) the basket, the responses of the two groups of children differed. The Danish children responded in a way which was consistent with the canonical function of the basket as a container object, thus when initially presented to the basket in an upright and canonical orientation, 59% of the Danish children's responses consisted of erroneous placing the corn-maize inside the basket. Contrary to this response strategy, only 46% of the Zapotec children's responses to this item consisted of the children inverting the basket in order to correctly place the corn-maize ON the surface region of the basket. This suggests that the Zapotec children managed, to a larger degree, to disregard the perceptual-based canonical property of the basket as a container object. When presented to the two language prompts that referred to the notion of a support relationship only and with the basket initially presented in an inverted-initial orientation, the Danish children produced relatively the same amount of IN errors as the Zapotec children produced UNDER errors. Again this suggests that the Danish children were influenced to a larger degree by the basket as a container object, than was the case of the Zapotec children. Hence, there was a clear discrepancy in the nonlinguistic strategies employed by the two groups of children mirrored by the different types of error strategies produced by each language group. Also to the instruction LÁANI (inner region) the Zapotec children produced relatively and significantly more UNDER responses than the Danish children did to the instruction I (in). Even when presented with the initial-inverted orientation of the basket, which was expected to be the orientation least motivating an IN-response, the Danish children still mainly turned the basket upright placing the maize inside it, while they hardly ever placed the corn-maize under it. In contrast to this strategy, a similar number of the Zapotec children produced UNDER as IN responses to this trial suggesting that their overall understanding of the meaning of the term LÁANI was less dependent on the canonical function of the basket as a container object (see figure 5.4).

As a whole, the linguistic guidance of the children's object manipulation proved to have a larger impact than the imitative instructions on the two groups of children responding in 'opposite' directions when manipulating the container object. This difference demands further examination, and may at a first glance seem directly accountable for by the above illustrated differences concerning the semantic partitioning of the spatial array within each of the respective languages. The explanation would then follow that, since Danish, at the lexical level, offers a clear distinction for identifying the spatial relationships of IN versus UNDER this may serve the Danish children as a 'hint' about which type of response might be expected of them. In the case of the Zapotec children, however, the term LÁANI does not distinguish semantically between an IN versus an UNDER spatial configuration and thus only indicates that the object should be placed in an inner region, with no attention paid to the orientation of the basket. This prediction was in part confirmed.

Thus, when only viewing the between group differences at the linguistic level, the semantic structuring seems to explain the differences entirely. However, such an explanation in terms of linguistic relativity tends to leave out the important

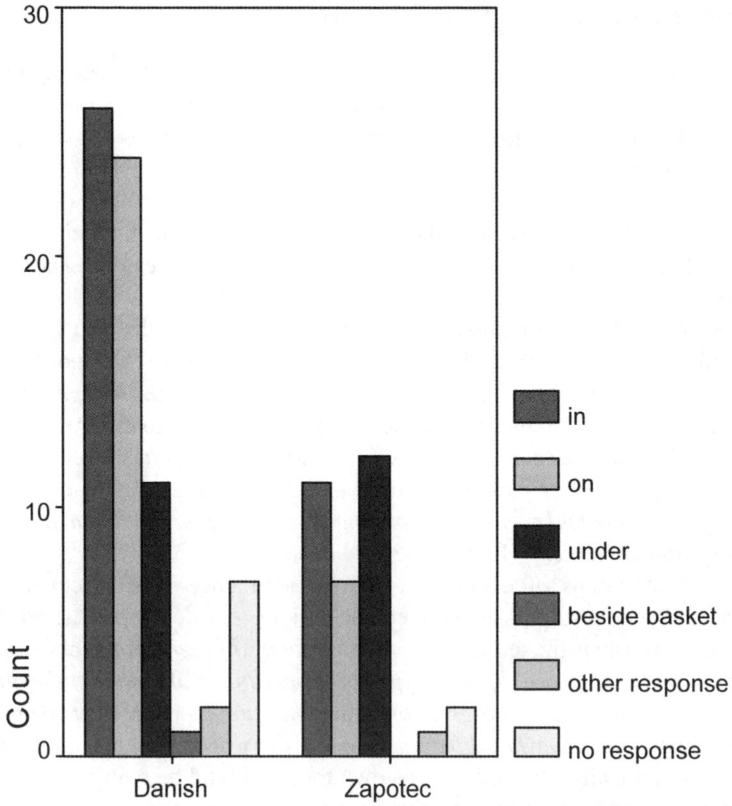


**Figure 5.4 Responses by language group to the I/LÁANI configuring linguistically-guided object manipulation for the Initial-Inverted basket**

role of the cultural differences present in the distinction between the one-to-many versus many-to-one functionality as part of the socio-cultural profiling available to each of the groups of children. If this cultural difference in object manipulation is viewed as an influencing factor, then it might instead suggest that children's acquisition of language, parallel to their acquisition of meaningful and socio-cultural manipulations of objects, are best acknowledged as mutually influencing each other during ontogenesis (Sinha & Jensen de López, 2000). Thus, the different response strategies produced by the two groups of children in the imitation task and in the language task were mutually due to the ecological and environmental constitution of how objects are used in each culture, *and also* by how the languages as a tool serves to mediate cognition in partitioning spatial relationships between objects. Hence it may not be the language *per se* that is responsible for the differences, but the semantics as part of the children's socio-cultural environment that seems to motivate the two language groups in different directions.

## Linguistic Relativism

The conclusion from this study indicates that children's early non-linguistic and linguistically guided object manipulation for basic spatial relationships between two objects is determined by their culture-specific cognitive habitus and by language-specific cognitive strategies. As mentioned briefly, there exist several other possible interpretations of the results, which are in part similar to my view. First of all, in accounting for the differences in the linguistically guided manipulation task only, the view of linguistic relativism serves as one means of interpretation. The American anthropological linguist Whorf, benefiting from Sapir and indirectly from Boas, launched the notion of linguistic relativism. Whorf argued that the language we speak influences our thought. However, according to Whorf it was not all thought as an absolute and determining property that should be expected to be influenced by language. Instead he hypothesized a specific type of thought to differ in accordance with one's language structure, namely what he called *habitual everyday type of thought*. Lucy describes habitual thought in terms of *'everyday, routine ways of attending to objects and events, categorizing them, remembering them, and perhaps even reflecting upon them'* (Lucy, 1992, p. 7).

From observations of exotic languages – a practice Whorf actually argued necessary in order to surpass our own ethnocentricity – he developed the principle of linguistic relativism in the sense of *'users of markedly different grammars are pointed by their grammars toward different types of observations and different evaluations of externally similar acts of observation, and hence are not equivalent as observers, but must arrive at somewhat different views of the world'* (Whorf, 1956, p. 221). Whorf even, critically, stressed that his own theory should be seen as also applying to the premises of science and its ethnocentricity in respect to non-Western modes of conceptualization. Consequently, he stated that *'no individual is free to describe nature with absolute impartiality, but is constrained by the modes of interpretation even when he thinks himself most free'* (Whorf, 1940, p. 214, cited in Lee, 1996). A modern and perhaps more dynamic view, which is similar to that of Whorf, is the one expressed by Slobin (1996) in what he refers to as the active process of 'thinking for speaking', an activity in which the individual is forced to take a specific world view. Also Tomasello's (1999) view of language usage as perspective-taking resembles the idea that language is a tool for thought. Supporting these views, the recent cross-linguistic studies by Bowerman (1996) and Jensen de López' (2002) suggest that children's linguistic conceptualizations are influenced from the onset of language acquisition by the specific semantic structure of their native language, hence, even if children possess 'true' concepts concerning the physical properties of objects, these should be viewed as readily open to language and cultural readjustments during ontogenesis.

This notion of language as a mediating tool and also the notion of intentional actions as mediating signs, although widely associated with Vygotsky (1978), was similarly addressed by Sapir. He drew a parallelism between actions and language as mediating signs of yet other acts and viewed language *per se* as an act. He stated that *'a vast number of acts are language.....That is they [acts/language] are not important to us because of the work they immediately do, but because they serve as mediating signs of other important acts'* (Sapir, 1949, p. 146, in Duranti, 2000, p. 43). Hence in Sapir's view language does not only serve an immediate purpose, it also packages information concerning socio-cultural practices and values. Language, as a mediated tool, serves children in acquiring such socio-cultural practices and values, but at the same time these particular practices and values also serve as a tool for learning one's language as a semiotic system.

## Cultural Embodiment and Intentional Affordances

The notion of linguistic relativity can only partially account for the cross-cultural differences expressed by the Danish and Zapotec children. Unless, following the strong and deterministic interpretation of the linguistic hypothesis, the language differences in themselves do not explain the cross-cultural differences appearing in the imitative object manipulation task. In order to account for both the cross-cultural and cross-linguistic differences children's non-linguistic and linguistically guided performances must be viewed as culturally embodied within intentional and purposeful social practices, as argued by Sinha and Jensen de López (2000). A view similar to that of Sihna and López (although relying on formal rather than on cognitive semantics) is expressed by Hanks (1990) in his extensive analysis of the spatial items known as deixis ('here', 'there' etc) in Yucatan Mayan. Through his analysis he illustrates that the conceptualization of the human body as a corporeal field is habitually used by Mayan speakers to interpret speech as situated within culturally defined living space. In doing so Hank integrates formal semantics with phenomenological characterizations of the human body as a crucial mediator of our relation of the world of objects around us (Duranti, 2000). Discourse about space involves self-awareness or taking the perspectives of others. In describing this, Hanks relies on what Merleau-Ponty calls a *prise de conscience* by the speaker in relation to the listener (Hanks, 1996). Hence to understand an utterance one must be aware of the perspective of both oneself as well as that of the listener grounded in the social values, practices and habitus of the individuals. Hanks' view may also be extended to account for children's early manipulation of objects. Thus, the Zapotec children, in responding to the spatial relational imitation task might be said to be responding from a multi-functional cognitive habitus or habitual thought concerning the canonical functions of the basket. This specific kind of cognitive habitus is what influences these Zapotec children to differ in their response strategies from what is well reported for Western children's responding from a uni-functional cognitive habitus concerning object use.

The child's development of non-linguistic and linguistically guided object manipulation, thus becomes incorporated within a whole series of social abilities. These are constrained by the mediation of cultural practices, different types of profilings, of which many are socially constructed within the specific environment within which the child is situated (Sinha & Jensen de López, 2000). The parallel between children's acquisition of the intentional/canonical affordances of objects and that of the canonical affordances of linguistic concepts rests on the notion of children perceived as enmeshed in a specific environmental and cultural surrounding (Sinha & Jensen de López, 2000). In addition it also relies on the universal ability of infants to place themselves in the intentional space of the others – discerning the user's intentional goal (Tomasello, 1999) – an ability known as joint attention and which develops between the age of nine to twelve months (Carpenter, Nagell and Tomasello, 1998). The present study suggests that the embodied culturally mediated habitus of young children influences both their early object manipulation and their early linguistic conceptualization of spatial relations in parallelism during ontogenesis, suggesting a mutual manifestation in an entire matrix of cultural practices or habitus.

Serving as a closing remark, Wittgenstein's view concerning the meaning of words expressed in *'One cannot guess how a word functions. One has to look at its use and learn from that'*. (Wittgenstein, 1958: 109, § 340, cited in Duranti, 2000), should in my view thus, be reformulated and extended as *one cannot guess how a word nor an object functions. One has, culturally and embodiedly to experience how either a word or an object functions in a specific culture.*

## References

Aguiar and Baillargeon (1998): Eight-and-a-half-month-old infant's reasoning about containment events. *Child Development*, *69*, 636–653.

Bremner, J.G. (2001): *Infancy*. (2nd ed.) Oxford: Blackwell.

Bowerman, M. (1996). The origins of children's spatial semantic categories: cognitive vs linguistic determinants. In J. Gumperz and S. Levinson, (Eds.), *Rethinking linguistic relativity*. Cambridge: Cambridge University Press.

Brugman, Claudia, (unpublished manuscript). Metaphor in the elaboration of grammatical categories in Mixtec.

Bourdieu, P. (1997). *Outline of a theory of practice*. Cambridge: Cambridge University Press.

Caron, A.J., Caron, R.F. & Antell, S.E. (1988). Infant understanding of containment: an affordance perceived or a relationship conceived. *Developmental Psychology*, *24,* 620–627.

Carpenter, M. Nagell, K. Tomasello, M. (1998). Social cognition, joint attention, and communicative competence from 9 to 15 months of age. *Monographs of the Society for Research in Child Development*, *63*.

Chomsky, N. (1980): Rules and representations. *Behavioral and Brain Sciences*, *3,* 1–61.

Clark, E. (1973). Non-linguistic strategies and the acquisition of word meanings. *Cognition*, *3*, 161–182.

Clark, E. (1993). *The lexicon in acquisition*. Cambridge: Cambridge University Press.

Cole, M. (1996). *Culture psychology: A once and future discipline*. Cambridge, MA: Harvard University Press.

Costall, A. (1995). Socializing affordances. *Theory and Psychology*, *5*, 467–481.

Duranti, A. (2000). *Linguistic anthropology.* Cambridge: Cambridge Textbooks in Linguistics.

Fodor, J. (1983). *The modularity of mind.* Cambridge, MA: MIT Press.

Freeman, N.H., Lloyd, S. & Sinha, C. (1980). Infant search tasks reveal early concepts of containment and canonical usage of objects. *Cognition*, *8*, 243–263.

Hanks, W.F. (1990). *Referential practice: language and lived space among the Maya*. Chicago: University of Chicago Press.

Hanks, W.F. (1996). *Language and communicative practices*. Chicago: University of Chicago.

Ingold, T. (1992). Culture and the perception of the environment. In E. Croll and D. Parkin (eds.), *Bush base: forest farm – culture, environment and development.* London: Routledge.

Jensen de López, K. (1998). Organizing space by use of prepositions, body-part terms and dispositional verbs. Paper presented to the Second Conference on Conceptual Structure in Discourse, Atlanta, October 1998.

Jensen de López, K. (2001): Sociodramatic play in a Zapotec Indian Community. Paper presented to the Tenth European Conference on Developmental Psychology, Uppsala, Sweden, August 22–26.

Jensen de López, K. (2002): Language-specific patterns in lexical acquisition of Danish and Zapotec spatial grams. Electronic proceeding from the Stanford Child Language Conference, April 12–14, Stanford Uninversity: 50–59.

Jensen de López, K. (2003). Baskets and Body-Parts: A Cross-cultural and Cross-linguistic investigation of children's Development of Spatial Cognition and Language. Ph.D. Thesis. Institute of Psychology, Aarhus University, Denmark.

Karpatschof, B. (2002). *Activity, tool and meaning.* Paper presented at The Second Conference on *Doing Things with Things: The Design and use of objects*, University of Copenhagen, November, 2002.

Lakoff, G. (1987). *Women, fire and dangerous things: what categories reveal about the mind.* Chicago: Chicago University Press.

Lee, P. (1996): *The Whorf theory complex*. Amsterdam: John Benjamins.

Levinson, S. (1996): Frames of reference and Molyneux's question: Cross-linguistic evidence. In P. Bloom, M. Peterson, L. Nadel & M.F. Garret (eds.), *Language and Space* (pp. 109–169). Cambridge, MA: MIT Press.

Lucy, J. (1992a). *Language diversity and thought: A reformation of the linguistic relativity hypothesis*. Cambridge: Cambridge University Press.

Lucy, J. (1992b). *Grammatical categories and cognition: a case study of the linguistic relativity hypothesis*. Cambridge: Cambridge University Press.

Luria, A.R. (1979/1984). *Sprog of bevidsthed.* Translated from Jazyk i soznanie. Nyt Nordisk Forlag.

Mandler, J. (1996). Preverbal representation and language. In P. Bloom. M. Petersen, L. Nadel & M.F. Garret, (Eds.), *Language and space*. Cambridge, MA: MIT Press.

MacLaury, R. (1989). Zapotec body-part locatives: Prototypes and Metaphoric extensions. *American Linguistics*, *55*, 119–153.

MacLean, D.J. & Schuler, M. (1989). Conceptual development in infancy: The understanding of containment. *Child Development*, *60*, 1126–1137.

Mauss, M. (1979). *Sociology and psychology: Essays*. London: Routledge & Kegan Paul.

Pieraut-Le Bonniec, G. (1985). From visual-motor anticipation to conceptualization: reaction to solid and hollow objects and knowledge of the function of containment. *Infant Behavior and Development*, *8*, 413–424.

Palmer, G. (1996). *Towards a theory of cultural linguistics*. Austin, TX: University of Texas Press.

Rofhling, K. (2002). *UNDERstanding: How Infants acquire the Meaning of UNDER and Other Spatial Relational Terms.* Doctoral Dissertation Thesis, Faculty of Linguistics and Literature, University of Bielefeld, Germany.

Slobin, D. (1996). From 'thought and language' to 'thinking for speaking'. In J. Gumperz and S. Levinson, ed., *Rethinking linguistic relativity*. Cambridge: Cambridge University Press.

Sinha, C. (1982). Representational development and the structure of action. In Butterworth, G. and P. Light (eds.), *Social cognition: Studies in the development of understanding* (pp. 137–162). Brighton: Harvester Press,.

Sinha, C. (1999). Situated selves: learning to be a learner. In Bliss, J., Säljö, R. and Light, P. (Eds.). *Learning sites: Social and technological resources for learning* (pp. 32–46). Oxford: Pergamon.

Sinha, C., & Jensen de López, K. (2000). Language, culture and the embodiment of spatial cognition. *Cognitive Linguistics*, *11*, 17–41.

Spelke, E. (1991). *Physical knowledge in infancy: Reflection on Piaget's theory*. In S. Carey and R. Gelman (eds.) *The epigenesis of mind: Essay on biology and cognition* (pp. 133–169). Hillsdale, NJ: Lawrence Erlbaum Associates, Inc.

Spelke, E., Breinlinger, K., Macomber, J. & Jacobson, K. (1992). Origins of knowledge. *Psychological Review*, *99*, 605–632.

Tomasello, M., Kruger, A.C. & Ratner, A. C. (1993). Cultural learning. *Behavioral and Brain Sciences*, *16*, 495–552.

Tomasello, M. (1999). *The cultural origins of human cognition*. Cambridge, MA: Harvard University Press.

Ulvund, S.E. (1983). The canonicality effect in search for the hidden object. *Scandinavian Journal of Psychology*, *24*, 149–151.

Vygotsky, L. (1978). *Mind in society: The development of higher psychological processes*. (M. Cole, editor) Cambridge, MA: Harvard University Press.

Vygotsky, L. (1986/1994). *Thought and language*. (A. Kozulin, editor). Cambridge, MA: MIT Press.

Whorf, B.L. (1956). *Language, thought and reality*. Cambridge, MA: MIT Press.

Wilcox, S. & Palmero, D.S. (1974). 'In', 'on', and 'under' revisited. *Cognition*, *3*, 245–254.

Wood, D., Bruner, J. & Ross, G. (1976). The role of tutoring in problem solving. *Journal of Child Psychology and Psychiatry*, *17*, 89–100.

# PART III
# Transformation and Things

Chapter 6

# The Cognitive Biographies of Things

David de Léon

We are currently seeing an increasing awareness in the cognitive and mind sciences of the importance of physical structure for cognition. The old view of cognition as something that takes place only in the head has been replaced (or at least tempered) by a view that recognises the roles played by physical and social structures. The environment, it turns out, is not just an arena for action – a playground for problem-solving and plan constructing minds – but is intimately implied in many, if not all, cognitive processes.

There are several different ways of advancing this claim, but most would agree that physical structures in the world can, at least, act: as an extension of memory (Hutchins, 1995b; Beach, 1988; Norman, 1988), to simplify choice, perception and internal computation (Kirsh, 1995; Clark, 1997), to constrain and even determine cognitive behaviour (Zhang & Norman, 1994), and to transform tasks in ways that better harmonise with our cognitive competencies (Hutchins, 1990, 1995a; Norman 1991).

Once this basic idea has been accepted it should be natural to ask *how* these kinds of physical structures come about. After all, if physical structure can be an intimate and integral part of cognition, more so than previously recognised, then asking questions about the growth, development and appropriation of these structures should be as natural as asking age-old questions about learning and development. In fact, both learning and development need to be understood afresh in the light of these emerging insights. The genesis, evolution and adjustment to cognitively significant structure ought to be viewed as an essential aspect of most, if not all, of our cognitive achievements.

Most of the authors cited above *do* acknowledge that there are interesting processes responsible for the build-up of cognitively significant physical structure, but these processes then figure to a negligible extent in their accounts.

Hutchins (1995a), for instance, gives truncated histories of the astrolabe and the compass rose (both ancient navigational instruments that significantly transformed the cognitive task of ship navigation), but then simply concludes that practice can be 'crystallised' into things, without discussing the process of crystallisation itself.

Kirsh (1995) acknowledges that the interaction of agent and environment can be studied along different time scales, and does an admirable job of looking at medium and short-term mechanisms of how people set up their workplaces for particular tasks. However, the issue of how the workplaces themselves evolve is not addressed.

Bærentsen's (1989) work on the evolution of the rifle is an inspirational exception which explicitly deals with the influence artefacts have on the cognitive demands of task performance, and the influence of cognition on artefact development. Although a bold and innovative attempt, Bærentsen's analysis relies on an unanalysed notion of cognitive processes being built into things (see de Léon, 1999).

Activity theory (the tradition in which Bærentsen's paper is written) places great emphasis on the historical and cultural foundation of thought and artefacts and would therefore seem an ideal place to find the kind of analysis sought for. The activity theoretical concepts of *externalisation* and *historicity* also seem to capture the concerns discussed. However, as Engeström (1999) has noted, there seems to be a general paucity of work in activity theory on these very topics.

A part of the reason for this neglect is no doubt connected with the difficulty of reconstructing what are primarily historical processes. Unless we limit our interest in the ways in which artefacts and practices co-evolve to very short time scales (for a nice study in this vein see Agre & Shrager, 1990) we have to choose between longitudinal studies and historical reconstructions. Of these two options a longitudinal approach may, initially, seem preferable, as we avoid much of the speculation and conjecture required in a reconstruction. However, longitudinal studies demand great effort without guaranteeing results: we cannot know beforehand that anything of interest will turn up at a chosen site or during the time-frame selected. In many cases the sheer scope and intrusiveness of longitudinal projects also make them unfeasible.

Although less controlled and more speculative than a longitudinal study might be, reconstructions permit us to explore sites where the occurrence of significant artefactual change has already been established. They also present an opportunity to investigate real-life events and changes that span durations for which a longitudinal approach would be impractical. These particular characteristics make reconstructions, despite the aforementioned methodological concerns, a compelling and intriguing possibility – a possibility that has, to date, been insufficiently explored.

In the rest of this paper I will take a shot at constructing what I like to call a cognitive biography, tracing the life-history of a particular artefact and its use over a period of roughly three decades, and detailing the mutual influences between cognition, activity and changing physical structures. In contrast to reconstructions of events taking place over several lifetimes (cf. de Léon, 1999) the present biographical time scale makes ethnographic methods and structured interviews part of the available methodological arsenal.

The artefact in question is an unusually large spice shelf that I encountered whilst conducting a cognitive ethnography (Hutchins, 1995a, 1995b; Lave, Murtaugh & de la Rocha, 1984) of people cooking at home in their kitchens (see de Léon, 2003). Each of the participants of the cooking study were video filmed whilst preparing dinner and later interviewed about the organisation of their kitchens and about the origins of their tools and cooking practices. One of the participants of the study was Robert, a man in his mid-fifties. It is in his home that the shelf described in this paper resides. Based on the interview conducted at the time of the study I have attempted a reconstruction of the genesis and evolution of the shelf and pieced together a credible story of the underlying factors behind the various changes to the shelf, as well as their probable cognitive consequences. The reconstruction was continuously checked against the tape I had of Robert cooking and a number of supplementary interviews. The shelf did not always appear as it does now. The collection of spices has been stored in a manner of different ways and the actual shelf makes its appearance fairly late in the story. Although I speak of the evolution of the shelf it is really the history of a constellation of artefacts and practices.

This paper is thus an experiment in reconstructive cognitive biography. The result is an unusual hybrid: on some occasions I use data from the case study to make particular claims, at other times I introduce extraneous theories and observations to bear on the case in question and to explain my observations. I hope that the attempt might give some indication of what a cognitive biography might look like, and what sorts of things we might learn by constructing them.

## A Cognitive Biography of a Shelf of Spices

First I will give a brief description of the shelf and then outline some ways in which its current structure and organisation supports Robert's cognitive activity whilst cooking. This is followed by a reconstruction of the shelf's history.

### *A brief description of the shelf*

Most of the spices in Robert's kitchen are kept on a tall shelves fixed to a wall, a few steps from the stove and workbench where the main activities of cooking take place (see Figure 6.1). The shelf consists of two prefabricated units bought at IKEA (a ubiquitous Swedish furniture store) that have been placed one above the other.

Each shelf is just deep enough to accommodate one spice jar and wide enough to accommodate a row of about ten jars. All jars have been labelled with embossed plastic strips and are neatly aligned along the shelving. Almost all are of identical size, row upon row of yellow plastic lids divulging their origins as reused Coleman's mustard jars. Dispersed among these are a couple of tins, a few brand name spice jars and two pepper mills of disparate design. Through the clear glass of the jars various dry powders, seeds, flakes and roots can be seen, their colours ranging from beige to brown.

In the narrow space between the two units that make up the shelf – too narrow to accommodate an additional row of jars – lies a bulldog clip, some rubber bands, a small pile of paper twist ties, and a paper packet of black pepper. Along one side of the shelf hangs a decimated garlic braid.

In all, almost exactly one hundred jars and containers are kept here. This constitutes an unusually large and impressive collection.

**Figure 6.1 The shelf (to the left of the door), sink and plate rack (far left of picture) and corner of fridge (far right side of picture). Part of the dining room can be seen through the kitchen door**

*The organisation of the shelf*

Robert's cooking encompasses Western as well as more exotic cuisines. About a third of the spices found on the shelves (the lower three shelves) are endemic to French and Italian cooking, the remaining shelves being devoted to spices used in Indian, Middle Eastern, Chinese, Japanese, Indonesian and Thai dishes.

The spices are organised into categories according to a number of different principles (see figure 6.2 for the basic categorisation of the shelf).[1] The top shelf, for instance, contains various hot spices, such as chilli and cayenne. Here it is taste and function that determines placement. Another section contains different kinds of dry leaves used in South and East Asian cooking, and is thus loosely organised by the *form* in which the spices are found. A less obvious category is the group of spices placed together because of their modest application, being dubbed 'by-the-pinch spices' by Robert; the principle governing this particular categorisation being the manner in which they are applied. There are also several sections in which the spices

1 The categories in figure 6.2, and in the text that follows, are Robert's own and were taken from a picture of the shelf which he had annotated. In the interview Robert also explicated some of the uses to which he put the spices.

are grouped together because they are used together in a particular style of cooking. There are prominent sections with spices used in, for instance, Indian and Chinese cooking.

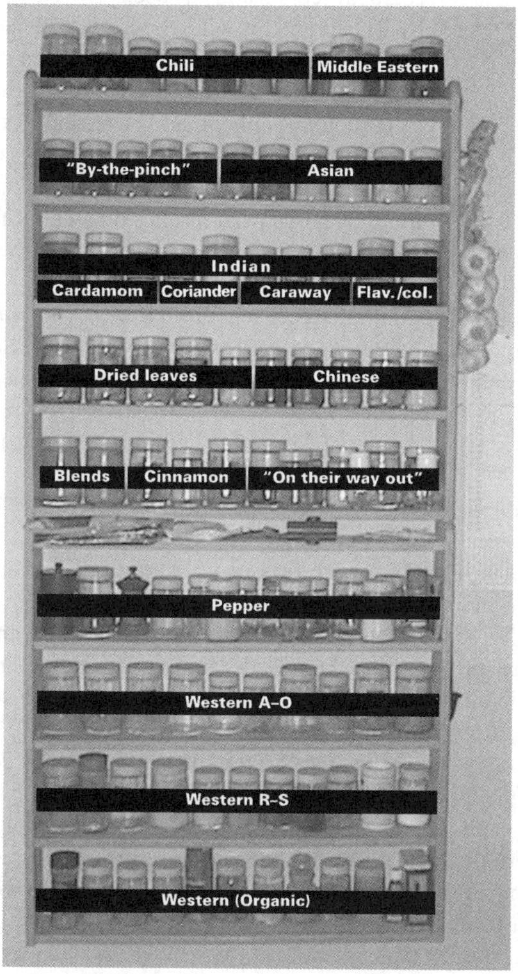


**Figure 6.2 Basic categorisation of the shelf**[2]

2 The fastidious reader might note a slight discrepancy between the labels in the picture and the description of the categories given in the text. The figure is based on a picture taken a year after the original study and in the interim the organisation of the shelf changed somewhat (more on this below).

In those cases in which a particular spice is found in more than one form (e.g. whole and ground) these have been placed adjacent to one another.

The bottom three shelves are home to more familiar spices used in Western cooking. This is the largest regional section and has been arrayed alphabetically. The spices kept here are shared by Robert and his wife. Since his wife lacks his penchant for spicy and exotic food this is the only part of the shelf that she ever uses. As she is also substantially shorter than her husband the placement of the spices, in this mutually accessible region, is particularly felicitous. The reason Robert gives for the alphabetical ordering of these shelves is that it was the only obvious categorisation to present itself that would serve two people. It is instructive to note that the only region of the shelf that is used by more than one person relies on a culturally conventional system of categorisation. Alphabetisation ensures a clear, mutually intelligible, and maintainable order.

There is also a small section of spices that are 'on their way out'. According to Robert these are spices that will be sacrificed as space is required. Some of these are spices that Robert once bought out of curiosity, or that he has finished experimenting with, or for which he has recently found better alternatives (for instance, access to fresh spices that were only previously available in desiccated form).

*Some ways in which the shelf currently supports cognition*

Since each shelf is only deep enough for one jar, almost all the jars can be seen at any given time; of the roughly one hundred jars that stand here only a handful are blocked, or partially obscured, from sight. The jars are labelled and their contents can be clearly seen through the glass, both label and content contributing to the ease of identification of a particular spice. We might think of the shelf as a kind of conceptual model, a physical structure embodying the basic spice combinations of some of the most common, Asian and Western dishes, as well as certain aspects of Robert's cooking practice and his personal way of conceptualising cooking.

We should be cautious, however, lest we view the shelf simply as a reflection, projection, or externalisation of Robert's inner representations of spices and cooking. For one, the genesis of the shelf belies such an interpretation. As we shall see in the following, there are several determinants of the shelf's structure and organisation that are incidental, rather than intentional. Moreover, to whatever extent (and in whatever form) the structure and content of the shelf is actually represented by Robert, this will have been repeatedly shaped by the presence of the shelf itself.

The visible thematic spice groups arguably function to support Robert's memory in a number of different ways. Assuming that he knows what spice he is looking for, a problem then facing him is locating the appropriate jar on the shelf. Instead of having to scan the entire shelf for the spice in question, the thematic groups focus his search to a particular area (obviating the need for knowing the exact location of every spice). For example, just knowing that a spice is, or is not, used in Western cooking removes a large part of the shelf from consideration. That the organisation of the shelf is consonant with his own idiosyncratic categorisations, conceptualisations and habits of cooking also makes the regions more easy to locate.

Even the relationship between the form of his body and the position and organisation of the shelf comes into play here. The spices that are most frequently used (the Indian spices, according to Robert) are within easy reach, whereas slightly less frequently used spices (such as the Middle Eastern spices) require him to stretch upwards, or (in the case of Western cooking) to bend down. The placement of the various groups of spices is not only a question of physical effort and comfort, but ensures that the customary position of Robert's body when facing the shelf presents him with the most regularly used sections of the shelf. The same holds true for Robert's wife, whose height constrains which shelves she has easy access to. This is a very straightforward and clear example of the role of embodiment for cognition (for a critical review of the concept of embodiment see Clark, 1999).

These, then, are some ways in which the shelf can support the task of locating a particular spice. When cooking a dish from memory an occasional problem is actually remembering which spices to look for in the first place. In such a case, all Robert needs to know is what *kind* of spices he is searching for. Looking at the appropriate area of the shelf he need then only recognise the spices required – a far easier task than recalling them (for a primer on recognition and recall see Baddeley, 1997).

The co-location of spices that are commonly used together also serves as a reminder, throughout the cooking session, of spices still to be applied. Anytime a spice jar is replaced on its shelf, neighbouring jars can jog Robert's memory.

There is also an interesting structural feature of the shelf that supports the replacement of spice jars. Since the spices are stored on the shelf one jar deep, and each plane is completely full, the removal of any jar leaves a clearly visible gap. This gap can then function as a perceptual place marker. Again, this saves Robert from having to remember the exact locations of where particular spices are stored: he has only to look for a break in the array to know where to replace a jar. Of course, should Robert pick out several jars together, he would be left with the problem of pairing the correct jars with the appropriate gaps when time comes to replace them. This is not an insurmountable problem and would still be easier than having to remember the exact locations. However, as seen on the video of him cooking, Robert only picks out and uses one jar at a time, replacing it before picking out the next one, thus ensuring that there is no confusion as to which jars belong in which gaps. There are several ways in which the shelf could potentially be used, but significantly, Robert has settled on a strategy that *permits* the physical structure to simplify the cognitive demands of correctly replacing used jars. It is well to point out that it is the *combination* of techniques, procedures and/or habits, with particular artefacts and task environments, in relation to specific tasks, that determines the cognitive congeniality[3] of an activity.

---

3 Kirsh (1996) calls the measure of how cognitively hospitable an environment is its 'cognitive congeniality.' A cognitively congenial environment is one that reduces 'the number

## The History of the Shelf

If we want to understand how the shelf came to have its present structure and use, we must go back in time to the late sixties, to the spice shelf in one of Robert's previous homes, and then trace the development of the shelf back to the present. And this is what I will attempt next, reconstructing the genealogy of the shelf with Robert's help.[4]

In the first kitchen that Robert remembers having (in a flat in Stockholm, Sweden) the spices were kept in no determinate order, and on a single shelf next to a stove (see step 1 of figure 6.3). At that time his collection was considerably smaller, consisting of only a few conventional Western spices, and could fit snugly on a single shelf. Robert had yet to develop the intense, and broad, interest in cooking that he has today, and exotic food was still something that was only occasionally sampled in one of Stockholm's few Chinese restaurants (in the late sixties Stockholm had only two, or possibly three, of these).

Although there was no intentional order to the arrangement of the jars at that time we can speculate that there may have been some incidental grouping resulting from the handling of the jars. In the kind of arrangement described, spices that are often used together will tend to gravitate towards each other. There are several ways in which they may do this. If all, or some, of the spices used in a particular dish are taken off the shelf and put back at the end of a session of cooking, spices that often occur together will tend to end up in close proximity. Or, if spices are placed at the front of the shelf immediately after use, more commonly used spices will be found near the front, whilst spices in less demand will be gradually pushed towards the back wall. Needless to say, this kind of grouping would have aided the location of common, and even uncommon, spices. With just a few spices in the collection there would have been little incentive to organise them further.

These kinds of processes, in which the repeated performance of an activity shapes the environment in which that activity takes place, are an important source of supportive structure.[5] The spatial redistribution of artefacts is one basic mechanism which we have already encountered. In the same way that spice jars can come to be functionally grouped through their use, so may other artefacts employed in the kitchen. During my study of cooking, from which this case is taken (de Léon, 2003), I noticed several of the participants making frequent trips to the plate rack in order to fetch common objects. Implements that are routinely required are likely to have been recently used and cleaned.The plate rack is therefore the most probable place to

---

and cost of mental operations needed for task success,' 'reduces cognitive load on working memory' and increases 'the speed, accuracy or robustness of performance' (Kirsh, 1996). The use of the term is extended here (for reasons outlined in the above paragraph) to cover activities as well as environments.

4 I have taken some liberties in truncating the history of the shelf and excising portions that add little, from the point of view of the reader.

5 Barker (1968) calls this kind of relation between behaviour and environment 'behaviour-milieu synomorphs'.

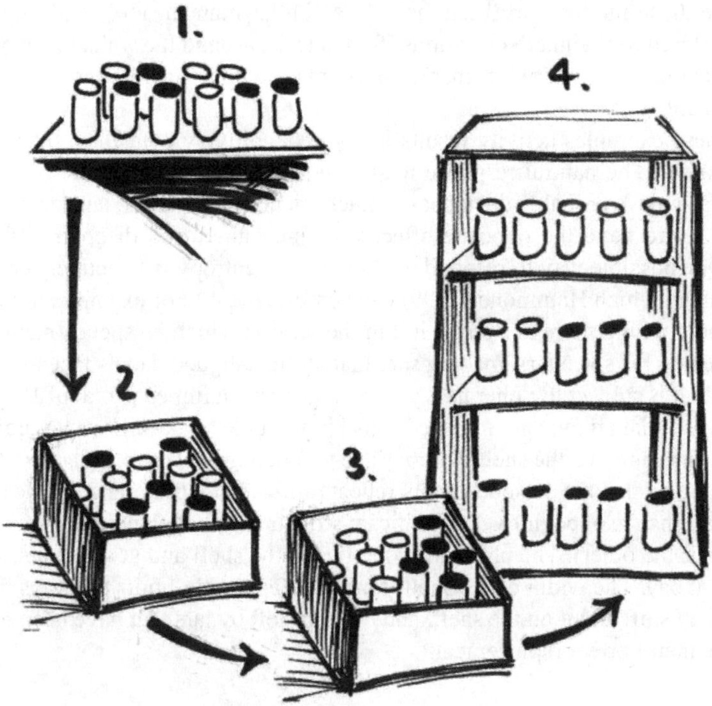


**Figure 6.3 A schematic history of the shelf**

find them. In addition, the rack is also conveniently placed in most kitchens and its contents visible. The processes of using and cleaning kitchen implements, therefore, sorts out, and makes readily available the most frequently used implements.

Note that this particular use of the rack also conserves effort, the effort of emptying the rack and replacing the things kept there. The rack is cleared almost as a by-product of the activity of cooking.[6] Much of human activity is like this, with actions having multiple reasons and serving multiple simultaneous purposes (cf. Wertsch, 1998).

Basic wear and tear is another mechanism that can generate supportive structure. For example, think of a footpath kept clear through use (Barker, 1968), or the growth of meaningful pathways between buildings (see Ribeiro, 1996). Or, consider how repeatedly opening the phone book to the same section (for instance, the pages containing your local pizzerias) can weaken the spine of the book making it easier

6 Reading an earlier draft of this paper one of my colleagues pointed out an important exception to this way of using the plate rack. Although she recognised the use of the rack described here, she mentioned that she will sometimes leave the rack untouched for a period of time after washing up so that the full extent of her domestic efforts might be recognised, and appreciated, by her partner.

to locate those numbers in the future.[7] In a similar manner, tools and implements that are stored in designated locations (for instance, around the walls of a workshop) can discolour, or otherwise mark, those places, thus facilitating their correct replacement.

In these examples activity results in some cognitively congenial change to the environment. The natural response to such change is compliance; the net effect is beneficial and we probably do not pay it much attention. However, it is more common for activity to have the opposite effect, creating clutter and disorder, rather than order. One possible way to respond to encroaching entropy is to actively counteract it, a strategy which Hammond (1990) calls enforcement.[8] For example, in the video of Robert cooking there is a slight lull in the session which he spends meticulously straightening his spice jars, making sure that all 'misaligned' labels face to the front. As the shelf is subject to rather heavy use (in the session filmed a total of 18 different spices were taken down and replaced) this kind of upkeep becomes a natural part of activity, ensuring that the shelf can continue to function as it does. Of course, it could also be argued that the episode simply reflects an aesthetic preference or ideal, rather than maintenance of cognitively significant structure (although neither interpretation invalidates the other). The physical properties of the shelf and jars also help to keep entropy at bay. The width of the shelf, for instance, greatly limits the ways in which the jars can shift about on the shelf, and the gaps left by jars that have been removed facilitate their correct replacement.[9]

### *The collection grows*

Towards the beginning of the seventies Robert starts to experiment with Chinese food in an attempt to recreate some of his favourite restaurant meals. There are, as yet, no Chinese cook books available in Swedish (and books in English are still hard to come by). However, the Swedish-Chinese Association publishes a small pamphlet that Robert procures. Through an acquaintance (a supplier to some of Stockholm's delicatessens) Robert buys exotic spices in small yellow stackable tins. Throughout

7 This is why your avant-garde books always seem to fall open at the raunchy episodes in the hands of any guest browsing your bookshelves.

8 Hammond (1990) and Hammond, Converse and Grass (1995) take enforcement to be an *active* strategy of order imposed on the environment. It is interesting to note how, in the present case, enforcement is sometimes *incidental* (recall how clearing the plate rack can be a by-product of other activities).

9 It would be interesting to analyse and compare the various artefactual and procedural means that have been devised to resist entropy. What technical solutions are there? For what kinds of task is artefactual stability (taken to mean something other than plain robustness) a desiderata? Does stability stand in the way of other functional aspects? If so, what kinds of trade-offs are there (cf. Bleed (1986) on the trade-offs between reliability and maintainability in hunting weapons)? An obvious place to start would be to look at collections and catalogues and how these are used, and how they have evolved. Another would be to study how surgical instruments are handled and cared for.

the seventies Robert's spice collection grows, in concert with his steadily increasing knowledge and interest in cooking. Robert and his family move a couple of times and at some point Indonesian dishes are added to the repertoire. The small yellow tins are gradually abandoned as spices become more readily available from other sources. The spices, that are now bought by weight, are transferred to recycled Coleman's mustard jars (these are the jars that can be seen in figures 6.1 and 6.2).

### *Spices in a box*

In 1979 Robert and his family move from Sweden to England. An extended period followed in which they lived in a succession of more temporary settings: a van, a trailer, a couple of rented apartments. During this transitional period Robert kept his spices in a low box (see step 2 of figure 6.3).

Looking down into the open box only the lids of the spice jars could now be seen, the many identical lids exacerbating the difficulty of distinguishing one spice jar from another. To find a particular spice, Robert had to rely on his memory and/or make an educated guess. To determine whether or not the jar selected was the one actually sought for he would have to lift it above its neighbours to be certain of its identity. Some of the incidental ordering on the shelf may have survived the transfer to the box, but may also have been broken up. Assuming that at least some of the ordering of the spices made it into the box an incorrect guess might still give a clue to whether he was searching in the right area of the box. Again, just using the box may have bought some gradual ordering to the spices.

The temporary solution, as so often is the case, turned out to be less temporary than initially expected. Eventually tiring of the impracticalities of the arrangement Robert decided to order the spices into thematic groups (see step 3 of figure 6.3). To locate a jar he would still have to rely on memory. Nevertheless, the organised box was an improvement over the earlier, mostly haphazard, distribution.

This is the first full and deliberate ordering of the spices undertaken. If there was already some order in place, as I have suggested, we can speculate that that order may have influenced the subsequent intentional organisation, perhaps serving as a rough guide. Any ordering that is conserved through this kind of process corresponds nicely with the way that the spices are used.

### *From box to shelf*

In England Robert discovers Indian cooking. For obvious reasons to do with the country's colonial past, Indian cook books, restaurants and spices were all readily available. More spices were brought and Robert's collection started to spill over into various drawers in his kitchen.

In 1982 the family buy a house and Robert purchases a small shelf for the new kitchen. The jars in the box were transferred to the shelf and placed in the thematic categories that had crystallised over the years (see step 4 of figure 6.3). Although this particular shelf is not the same shelf as the one described earlier in the paper

**Table 6.1 Summary of main cognitive differences between using the box and using the shelf**

| |
|---|
| **Remembering which spices to use**<br>A cursory scan of the shelf can trigger memory of the spices included in a particular dish. When taking or replacing a jar on the shelf during cooking, adjacent jars may serve as reminders of spices still to be applied. In contrast, the content and labels of the jars kept in the box are not visible. |
| **Finding a sought for spice jar**<br>A guessed at location of a particular spice is easier to confirm using the shelf, since feedback is instantaneous and category boundaries more distinct. Erroneous guesses are more costly when using the box. |
| **Correct replacement of spice jars**<br>Gaps are easier to spot and fill on the shelf and neighbouring jars also help to establish correct replacement. In the box there is a greater risk that jars will shift about, thus breaking up thematic groups. |

(that one still being many years, and many meals, away) it can be assumed that it supported Robert's cooking in ways similar to the present day shelf.

In the transition from box to shelf there is a noteworthy qualitative shift that occurs. Whereas the chief function of the categories in the box was to aid Robert in locating specific spice jars (remember, only the top of the lids could be seen when the jars were in the box), the visibility afforded the jars when placed on the shelf gave rise to new, unplanned for, and unanticipated functionality, in addition to a general improvement of the previous functionality.[10]

Let me briefly outline some of the consequences of combining the categories of the box with the structural features of the shelf (the main differences between using the box and the shelf are also summarised in Table 6.1).

Finding a sought for spice on the shelf has some similarity to finding it in the box: in both cases Robert is required to know the relevant category to which the spice belongs as well as the rough whereabouts of that category. One of the things that differentiates the two cases, however, is the ease with which the supposed location of the spice is then confirmed. On the shelf, feedback is almost instantaneous, the jars are stored one jar deep and can be easily scanned (compare this with the shelf in his first kitchen which was just a single plane). In the box, a jar has to be lifted before its identity can be confirmed. Not only is it easier to locate a particular jar on the shelf, but the cost of a faulty guess is much less compared with the extra effort

10 Those with a fondness for evolutionary metaphors of artefact development (see e.g. Basalla, 1988; Ziman, 2000) might like to think of this event as a case of exaptation (Gould & Vrba, 1982). That is, as a feature which currently enhances fitness (i.e. cognitive congeniality), but which was not originally built for the role it now plays.

incurred when picking out the wrong spice from the box. The categories in the box also have looser boundaries and are harder to pinpoint than the more rigid categories on the shelf. From just looking at the box the various thematic groups are not readily apparent and there is the constant risk that the location of particular jars will shift about during prolonged use of the box.

The removal of a jar from either box or shelf leaves a gap that can later aid in the replacement of the jar. On the shelf the gap is easy to spot and fill, and the visible identity of adjacent jars can confirm a correct replacement. In addition, adjacent spices can serve as reminders of spices still to be applied. In the box the identity of neighbouring jars can only be established by lifting them up above the level of the box.

Earlier in the paper it was noted that the vertical positioning of the shelf (in relation to Robert's body) also contributes to the ease with which particular spice jars are found and retrieved.

*Reaping the benefits*

The ways in which the shelf supports cognition is a, mostly, unanticipated result of the combination of the categorisation of the spices contained in the box with the structural properties of the shelf. The claim made here is that the improved cognitive congeniality of the shelf is partly accidental, and historically contingent. However, the new ways of working afforded by the shelf are not automatically achieved. Although there are cases where a change in the material means of an activity entail a concomitant change in procedure, in this instance some adjustment had to be made before the benefits of the new set-up could be reaped. There may be many ways in which the shelf could potentially be used, but only some of these are an improvement over the previous use of the box. It is by using the shelf in particular kinds of ways that it is able to scaffold cognition. An example given earlier in the paper is a good illustration of this. You might recall how Robert's strategy (or habit) of taking down and replacing spice jars one at a time permitted the shelf to simplify the cognitive demands of the task. If several jars were instead taken down together, then Robert would be faced with the additional chore of pairing each of the jars with the appropriate gap.

The transition from spices kept in a box to having them arrayed on a shelf, the adjustments to, and appropriation of the resulting structure by Robert, is an interesting case in which an artefact (or artefactual complex) grows and develops in cognitively congenial ways. Needless to say, all artefactual change does not lead to improved functionality or to cognitive congeniality. Nevertheless, the process described may have greater generality than this single case.

Similar mechanisms can be found in, for instance, the gradual co-evolution of the form of books and bookcases (Petroski, 1999). Before the advent of the printing press, books were rare and expensive luxuries, either locked up or chained to their bookcases. As they became more numerous, vertical partitions were introduced to the then standard bookcase design in order to prevent the shelves from sagging.

Although the motivation for these partitions was originally structural the partitions later came to play an important role in locating books. Catalogues, usually posted on the end of a bookcase, grouped the books in accordance with the partitions that contained them. Even as late as 1749 catalogues were still not alphabetical, but based on these tables of contents.[11]

*Concluding the story*

In 1988 Robert and his family moved back to Sweden. During the summer of their return they lived in a caravan and a selection of the spices were again back in a box. Later, when Robert and his wife moved into a flat, Robert put in an order for a new shelf. In 1990 they finally bought a house and the two IKEA shelves, described at the beginning of the paper, were purchased.

At present almost all spices have been transferred to recycled Coleman's mustard jars. One could argue, from a cognitive standpoint, that a mix of jars, of varying appearance, would have been better (providing redundant cues as to identity), but here Robert prefers to let æsthetic concerns take precedence. Cognitive congeniality is, after all, but *one* factor that governs the shaping of our environment.

Today Robert has set a self-imposed limit on the continued growth of the shelf. He confesses to having been 'a bit of a collector' in the past, buying spices in order to learn about them. Now he knows more about his needs and there is also a greater pressure on available space with Japanese and Thai cooking having been recently added to his repertoire.

Since the time of the original study, and the last and most recent interview with Robert, the shelf has undergone further change and is still in flux. Since the initial study was conducted Robert's wife has converted to using organically grown spices. As a consequence the bottommost shelf has been cleared for that use (as seen in figure 6.2). The two shelves above it now house Western spices used by Robert alone. However, a short while after Robert's wife converted to organically grown spices many shops in Sweden ceased stocking them and they have become increasingly difficult to buy. Robert's wife confesses to now using the ordinary spices on the shelves above hers to 'top up' her own jars.

Will the organisation of the bottommost shelf persist, as a vestige of an ephemeral fad for organic spices, or will the organisation of the shelf eventually return to the one described in the text? One thing is certain, the present shape and organisation of the shelf is unlikely to end here and will undoubtedly continue to change, in concert with Robert's unabated interest in cooking and in response to ever changing circumstances.

11 For some other interesting types of interactions and exchanges between co-located artefacts see de Wit et al. (2002).

## Discussion

The story told here is a reconstruction of events taking place during a period of roughly thirty years. As we have seen, the evolution of the shelf is intimately tied to the changing circumstances of Robert and his wife, Robert's intensified interest and growing knowledge of cooking, and even to changes at a societal scale in eating habits. The biography of the shelf and its use has allowed us to glimpse some interesting things, a few of which I think bear repeating.

One important insight is the realisation that much of the structure that supports cognitive activity may have partially *non-cognitive origins*. At least some structure seems to be the result of chance, circumstance, compromise, surrounding agents, and the shaping force of repetition. Perhaps the most significant moment in the present case study is the emergence of new and unanticipated functionality from the combination of previously unrelated structures.

I believe that insufficient attention has been paid to these sorts of processes and their impact on tasks and task environments. We need to continue to explore and expand our catalogue of these phenomena, but more pressing, perhaps, is the work of disentangling and understanding their interplay with other, more purposeful and intentional, processes. Some changes to an artefact or task environment can impact the cognitive ease with which a task is performed without any major changes in procedures or techniques, whereas other changes are accompanied by a concomitant transformation in the way a task is carried out. How people adapt to a new structure, and appropriate and incorporate it into more congenial forms of a task, is a key part that needs to be properly worked out.

A better understanding of these phenomena may also serve as an important corrective to theories of design, production and artefact functionality, that are excessively intentional.

Another important and related point is the significance of use. One thing that has been demonstrated in this paper is that the cognitive congeniality of an environment is as much a function of an agent's particular use of that environment as it is a function of the environment itself. It is the particular ways in which things are used that *permits* them to contribute in cognitively beneficial ways. Cognitive congeniality is a relational property, and cognitive biographies must include both the changing forms and shifting uses of things.

As was noted in the introduction, the reconstructive nature of cognitive biographies may be the cause of some concern. The way that the present biography was created, for instance, was through repeated interviews coupled with study of the contemporary form of the artefact and associated activities. The biography is, by necessity, constructed after the fact; consequently there are aspects of it that are based on conjecture. Though cognitive biographies have some distinct advantages they also open the doors to speculation and presupposition.

This problem, however, is not unique to the present endeavour. There are a number of related enterprises that have learned to deal with similar issues. There is much that we may learn, for instance, from the history of technology (for reviews see Staudenmaier, 1984, 1990), the anthropology of technology (e.g. Lemonnier, 1986, 1992; Pfaffenberger, 1988, 1992), social construction of technology studies and actor-network theory (for a review of both see Bijker, 1994), as well as the diverse and numerous branches of archaeology. None of these disciplines (and there are more than those listed here) are specifically focused on cognition, but all are concerned with the processes behind changes in material culture. These areas may provide us with supporting evidence, complementary perspectives and methodological innovations and insights.

Recent focus on cultural biographies of objects (e.g. Appadurai, 1986; Kopytoff, 1986; Gosden & Marshall, 1999) is an interesting example, not only for the partial neologistic parallelism, but because of shared methodological issues. Both kinds of biographies seek to retrace sequences of relations between people and things. In the case of cultural biographies of objects it is a sequence of shifting meanings that is the elusive quarry, in the present case it is a sequence of uses and cognitions that needs to be reconstructed. Each quarry is as intangible and ephemeral as the other and we might find that there are methodological solutions to be shared.

Although interpretative science is difficult there are some potential rewards to be had. Cognitive biographies allow us, for instance, to explore real life events and changes spanning long time periods. And they allow us to concentrate our efforts on sites where significant change has already been established. But there is a further, fundamental reason for constructing cognitive biographies of things.

Tracing the history of a thing and its use can help us understand the present use of that thing. A cognitive biography allows us to better discern the cognitive roles currently being played by an artefact. Against the backdrop of earlier incarnations of an activity, and previous forms of an artefact, the cognitive functions of a thing are able to stand out in relief. For example: a feature of an artefact may be the result of a response or adjustment to problems inherent in previous versions of a task. Knowing about these earlier phases, enables us to discern (or, at least, to explore) the current roles being played by this feature. Overlaying succeeding phases of an activity with preceding ones can often point us to possible areas of cognitive significance.

A disregard for the developmental trajectories of environments, tasks and people, will therefore lack some of the essential ingredients necessary for a genuine understanding of the cognition of task performance.

## Acknowledgements

I would like to thank the participants and organisers of the Doing Things with Things workshop in Copenhagen for their reactions to the ideas that eventually became this paper, and the participants of the Lund University Cognitive Science seminar for their comments on an earlier draft. I am also grateful to Björn Nilsson for numerous suggestions, and Pieter Vermaas for some particularly cogent points of criticism. Thanks are also due my informant Robert for his help, as well as for his delicious cooking. This work was supported by the Swedish Foundation for Strategic Research.

## References

Agre, P. & Shrager, J. (1990). Routine evolution as the microgenetic basis of skill acquisition. *Proceedings of the 12th Annual Conference of the Cognitive Science Society.* Hillsdale, NJ: Lawrence Erlbaum.

Appadurai, A. (1986). Introduction: commodities and the politics of value. In A. Appadurai (Ed.), *The social life of things* (pp. 3–63). Cambridge: Cambridge University Press.

Baddeley, A. (1997). *Human memory: Theory and practice, 2nd ed*, Hove, UK: Psychology Press.

Barker, R. (1968). *Ecological psychology: Concepts and methods for studying the environment of human behaviour*. Stanford: Stanford University Press.

Basalla, G. (1988). *The evolution of technology*, Cambridge: Cambridge University Press.

Beach, K. (1988). The role of external mnemonic symbols in acquiring an occupation. In M.M. Gruneberg, P.E. Morris and R.N. Sykes (Eds.), *Practical aspects of memory: Current research and issues, Vol. 1: Memory in everyday life*. Chichester, UK: Wiley.

Bijker, W.E. (1994). Sociohistorical technology studies. In S. Jasanoff, G.E. Markle, J.C. Petersen and T. Pinch (Eds.), *Handbook of science and technology studies*. Thousand Oaks: Sage publications.

Bleed, P. (1986). The optimal design of hunting weapons: Maintainability or reliability, *American Antiquity*, *51*(4), 737–747.

Bærentsen, K.B. (1989). Mennesker og maskiner. In M. Hedegaard, V.R. Hansen & S. Thyssen (Eds.), *Et virksomt liv: Udforskning af virksomhedsteoriens praksis* (pp. 142–187). Aarhus: Aarhus Universitetsforlag.

Clark, A. (1997). *Being there: putting brain, body, and world together again*, Cambridge, MA: MIT Press.

Clark, A. (1999). An embodied cognitive science? *Trends in Cognitive Sciences*, *3*(9), pp 345–351.

de Léon, D. (1999). Building thought into things, *Proceedings of the 3rd European Conference on Cognitive Science*, pp. 37–47.

de Léon, D. (2002). Cognitive task transformations, *Cognitive Systems Research*, *3*(3), 449–459.

de Léon, D. (2003). Actions, artefacts and cognition: An ethnography of cooking. *Lund University Studies*, 104.

de Wit, O., van den Ende, J., Schot, J. & van Oost, E. (2002). Innovation junctions: Office technologies in the Netherlands, 1880–1980, *Technology and Culture*, *43*, 50–72.

Engeström, Y. (1999). Activity theory and individual and social transformation. In Y. Engeström, R. Miettinen and R.-L. Punamaki (Eds.), *Perspectives in activity theory* (pp. 19–38). New York: Cambridge Univeristy Press.

Gosden, C. & Marshall, Y. (1999). The cultural biography of objects, *World Archaeology*, *31*(2), 169–178.

Gould, S.J. & Vrba, E. (1982). Exaptation–a missing term in the science of form, *Paleobiology*, *8*(1), 4–15.

Hammond, K.J. (1990). Learning and enforcement: Stabilizing environments to facilitate activity. In B.W. Porter and R.J. Mooney (Eds.), *Proceedings of the seventh international conference on machine learning* (pp. 204–210). San Mateo, California: Morgan Kaufman.

Hammond, K.J., Converse, T.M. & Grass, J.W. (1995). The stabilization of environments, *Artificial Intelligence*, *72*, 305–327.

Hutchins, E. (1990). The technology of team navigation. In J. Galegher, R. Kraut & C. Egido (Eds.), *Intellectual teamwork: Social and technical bases of collaborative work*. Hillsdale, NJ: Lawrence Erlbaum Associates.

Hutchins, E. (1995a). *Cognition in the wild*, Cambridge, MA: MIT Press.

Hutchins, E. (1995b). How a cockpit remembers its speed, *Cognitive Science*, *19*, 265–288.

Kirsh, D. (1995). The intelligent use of space, *Artificial Intelligence*, *73*, 31–68.

Kirsh, D. (1996). Adapting the environment instead of oneself, *Adaptive Behavior*, *4*(3/4), 415–452.

Kopytoff, I. (1986). The cultural biography of things: commoditization as process. In A. Appadurai (Ed.), *The social life of things* (pp. 64–91), Cambridge: Cambridge University Press.

Lave, J., Murtaugh, M. & de la Rocha, O. (1984). The dialectic of arithmetic in grocery shopping. In B. Rogoff and J. Lave (Eds.), *Everyday cognition: its development in social context* (pp. 67–94). Harvard: Harvard University Press.

Lemonnier, P. (1986). The study of material culture today: toward an anthropology of technical systems. *Journal of Anthropological Archaeology*, *5*, 147–186.

Lemonnier, P. (1992). Elements for an anthropology of technology. *Anthropological Papers, 88.* Ann Arbor, Michigan: Museum of Anthropology, University of Michigan.

Norman, D.A. (1988). *The design of everyday things*. New York: Doubleday Currency.

Norman, D.A. (1991). Cognitive artifacts. In J.M. Carroll (Ed.), *Designing interaction: Psychology at the human–computer interface.* Cambridge: Cambridge University Press.

Petroski, H. (1999). *The book on the bookshelf*, New York: Alfred A. Knopf, Inc.

Pfaffenberger, B. (1988). Fetished objects and humanized nature: Towards an anthropology of technology. *Man*, New Series, *23*(2), 236–252.

Pfaffenberger, B. (1992). Social anthropology of technology, *Annual Review of Anthropology*, *21*, 491–516.

Ribeiro, G. (1996). Situating action III: Acting, dwelling, and squatting: An ecological approach to the relation between person and urban environment, *Ecological Psychology*, *8*(2), 131–151.

Staudenmaier, J.M. (1984). What SHOT hath wrought and what SHOT hath not: Reflections on twenty-five years of the history of technology, *Technology and Culture*, *25*(4), pp. 707–730.

Staudenmaier, J.M. (1990). Recent trends in the history of technology, *American Historical Review*, *95*(3), 715–725.

Wertsch, J.V. (1998). *Mind as action*, Oxford: Oxford University Press.

Zhang, J. & Norman, D.A. (1994). Representations in distributed cognitive tasks, *Cognitive Science*, *18*, 87–122.

Ziman, J. (Ed.), (2000). *Technological innovation as an evolutionary process*, Cambridge: Cambridge University Press.

Chapter 7

# The Woman who used her Walking Stick as a Telephone: The Use of Utilities in Praxis[1]

Hysse Birgitte Forchhammer

Many resources are spent on developing, issuing and adjusting utilities[2] in order to support and help handicapped people overcome their disabilities in every day life activities. But in practice these technologies do not always fulfill their purpose of improving the everyday life of the user. Utilities sometimes get in the way of the user, and they can prove impractical or even useless! A utility might be designed in an impractical way, so that the user literally bumps into it, falls over it or lacks the mental or physical capacities to us it. At other times, utilities are used in new, unplanned and creative ways to deal with an unexpected problem, as when a stick is used as a 'telephone' when an old woman wants to contact her neighbors by knocking on the ceiling. The use of utilities cannot fully be understood as a function of design. Utilities – and other things – are used in complex social practices: complex arrangements of people and material surroundings, imbedded in larger contexts of other societal practices and discourses. And, furthermore, the use of things is an ongoing practice. The things and the people involved, as well as their interrelationships, change, develop and deteriorate over time.

The aim of this paper is to take a closer look at how utilities are used in everyday practice by people with different degrees of physical and cognitive handicap. I will argue that the focus of analysis must be the interrelations between utilities, the people and situations involved, defined by the actual activities pursued.

## What are utilities? – Theoretical references

In professional practice, utilities are defined as those objects that are offered to patients in order to ease their daily lives by compensating for disturbances in certain functions. Thus, the concept is operationally defined with reference to the *intended technological use*. This definition, however, is restricted to only those objects that

1 With apologies to Oliver Sacks (1987).

2 The term 'utility' is used instead of 'disability-aids'. 'Utility' refers to all kinds of things *used* as aids, and not only objects that are deliberately produced for that purpose.

are made in the technological industries and designed with a certain purpose. Since my aim is to study how utilities are used in practice, the concept of utilities must be widened to also include things that patients themselves create or use *as if* they where utilities. Furthermore it will be necessary to clarify how the concepts of *practice* and *technology* are interrelated. I will briefly present how these concepts and their interrelationship are defined in the following analyses.

Consistent with the approach of *critical psychology* (Holzkamp, 1983, Dreier, 1993, Forchhammer and Nissen, 1994) the following reflections will be based upon an analytical definition in which utilities are regarded as*: technologies – strategies or objects– that are (intentionally or unintentionally) used in practice by different parties in order to alleviate a problem that has arisen in connection with the patient's illness.*

In this way I will be using 'technology' as an inclusive term for different degrees of materialized strategies and procedures,[3] objects and artifacts. A walking stick and a bed lift have a tangible material form, whereas a strategy for putting on socks with only one hand or mnemonics may be considered as objectified but not materialized in the same sense. A cognitive strategy such as calculation is an example of a socio-historically developed objectified strategy we are able to relate to almost 'as if' it was given to us in materialized form. In the following analysis, I will primarily focus on utilities in actual materialized form.

Technology is thus a socially produced object or strategy. Utilities can be used for many things and assigned many different meanings. Their function can be *transformed* into new and different functions that were not thought of before. Technologies are, nonetheless, often characterized as being designed in a certain context, by someone, with certain goals in mind. But it is a theoretical challenge to grasp the dialectics of predetermination and open-endedness in the use of technologies. I try to handle this problem by using the concepts of *objectification* and *subjectification. Objectification* is a concept, rooted in Marxist inspired thought (Leontjev, 1981, Heller, 1981), and is used to describe not only the specific condition in which technology is socially produced, but also how technology in one way or another represents specific meanings and functions. Objectification may be an expression used to describe how objects – possibly over thousands of years – are designed, developed, and adapted by and for people in order to fulfill specific purposes in the socio-historically organized (re-)production of living conditions. For example: a knife as a cutting tool or multiplication as a tool for calculating. We are in our practice as human beings usually able to grasp that meaning, though not necessarily in a merely reproductive way. We grasp the meaning by a process of subjectification, in which the common meaning becomes concrete and subjectively

3 A 'strategy' is the verbalized and consciously mediated way of solving a problem by implementing a specific way of doing it. 'Procedure' refers to the actual way of performing this specific task in practice. This way of using the term 'procedure' resembles the term of 'procedural memory' in cognitive neuropsychology (Gazzaniga, 1999). The distinction between 'strategy' and 'procedure' will be explained further in one of my later examples.

relevant. In this process, the common meaning may be realized, but may, instead, be transformed into a new meaning. In this way, the dual character of the process is also revealed. The process of using technologies is both a process of *subjectivation*, making sense in practice, and also of *objectivation*, producing (new) meaning that potentially can transform the concrete situation and be related to by others. The processes of subjectivation/objectivation come into play when an object, that may have had a different function in another context, is used as a utility and is assigned meaning as a utility by the user(s) in a different context, as when two phone books are used to raise the seat of a wheelchair.

Objectification/subjectivation is the *process* through which the socially produced character of technology is mediated through the use and ascription of meaning. Subjectivation is hence the process in which an object is used with a specific purpose in mind, being something that I/we can use for my/our particular goal, e.g. when a rock that happens to be lying on a beach is used as a seat on which I can rest. But this process of ascribing new use does confront limits. Not only do the physical characteristics of the object thus place constraints on how the object may be used, but also societal thought forms, discourses, ideologies and power-relations are manifest in the concrete use of technologies. The different discourses of how, where, and by whom, utilities should be used, are a concrete condition in the use of utilities.

Another concept, that of *everyday practice,* also mainly derives from critical psychology (Holzkamp, 1995). The concept of the subject as participating in the societal praxis is fundamental to being human. The subject is seen as a mediating authority who transforms the objective sociohistorical action conditions into subjective meaning and concrete action. The social life is organized into different action contexts and the participants move between several of these contexts. The contexts are limited by different relatively well-defined goals and means.

Most of the participants in my research live their lives in relatively limited geographical frames. Most of them seldom leave their apartments. Movements between different contexts nonetheless, characterize their lives. They move between their home and different institutions, e.g. hospitals, doctors, rehabilitation center, etc. New action contexts are continuously created as the 'domestic carer visits the participant to help with personal hygiene' or when 'a family member comes to visit and drink coffee', etc.

Life is thus structured in and around action contexts that are relatively delimited units, but life is also a continuation through these different contexts. Consequently, *daily life* is both homogeneous and heterogeneous, i.e. both continuous in terms of a series of more or less reflective, goal-oriented, actions and at the same time split up into smaller units of different routines, relaxation and 'doing nothing'. A standard reading of Holzkamp would lead us to think that only activities that contributed directly to 'the widening of societal production and widening of societal action potency' would count as 'real human activities' (Dreier, 2002, Huniche, 2002). According to such an interpretation, the theoretical understanding of everyday life presented by Holzkamp (1995) would give rise to an almost normative distinction between real goal-oriented activities, on the one hand, and less important, daily routine hurly-burly, on the other.

While looking at human practice as organized in activity contexts has its value, this theoretical perspective fails to grasp the entire complexity of human practice. Everyday life is also characterized by non-goal oriented activities. Concepts like procedural and routinized activities encompass other aspect of activities. But also concepts of *playing* (Keller, 2005), *relaxing* and *doing nothing* obviously must be considered as important to understanding this non-goal oriented forms of activity that form the complex whole of everyday practice.

Finally, I will argue that human everyday practice is *social*. As will be shown later in the empirical examples, the everyday use of utilities is socially distributed. Even though utilities are often designed for individuals, they are often used by, or involve, a number of other people or institutions. Human practice is also socially organized from a genealogical perspective (Foucault, 1987): every practice has a history and is embedded in, and related to, other layers of socio-historically developed practices. Although such a genealogical analysis will not be central to this paper, I will in some of the examples refer to historically developed thought forms or discourses on handicap and rehabilitation with reference to other genealogically based analyses of the field.

## The empirical study

The following examples are based on interviews and observations of a group of 25 stroke victims focusing on their use of handicap-utilities. Twenty-five participants were selected from the larger group of 150 patients who participated in a study of stroke and functional ability (Andersen, 2000). According to the standardized medical rating-scales, the 25 participants were all suffering from mild to severe symptoms following their cerebral stroke. They had all been hospitalized for 12–24 months before the interview. At the time of discharge from the hospital, all received one or more specially designed handicap utilities. In most cases, technologies to facilitate walking, such as a stick, a walking-frame or a wheelchair, or grips and handles had been installed in their apartment.

As all the participants had undergone a standardized medical and neuro-psychological test both at the time of their discharge from hospital and 6 month later, it was possible to select a sample that varied in respect to age, gender, social-status, functional and medical status and level of cognitive disabilities.

The participants gave their written consent to participate in the interview. Furthermore, it was suggested that a close friend, a care giver or some other person involved in the everyday life of the patient should also take part in the interview. In this way, the socially distributed aspect of use could be included in the study. But, in addition, the companion would also be able to assist in the interviews themselves given that some of the participants, due to their aphasia, had problems communicating (Forchhammer, 2001). With few exceptions, the interviews took place in the homes of the participants. All interviews were taped and transcribed. Furthermore fieldnotes were taken at all visits. The interview sessions varied from 30 minutes to 3 hours.

*Analysis of daily life with utilities – when utilities are not used in the intended way*

Although, utilities are supplied in terms of one or more functions, sometimes these functions are not fulfilled. In the participant group, I found several examples of utilities that were not used but rather were hidden away or seen as disturbing to the daily life activities of the patient. In a large 'functionalist' apartment complex in Copenhagen, an 82-year-old woman lives with her husband. She had suffered a stroke. Ever since the apartment was built in the 1930s, the couple had lived in the same apartment with a balcony. When their two children lived at home, the apartment seemed too small, but now the husband and wife live alone, and they are comfortable with the space in the apartment. The woman has a right-side paralysis and global aphasia, i.e. she has extensive difficulties with speech, writing, reading, and the comprehension of language and symbols. She can only move around by using a wheel chair and she needs assistance when she has to move from her wheel chair. Her husband takes care of almost all the domestic work, and so the need for home care is minimized. The woman had been supplied with a wheel chair when she was discharged from the hospital, but now the wheel chair had been left in the corridor taking up space. The problem was that new doors had been installed in the apartment shortly after the woman came home from the hospital, and now the wheel chair could no longer pass through the doors.

The patient's daily life situation had changed in such a way that the utility could no longer be used as planned. Small changes in the home, such as a new balcony door, changed flooring, or new furniture, can disable the functionality of the utility. In some instances the errors are made from the outset: if a handle has been placed in the wrong place or in an impractical place, then it may not used at all. Officially, it is the responsibility of the local authority, as represented by the domestic help or nurse, to report about the lack of use of utilities to the primary sector. In praxis, this system seldom works. The professionals who work in the home usually have other primary tasks to perform, e.g. cleaning, helping with personal hygiene, or nursing wounds. In praxis, the helper adapts to the impractical placement of a handle by supporting the patient and developing different compensatory strategies to make up for the lack of a practical utility. The formal goal of helping the patient wash herself is thus fulfilled. However, the rehabilitation element of helping the patient to be able to cope with the task herself has been placed in the background. Maybe the helper fails to appreciate the double function of the handle. Maybe the helper is unaware of the possibilities of changing the position of the handle or of other products on the market. It can also be a question of the frequent use of substitutes and the turnover of staff so that no domestic helper is ever in the same home over a sufficient period of time to be able to obtain extensive knowledge of the participants' special rehabilitation needs.

We can, thus, identify a certain type of problems with the use of utilities, that is presumably common among most professionals, and which, in most cases, could be solved with relatively limited resources: through better evaluation of the utility in its concrete setting and also by the introduction of a more systematic and frequent re-evaluation procedure in which the actual functionality of the utility is evaluated and adapted.

In the example of the door handle, the utility had lost its practical functionality because of physical changes in the apartment. In other cases, the changes that occur concern the patient. It could for instance be that the functional aspect of the user's ability to act has changed, such as a physical deterioration in functioning so that they are no longer able to use the utility.

For example, a 62-year-old woman had developed a considerable spasticity in her paralysed hand and could no longer grab the handle on her walking tool. Consequently, she stopped using the walking support and instead now supports herself by holding onto different objects in her living room, thus increasing the risk of her falling.

*When use is context dependent*

Technologies can be more or less connected to a specific location or dependent on certain practical conditions, e.g. an electric toothbrush has to have electricity and is designed to be used in the bathroom, or somewhere at least where there is access to water and a drain. Other utilities are designed to be moved from place to place and to be used in different contexts, such as a walking frame.

When a utility is not used as planned, it may be a matter of changes in the physical environment, or else remission or changes in the participant's physical abilities. But it may also be because the particular utility has never been tried in, or adapted to, the specific environment in which the utility is to be used. For example, one woman had an emergency button installed, but this was placed on a table in the living room, thus preventing her from reaching it when she fell in the hall.

It can also be the case that training in the use of a tool is given in one context but the tool is actually going to be used in a different context. This kind of transfer can be especially problematic if the patient due to her brain damage has acquired specific problems of abstract thinking, memory or other specific cognitive disturbances. A participant learnt, for instance, how to put on a support sock whilst sitting on a hospital bed with a tall edge against which she could support herself. At home, however, she has a bed without tall edges, and so she had to re-learn the entire procedure. In this case, the patient had cognitive problems concerning abstraction and breadth of view and problems in visuo-spatial orientation, which made it difficult for her to apply the learning from one context to another context.

*When the utility is used in new and untraditional ways*

In a different case, the physical level of functioning of the participant had *improved*, so that she no longer used her utility in the traditional sense. A younger participant, who suffered a stroke at the age of 45, had to give up her former job and now receives disablement pension. She spends most of her time in her apartment and has taught herself to work with word processing and spreadsheets at the computer. Moreover, she is active in several associations where she writes summaries and balances the budget. Despite her activities, the days are still long. She watches TV and cooks her own breakfast and lunch. When she first arrived home from the hospital, she felt 'bound to the wheel chair'. Now she moves around in her apartment by supporting herself against different items of furniture, such as doors and window frames. She explains how she was told that she would never be able to walk again. However, she proved them wrong. She has always done more than she was 'permitted' by the personnel concerned with her treatment and rehabilitation. She claims that her tendency to cross the lines, placed by the professionals, is the reason that she has come as far as she has. It has, however, also been the reason that she has fallen a few times, and her friend claims that the participant often overestimates her own strength. She still has her wheelchair, but she no longer uses it as a wheel chair. She uses it, instead, as an 'office chair'. When she works at the computer, she is comfortable using the wheel chair as an office chair, because it enables her to drive around and change her positions in a way that she could not with ordinary office chairs. Furthermore, she uses the wheel chair as a 'launching pad' when she has to stand up. By having a wheel chair, on which she can lock the wheels, she trusts that the chair will not disappear under her when she has to stand up.

A couple of times a week, another participant gets help from the upstairs neighbor. He comes down to help with the shopping and to get a cup of coffee. They have arranged that the participant will use her walking stick to knock on the ceiling, whenever she is ready for a visit.

In the examples I have been discussing so far, such as the wheel chair and walking stick, the utility has continued to be used for its intended function, but also used for an 'improvised' function. In other cases, the technology of utilities far exceeds being a consciously used utility and is instead an ordinary household item. Things and objects that had originally been used to compensate for a function disorder have now become a part of the every day inventory, as when a specially designed chair for use in the shower is used as a flower-bench.

In other cases, the process is reversed. Ordinary pieces of furniture, or other items that the participant has always possessed, change their function and are used as utilities: furniture is used for support and take-off, books are used to raise and support, bath stools are used as steps or plant stands. Several participants reported that they have changed their procedures. They had, for instance, found a different way to put on their clothes than the procedure used in the hospital. The participants were, however, seldom consciously aware of the fact that they had created new utilities. That is, the participants had made small changes and adaptations – actions – probably without taking any notice of these changes. The participants did not mention these changes spontaneously, but the changes became clear the minute I asked the participants to *show* me how they used a particular item or how they followed a certain procedure.

*When we encounter limitations upon transformation and meaning ascription*

Things change meaning when they are used in new ways. There are, however, limitations on meaning ascription and transformation of use. Although it is difficult to *define* abstract limitations on the meanings that can be ascribed to the technology, the participants encounter such limitations in praxis every day. A person might well assign human traits to the walking stick, such as calling it a 'friend' or an 'enemy,' but when communicating with another person there has to be some agreement about whether or not the words are meant ironically, concretely or metaphorically with regards to the utility in question. An aphasic might find a situation such as this very difficult as a result of their problems with contextualization and framing of meaning ascription. The aphasic participant may appear childish or unclear when she identifies her walking-stick as the 'stupid, stupid, you know, that one'. The limitations of meaning ascription are thus not embedded in the technology itself but rather defined by the existing societal discourse and hence situationally defined.

The material characteristics of the technology might also set limits on what the object may be used for. The object may fall over, break, roll away, etc. At the same time, the specific shape of the object objectifies a more or less open potential of usage. The more advanced a technology, the more firmly defined is this potential. Transforming this potential of usage demands a certain competence on the part of the participant. Some technologies require far more competence than others do. An electronic bed, for instance, requires a certain amount of learning and conscious appreciation of the specific possibilities and limitations of the technology. But neither the competence nor the objectification of the usage potential is independent of the situation in which the technology is used. When a 95-year-old demented stroke participant is about to fall, he automatically reaches out toward his walking frame – and *not* the door handle. He cannot consciously explain this action. The act is rather an expression of a bodily learnt competence, a procedurally acquired, pre-reflexive, and automatic action sequence. In this situation, the usage potential of his utility is objectified as meaningful to him. The utility user's situational embeddedness helps 'redeem' different usage potentials of the particular technology but this never occurs independently of the subjective competence.

### *When the socially distributed usage of utilities is overlooked*

Utilities are not only used by the people who receive them. Some utilities, such as a lift, are designed to be a tool for the helpers, whereas other utilities are designed for the patients to use, as in the case of a support sock.

In praxis, utilities are used in various and frequently unpredictable ways, and often also in both social and distributed ways. The daughter of an 80-year-old demented woman has bought a calendar, which has been placed on the table next to the phone in the apartment. In order to make daily life easier for the mother, the domestic care bought yet another calendar, that the participant could carry around with her. The calendar by the phone has a page for each separate day. In this calendar the program of the day is recorded. In the carry-around calendar, birthdays and arrangements during the week etc. are written down. Although the patient is able to read and write in the calendar whenever she is encouraged to do so, she does not, however, use it spontaneously. Her daughter and the domestic care explain that it is a recurrent problem that they have to encourage the participant to use the calendar. The daughter worries that her mother is not oriented in time and place, and she views the calendar as a way of linking her mother to reality, so that, for example, she 'at least knows what day it is'.

Despite the fact that the mother never uses her calendar, it has become a utility that is frequently and collectively used: it has become a journal that carries messages between the different parties who come to visit or take care of the mother. Hence, the calendar fulfills several functions in her daily life of the participant. However, although it is used as a utility by all the people helping the participant in her daily life, it does not help the *participant* with her memory problem.

The old woman has a type of cognitive problem that makes it hard for her to use the utility in her daily life. When the utility is used in standardized conditions, for instance in the hospital guided by the occupational therapists, the patient has no problems using the calendar. At home, however, her lack of initiative prevents her from using her calendar. A 'hidden' disorder of the functional aspects of the activity hinders usage of the utility.

This example also illustrates that the utility objectifies a particular socially produced standard. The calendar is a product of a particular historical period, in which structuring daily life into units of time is a central part of the life conditions, and is also seen as central to the discourse on 'the good life'. The calendar is designed to be used by someone working an 8 a.m. to 5 p.m. day, as a tool for maintaining and recreating the daily life. Now, most people do not experience daily life as a homogeneous row of repetitions. Rather, they experience changes, unexpected events, etc. A calendar thus becomes a central element for instance for anyone in the process of 'returning back to daily life' after a disabling illness. The calendar is designed in such a way that appointments and special occasions can be noted, thus implying the routine of daily life and important changes and 'breaks' in daily life. Routine usage of a calendar provides the necessary background for making special occasions stand out. Notes in the calendar are supposed to be used as cues to perform certain actions and procedures; e.g. 'call my daughter to wish her happy birthday' or 'make myself ready to go to the day-care center', etc. These are sequences of action that go beyond daily life in the apartment. They presuppose and involve participation in other contexts.

### *Conflict, ideology and power*

In praxis, a (latent) conflict may exist concerning what kind of usage is the right usage. As we saw in the calendar-example, the daughter and the domestic help may have confused means and goal: the use of the calendar became a goal in itself. The goal of the participant may have been quite different, for instance to remember what she had forgotten. In this respect, the calendar was of no use to her. She not only forgot to use it but also the verbal cueing in the calendar did not help kick-start the expected action sequences. Because of her brain injury, there is only a weak connection between conscious, verbal planning and the actual execution of more implicit procedures/sequences of action. This latent conflict, concerning the mother's lack of use of the utility, embodies an element of unawareness of the character of the mother's cognitive problems. It is also an objectification of a certain societal discourse on memory as a social competence. Now, although having a bad memory, as such, is generally acceptable and something we can all relate to, it is, nevertheless, important to take care to respect the acceptable and available mnemonics of the culture. It is not normally acceptable to forget appointments, special occasions or social events. Yet, if seen as a sign of illness, decay, or senility, it is no longer regarded as unacceptable or even rude. However, framing the mother's behavior in this way emphasizes her deterioration and her loss of personal integrity and autonomy. Hence, one could claim that some utilities, in specific social contexts, objectify a higher status than others do. Or, in other words, technology often potentially objectifies a latent social conflict.

### *The neglected proficiency of 'disabled' action*

An important perspective is still missing in the analysis of the calendar-example: the participant's own experience of – and method of dealing with – her memory problem. Although the participant currently speaks of 'my memory problems', one has to wonder whether or not the participant would – independently of neuro-psychologists, domestic helpers, etc. – have ever referred to it as a *memory problem*? When asked about her daily life after leaving the hospital, she primarily focuses on her problems in maintaining her balance and not being able to move around freely. She is often in pain and it is difficult for her to get anywhere. She also explains that she has a tendency to forget things. When I asked her to expand on this, she found it difficult to say anything more specific. She suggests that I ask her daughter. Later on, she gets up and walks with a great deal of trouble out of the living room. I can hear that she turns around in the kitchen and comes back into the living room, only to turn back and go into the kitchen again. This happens repeatedly until she finally comes out with a bowl of sugar, which she places on the table. These acts illustrate that the participant – without being consciously aware of the fact – brings herself back to the situation in which the urge to act originated. Hence, she 'is reminded' of what she wanted to do. As a memory aid, she reconstructs the situation and it helps her to remember. This strategy seems to relieve her problem, but it does not address the fact that the people around her still regard her *real* problem as lacking a memory for time and place. The people in her immediate surroundings failed to notice the strategy that the participant herself had developed. Thus the participant's own definition of the problem and her own strategies of conduct have been overlooked and overshadowed by interpretations made of others in praxis. This has led to the choice of an inappropriate utility, i.e. the calendar.

### *Concepts of illness, health, and the good life*

In an interview, a 65-year-old man spoke about his problems in getting outside his apartment. He can move around *inside* his apartment, although with some difficulty, but he cannot walk outside alone. He has a daughter who comes to help him almost every day. The patient can walk with a little support, but because of his left-sided neglect, he keeps bumping into the person supporting him. The father and his daughter have borrowed a wheelchair a couple of times. This has increased the action radius of the patient considerably. Now, three years after two serious strokes, doctors and physiotherapists have given up on further rehabilitation. They tell me that the patient, however, does not want a wheelchair, and this decision is partly supported by his daughter. Accepting a wheelchair would be the same as resolving to give up on rehabilitation. For this participant, *not* using utilities is a part of the political struggle for rehabilitation.

The act of *not* using utilities received from the hospital may be experienced as an indication of improvement: an experience of being less disabled than before. To this participant in his daily life, the utility is a symbol of illness, an externalization of the inner, organic dysfunction. The utility symbolizes a need for help and support. This is seen as negative in this example, not because of a general aversion toward receiving help, but because the existence of the utility is a sign of 'somebody else' giving up on his rehabilitation. He has already had experience of the professionals making incorrect judgments, when they insisted to him that he would never walk again. Using utilities perpetuates the patient in a dependent relation to the judgments of the professionals. It objectifies a common assumption that functional disorders can only be rehabilitated within the first year; thereafter the disabilities are seen as permanent. By accepting the utilities, the participant feels he would surrender to this defeatist standpoint.

Paradoxically, the participant himself nevertheless reproduces this view of his illness as a temporary condition: something that has temporarily 'entered' into the body but will leave again when he gets well. Getting well is – in this understanding – the same as getting totally rid of the illness and returning to the normal condition (i.e. before the illness) without any injuries or signs of the illness.

To some extent, the participant shares this idealistic view of illness as an abnormal, deviating condition, which contrasts with the normal condition. But at the same time he states that he knows that he will need rehabilitation for his paralyzed leg and that his leg will probably never be the same again. These two very different views of the illness do not seem to represent a conflict for the participant. The idealistic view, i.e. that he will get completely well again, exists as a goal for the participant, even though he describes the paralysis of his leg as probably permanent. It seems, however, that the professionals, who have been in touch with the participant, have interpreted these apparently conflicting views of the illness as an expression of lack of realism and inadequate recognition of his own situation. According to the participant, the doctors and the therapists at the hospital tried to give him a more realistic view on his situation. But the professional discourse on illness is as contradictory and incoherent as the participant's. The concepts used in treatment and rehabilitation contexts, however, are just as different and contrary: illness can be seen as either chronic and life long, or else as a process or as an event (Stiker, 1999). The discourse can concurrently include defeatist, biological deterministic, optimistic or even unrealistic views of how the power of will and the specific abilities of the individual can cope with the illness (Rose, 1999).

The discourse of illness and rehabilitation is still being negotiated and further developed. What may seem a meaningless discussion of words may be important from a participant's perspective because it may be a matter of what rehabilitation offers or whether or not a participant gives up or feels renounced by others. Different parties participate in different contexts in which important decisions are made concerning further rehabilitation. Utilitarian considerations concerning the patient's possible gain from a particular rehabilitation program compared to other patients' gains are part of the professional perspective but do not make sense for the patient.

In short, although many patients and relatives have struggled long and hard to gain access to rehabilitation, the utilities themselves, that may sometimes be essential to the process of rehabilitation, may nevertheless come to symbolize quite the reverse. Thus, in praxis, the ascription of negative meaning to the utility may limit the action possibilities for the participant, even though it may feel like a victory to be able to put it aside.

### *Utilities as 'stigmata'*

In my analysis, I have emphasized how the use of utility technology is situated and how meaning and function is transformed and changed in the social praxis in which the participant acts. But my interviews and observations also describe another side of the utility user, that I have not yet discussed in this article. Some of the participants saw the utility as more static and constraining, a 'stigma', a negative sign of disability, helplessness and exposure (Goffman, 1969). For some of the participants this is not a temporary meaning ascription but rather an interpretation that is maintained across situations and different action contexts within which the participants move.

A 67-year-old woman, who now lives alone in her apartment in an old apartment complex, talked about her decision not to use utilities. Her late husband had a small business and, for most of her life, she had been part housewife, part helpmate. Following her stroke she has been able to manage almost without any help. In the past few years, however, she has experienced a growing problem with her balance. She fears that she might have had yet another small stroke. Her doctor has tried to comfort her and has started her up in treatment with Prozac. A domestic help, who comes every fortnight, arranged for the woman to be offered the chance of having a banister put up in the stairway. But the patient did not want a banister. During the course of the interview, the woman reported that she had not told any of the people living on the same stairway as herself about her illness. She did not want to 'expose' herself and she did not want strangers to take pity on her. The participant tried in several ways to conceal and cover up her disability. She views her functional disorder as a serious problem when meeting strangers in the street or meeting others living on the same stairway. Her unsteady gait – and its externalization in the form of an extra banister – becomes, in Goffman's terms, a socially constructed stigma. Once again, borrowing a term from Goffman, she tries to 'pass' by hiding her disability and thus turns down the use of utilities, such as the extra banister.

The concept of socially constructed stigma tends to imply that the freedom of action of the participant is limited by an independent and presupposed meaning ascription that she merely reproduces across the different contexts in which she participates. But such meaning ascription is not static nor independent of the particular situation. The participant can for instance live with – or, as she herself puts it, 'has learnt to live with' – the fact that the domestic help comes once every fortnight. One can interpret this situation in many ways. Her attitude might be attributed to a depressive state of mind, or as an attempt to hold on to a former definition of quality of life. Such interpretations would not, however, be appropriate to make on the basis of the interviews and observations that I have made. This example itself demonstrates that for some participants there is an on-going process of reification, in which the technology is objectified and ascribed relatively independent meanings of stigmatization. The participant tries to escape from being stigmatized, but paradoxically, the process of stigmatization is maintained and reinforced by the participant's attempts to cover up, hide and 'pass'.

As a contrast to the above example, another participant illustrates entirely different attitudes and action strategies: she uses a wheelchair and has had several different ramps installed so that she can get out of her first floor apartment with help from up to two people. When she has to get out of the apartment, she yells out of the window to contact her two neighbors working in a garage across the street. If they have time, they come over and carry her out of the apartment. Her contact with the world around her has been extended ever since she fell ill. The domestic help comes daily, her daughter calls frequently to make sure that her mother has not fallen or become ill, and the two neighbors carry her out of her apartment – all these contacts have been established or intensified as a result of her stroke. Her disability and the visible signs or stigmata have in some way been her gateway to a more extensive social life.

## Summing up

I have based this article on an examination and discussion of concrete examples of how stroke-patients use utilities in daily life. The research reveals that the utilities issued to such patients are not always used as planned. Such wrong, different or lack of usage is caused by different conditions. Often the utility is insufficiently designed for the specific context in which it is to be used. In other instances, certain (hidden) cognitive difficulties have been overlooked in the patient. Lack of information and training for the patients and helpers can also be a problem. Furthermore, the follow-up and re-evaluation of needs and tools does not always function optimally. In these latter cases the problems with the use of utilities are caused by poor evaluation of the patients' needs and changes in levels of function and/or changes in the surrounding environment.

I have also pointed to the fact that utilities are often used with entirely different purposes than those originally planned. This is not necessarily problematic. On the contrary, this new transformed usage can be more meaningful for the user. However, new transformed uses of a utility *can* be inconvenient for the patient or the helper. Moreover, it can be expensive and inappropriate if advanced and/or specially designed utilities are used as ordinary household items belonging to the user e.g. using the wheel chair as an office chair or the bath stool as a flower bench.

This analysis has shown how the use of utilities is socially distributed. Often many parties use the utilities. If this aspect is overlooked, the potential of this distributed use may also be forgotten. It can also be difficult to understand and solve the conflicts that can arise as a consequence of the collective or distributed use of the utilities. Different parties may have different – and not always explicitly defined – understandings of the participant's problems and need of utilities. If these differences are not acknowledged, conflicts can arise. Moreover, these differences in usage *may* lead to an overshadowing of the participants' own strategies of solution.

Utilities become, for some participants, a *symbol of illness*, and in some cases the termination of using the utilities is a sign of improvement and *getting well*. This act is seen as part of the battle to attain rehabilitation– in order to be acknowledged as a person with a potential to regain lost functions, and not just seen as a 'hopeless case'. In a few cases, the utilities are seen as stigmatizing, and the user may feel constrained and *choose not* to use the utilities.

The people involved in this research belong primarily to the group of elderly people with stroke. They are all retired and with a relatively low level of education and economic status. It is noticeable that the type of utilities offered to this group of people is a relatively simple, low technological tool. Apparently, this reflects the limited goal of ensuring a minimum level of functioning in their own home; it does not, however, ensure the patients' participation in leisure activities, and the resumption or development of new interests. In this article, however, I have not dealt with what wishes and/or needs this group of people formulate themselves for the *development* of the technology of utilities. Instead, I have focused on how the existing utilities are used and what problems these uses bring about.

In order to solve some of the problems discussed and take advantage of the potentials of distributed use of utilities, it is necessary to look at the concrete and situated use of utilities. It is hence necessary to examine the practical and individual barriers systematically, e.g. cognitive difficulties. Moreover, it seems necessary to develop a more systematic administration system that ensures evaluation and follow-up procedures regarding the utilities that have been issued. The administrative system must make sure that utilities are returned if the specific utility is no longer needed, or if an old utility is replaced by a new one. Thus, utilities are to be re-evaluated on a regular basis to ensure that the most appropriate utilities are issued and used. This evaluation process must be based on an analysis of the practical usage, i.e. analysis of how the utilities are used, who uses them, where they are used and what they are used for. As part of this analysis, considerations of the character of the problem, observations of users and their own solutions should be included.

In the development of new utilities, it is essential to take seriously the considerations of the users themselves regarding their needs, and the functionality and aesthetics of the utilties. But the analysis also points to the fact that some users do not like using the utilities because they symbolize disability and passivity and the abandonment of the very possibility of rehabilitation. It would therefore seem obvious to try to develop any utility so that it embodies an element of rehabilitation within itself.

## References

Andersen, H.E., Schultz-Larsen, K., Kreiner, S., Forchhammer, B.H., Eriksen, K. & Brown, A. (2000). Can readmission after stroke be prevented? *Stroke*, *31*, 1038–45.

Bech-Jørgensen, B. (1994). *Når hver dag bliver hverdag*. Copenhagen: Akademisk Forlag.

Dreier, O. (1993). *Psykosocial behandling. En teori om et praksisområde*. Copenhagen: Dansk Psykologisk forlag.

Dreier, O. (1997). *Subject and social practice*. Center of Health, Humanity and Culture, Department of Philosophy, University of Århus.

Dreier, O. (2002). Introduktion til Holzkamps arbejde om livsførelse. *Nordiske Udkast*, No. *2*, 3–5.

Foucault, M. (1987). *Sexualitetens historie I. Viljen til viden*. Humlebæk, Denmark: Rhodos.

Forchhammer, H.B. (1994). Psykologiske sunhedsbegreber i subjektvidenskabeligt perspektiv. In U.J. Jensen & P.F. Andersen (Eds.) *Sundhedsbegreber – filosofi og praksis* (pp. 139–179). Århus: Forlaget Philosophia.

Forchhammer, H.B. (2001). Interviewet som handlesammenhæng. *Nordiske Udkast*, 2001, no.1, 23–32

Gazzaniga, M.S. (1999). *The new cognitive neurosciences*. (2nd. ed.) Cambridge, MA: MIT Press.

Goffman, E. (1961). *Asylums*. London: Penguin Books.

Heller, A. (1981). *Das Alltagsleben.Versuch eine Erklärung der individuellen Reproduktion*. Frankfurt: Suhrkamp.

Holzkamp, K. (1983). *Grundlegung der Psychologie*. Frankfurt/M: Campus.

Holzkamp, K. (1995). *Alltägliche Lebendfürung als subjectwissenschaftliches Grundconzept, Das Argument, 37*(212), 817–46.

Huniche, L. (2002). *Huntington's disease in everyday life. Knowledge, ignorance and generic risk.* Institute for Psykology, Copenhagen University.

Keller, K.D. (2005). The corporeal order of things: The *Speil* of usability. *Human Studies*, *28*, 173–204.

Leontyev, A.N. (1981). *Problems of the development of mind*. Moscow: Progress.

Sacks, O. (1987). *The man who mistook his wife for a hat*. Copenhagen: Borgens forlag.

Rose, N. (1999). *Powers of freedom*. Cambridge: Cambridge University Press.

Stiker, H.-J. (2000). *A history of disability*. (trans. W. Sayers) Ann Arbor: University of Michigan Press.

# Chapter 8

# Politics of Things: Interplay of Design and Practice in a Design Workshop with Children[1]

Estrid Sørensen

In her book *Plans and Situated Actions*, Suchman (1987) shows how plans and other things become involved in practices as *resources* for the formation of actions. Plans are not prescriptive for action, she emphasizes. The same can be said about any thing, about any design. Designs engage *in* practice, they do not impose their order *on* practice. But what then, can we say about the interplay of design and practice? Does a fixed and standardised design result in a rigid practice, and does an open design bring along flexible practices? These are the central questions of the following chapter.

With inspiration from later developments within actor-network theory (ANT) (Mol & Law 1994; Law 1994; Law 2002) I use the term *ordering* to discuss two cases from a design workshop with fourth to sixth grade primary school children, who worked with an open-ended design of a 3D virtual environment. The ways in which children, design, computers, researchers etc. came to relate to each other formed different orderings. Talking about how human activity is ordered is in other words talking about *politics*. I argue that things have politics.

After first introducing the after-school project *Femtedim* I describe the design involved in this workshop. I describe how different orderings were inscribed (Akrich 1992) in the design, defining an open-ended activity. Secondly, I present descriptions from my fieldwork to illustrate how this open-endedness was continued into practice. I show that different orderings were at play and I conclude by discussing this more procedural way of understanding design compared to seeing design as a finished product, and compared to defining design as linked to designers' intentions.

1 I would like to thank the editors of this volume and several authors, who have been very helpful with comments on this chapter, as well as Jeannette Pols, John Law and Lucy Suchman, who have commented on earlier versions of the chapter.

## The design workshop

### *Participants and aim of the research project*

The design workshop called the *Femtedim project* was established in a 5th Dimension[2] after-school activity situated in an urban school in Copenhagen. Children from nine to twelve years of age attended the design workshop which ran once a week from September 2000 to June 2001. The children enrolled by giving their informed consent but participation was voluntary and although some of the children attended every time, others did so only irregularly. About 40 children passed through the Femtedim project of which 15-17 constituted the main group of regular attendants.

The aim of the design project was to create an open-ended design that kept the interaction between children, design and other resources evolving. The reason for experimenting with such an open-ended design was rooted in the general dissatisfaction with overly standardised educational practices that are not able to challenge and support children's individual potentials (Lee 2001). An open-ended design should not impose any *a priori* definition of children's needs, but be flexible enough to develop challenges and support along the way. Similarly, with the ambition to make the project take a point of departure in the children's own activities no learning goals were set. In this chapter, I will not go further into discussing the extent to which this aim was reached, but focus on how design can contribute to establishing such open-endedness.

### *The design concept*

In the *Femtedim project*, design is understood in a quite broad sense. It concerns partly the forming of an *interface* of a graphic 3D virtual environment program called Active Worlds,[3] partly forming the *practices* in the computer lab with and around the program. Design comprises more than the interface designers usually describe in their definition of design. Akrich (1992), Grinth & Woolgar (1997) among others have shown that even if these ideas are rarely accounted for in designers' descriptions of design, designers do indeed have ideas about users and users' activities with the technologies they are developing and these ideas guide the

2 5th Dimension is a concept for a joint computer based after-school activity for children and a research field for researchers studying child-computer interaction developed originally by Cole and Griffith in the mid-1980s (Cole 1996). It is traditionally based on an activity theory framework with a number of designed artefacts to support learning and development. During the past 20 years the 5th Dimension concept has spread to first various places in the USA, but later also to South America, Australia and Europe. At each place, the 5th Dimensions are locally adapted, meaning that they may involve different artefacts, different user groups, different research aims, theories etc. The cases described in this paper is a result of the establishment of a new 5th Dimension site in Copenhagen in 2000, partly financed by the EU 5th Frame program. For more information, see http://www.5d.org.

3 http://www.activeworlds.com

design process. It is simply impossible to design a technology without imagining something about the practice it is going to be part of. As Winner (1995) has explained the countless ways in which machines, instruments, and structures of common use were designed in the 70s – buses, buildings, pavements, plumbing fixtures, and so forth – made it impossible for many disabled persons to move about freely. These technologies were not designed strategically to exclude certain members of society, but, as Winner puts it, were instead the result of 'long-standing neglect' (p.32) in taking these people into account when designing infrastructures. Put differently, design processes implicitly referred to practices that involved 'able' citizens with full control over limbs and senses. Design is never just about making a technology but always also about designing practices, whether intentionally or not. This, I argue below, is a political endeavour.

My definition of design also implies more than what teachers and pedagogical professionals usually have in mind when talking about planning their lessons. Even though teachers do not generally talk about *designing* a lesson, central aspects of design such as organising and planning are indeed part of what teachers do prior to each lesson. What significantly distinguishes how teachers conceive of their job and how interface designers do is that the former mainly understand it as forming the *practice* of the class, whereas interface designers generally see their job as creating *technologies* leaving alone the specific practice in question. From this perspective, the teachers' designing activity can be said to be at the opposite end to the interface designers' on a continuum between designing technology and designing practice. In contrast, I argue that just as designers implicitly design *practices* as well as technologies, so do teachers implicitly design technologies when planning the practice of the class.

*Design of the interface and practice in the design workshop*

In our project, design was partly comparable to interface design, partly comparable to design of pedagogical practice. Let me be more specific. *Designing the interface* meant in this project designing the graphic appearance of the Active Worlds browser's 3D[4] virtual environment. Active Worlds is an Internet-based application which means that any computer user with access to the Internet can enter this virtual environment. There are various *worlds* in an Active Worlds *universe*, each having a different landscape: the terra-formed landscape of the 'Babel world' alluding to pre-historic sites found in the United Kingdom, the dimly lit theatre auditorium of the 'ENZO world', a gathering of historic villages in the 'Journeys world' etc. Based on Active Worlds technology, the Eduverse[5] universe is reserved for professional

4 Technically, Active Worlds is what is called 2½D. It is not based on 3D graphics, but to the naïve eye, it looks like a spatial 3D environment with height, length and depth, compared to flat 2D graphics like a html page.

5 Eduverse is one browser – one universe. Eduverse can be downloaded from http://www.activeworlds.com/edu/awedu_download.htm. The program is executed from a personal

educators and researchers of education. As educational researchers we had the opportunity to achieve a virtual world free of charge which my research team[6] did. We were now 'world owners' and we named our virtual world *Femtedim*.

It is up to the owner of the virtual world to design the landscape of the world.[7] The Active Worlds platform provides about 2000 pre-given *building* blocks which can be used to build up the houses, forests, rooms or whatever is wanted in the world, just as it is possible to design new objects. Designing a virtual environment is limited to designing the world, its graphic landscapes, architecture, navigation paths, etc.[8] The Active Worlds browser stays unchanged. The browser can be described as a frame you use to browse between different virtual worlds. It is set up with menus for defining the settings of the worlds, the perspective of the *avatar*[9], the range of sight etc.

Apart from designing the interface to the extent the Active Worlds platform and the time and skills of the world owners allowed, designing in the Femtedim

---

computer with Internet access.

6 Comprising Michael Aagaard, Nina Armand, Agnete Husted-Andersen and Tine Jensen.

7 The world can be designed with a flat ground surface or without such, in the latter case the experience will be like being in cosmic space. Furthermore, a horizon with for instance mountains, a cityscape, walls, stars, curtains, other things or just a colour can be installed, which will constitute the ever-present background of the world.

8 The virtual world can be described as a 'stage' for the activities taking place in the virtual world. Just as a theatre, a historic village etc. invite certain practices to take place it is possible to create signs with text, pictures, animations and video clips, which enable the designer through representations to instruct or inspire the users' activities. This can also be done by creating hyperlinks from objects in the virtual world to web pages on the Internet. This has the effect of opening a browser with a web page when clicking on or bumping into a hyperlinked object. This hyperlink functionality can also work to make an object appear or disappear when clicking on or bumping into another object, and thereby let doors open, make illusions of moving objects etc. just as it is possible to make hyperlinks that 'teleport' the avatar to another place. Put into sequences such design solutions allow the designer to make interactive environments that do not simply frame the practice, but that act on and react to the users conduct in the virtual world.

9 An avatar is a small figure that the user moves around in the virtual environment using the arrow keys or mouse. Having chosen a name and a look for her avatar, the user enters the virtual environment, which means she sees the avatar in the centre of the screen in the landscape of the virtual world. She can choose an isometric view, looking at her avatar from a bird perspective behind the avatar. The most used view, however, is the point-of-view. What the user sees on the computer screen in the point-of-view mode is the landscape of the virtual world as viewed 'through the eyes' of her avatar. To understand the feeling of navigating in the virtual environment, the closest analogy is hence our everyday bodily experience of being in a space, able to turn around 360 degrees in the environment we are in, and move in all directions. You can do the same in Active Worlds' graphic 3D virtual environment. Only, of course, your view is limited to the size and graphics quality of the program and computer monitor, and your movements are restricted by the rigidity of the input devices.

project also involved *designing pedagogical practice*. As is already obvious from my description of designing the interface design of practice cannot be sharply distinguished from designing the interface. There was more to designing practice, however, than designing the interface of our virtual world. We also created a frame story. It was about an avatar called *Avafar* who had lived all his life in the 3D virtual world Femtedim. We told the children that Avafar was getting old and with age he was losing his sight. Mysteriously, the story went, the Femtedim virtual world was disappearing at the pace of Avafar's sight failing. Avafar realized that he could not sustain the world anymore and he asked the children to take over. Melancholically but with faith in the children's ability to make the best out of Femtedim, he handed over the responsibility of rebuilding and maintaining the virtual world to the children. Avafar met the children in the virtual world, giving them assignments, helping them, discussing problems, engaging in small-talk, etc. Avafar was 'played' by our research assistant, who logged on to the Femtedim world every week at the same time as the children, but from a remote location.

Having introduced the design workshop, and having examined the concept of design and the two aspects of designing – interface and practice – I turn to analyse some specific details of the interplay of design and practice within the Femtedim project. First, however, we need a discussion of the metaphors that will be in play in the analyses of the empirical material.

## Analytic concepts

The central analytic concept in use in this chapter is that of *ordering*. Related to ordering is the issue of the *politics of things*.

### *Ordering*

In discussing the interplay of design and practice, I will with inspiration from Law (1994) use the term *ordering*. With this verbal mode of the noun 'order', which has long been of central focus in the social sciences, Law emphasises the study of ongoing processes rather than envisioning a fixed and essential structure. Whenever something is done, said, thought etc. elements of the world are placed in relations to each other, in patterns, and some of these patterns are repeated more than others forming stable orderings, while others are ephemeral and passing.

I have chosen the term ordering for my study of interplay of design and practice, because it leaves open for empirical investigation how the relations of design and practice may turn out. This implies not seeing humans and things or design and practice as separate actors 'doing things' to each other, but staying open to less clear-cut boundaries between these entities. Law and Mol describe rules for what constitutes objects and relations, the boundaries or transitions between them, etc. (Mol & Law 1994; Law 2002). Different orderings imply different rules.

Even though the term 'ordering' hints at somebody actively *making* an order, it is crucial for my analyses that this is not implied by the term. Note, how Pickering describes agency:

> One can start with the idea that the world is filled, not in the first instance, with facts and observations, but with *agency*. The world, I want to say, is continually *doing things*, things that bear upon us not as observation statements upon disembodied intellects but as forces upon material beings. Think of the weather. Winds, storms, droughts, floods, heat and cold – all of these engage with our bodies as well as our minds, often in life-threatening ways. The parts of the world that I know best are ones where one could not survive for any length of time without responding in a very direct way to such material agency – even in an English summer (never mind a Midwestern winter), one would die quite quickly of exposure to the elements in the absence of clothing, buildings, heating, and whatever. (Pickering, 1995, p. 6, emphasis in original.)

In my understanding of the term 'ordering' the study of the relationships of material forces of winds, storms, clothing, buildings and heating etc. is a study of *orderings of weather*. No matter how an ordering comes to be the way it is – as a result of strategic planning, of contingencies, of 'natural' occurrences or otherwise – it is an ordering.

In the following analyses I describe different *orderings* to characterise the different patterns of relations that emerge with the design solutions. I use metaphors suggested by ANT scholars.

### *Politics of things*

I am not simply interested in mapping orderings describing different patterns of relations between design and practice, but also in studying how a design may take part[10] in and form practices. In terms of the politics of artefacts, Winner (1999) discusses how the design of machines, instruments and structures set a certain order, which excluded disabled persons. Apart from how technical arrangements result in a form of social order, Winner describes a second way in which technologies may be political. This is not in terms of consequences of a technology, but in terms of a specific social order as prerequisites for the working of a technology. Because of the lethal properties of the atom bomb, Winner maintains, this technology demands a centralised agency controlling it, and 'a rigid hierarchical chain of command closed to all influences that might make its workings unpredictable. The internal social system of the bomb must be authoritarian' (op. cit. p. 34).

---

10 The formulation of 'taking part' is inspired by Dreier (1993; 1999), who emphasises that practitioners *part*icipate in practices, in the sense that they always only contribute to and have access to parts of practices, while other practitioners take up and contribute to other parts. I however extend the term to also apply to non-human participants of a practice. This move is inspired by studies of Science, Technology and Society (STS) in general, and by Haraway (1991) specifically, who talks about being *partial*, which I take to be the adjective of taking part or participating.

While Winner's discussion of whether artefacts have politics focuses on larger scale technological systems and their entanglements, Mehan (1993) discusses the 'politics of representations' on a more situational basis in terms of 'the competition over the meaning of ambiguous events, people and objects' (p. 241). Through the analysis of a meeting of an 'Eligibility and Placement' Committee discussing the possible placement of a boy into a program for the learning disabled, Mehan shows how negotiations and decisions about which terms to identify the boy results in the formation of a hierarchy (an ordering) in which one mode of representing the world gains primacy over others and eventually has decisive consequences for the boy's life.

Mehan does not talk about politics of technologies or things but of how representations may have political effects in terms of concepts assigned to events, people and objects. However, I will borrow Mehan's understanding of politics as the interplay taking place in micro-settings and merge it with Winner's ideas of politics of artefacts suggesting that it is not simply about humans assigning their own agendas to technologies, but that these technologies in their entanglements[11] indeed have their own politics.

In the following empirical analyses I describe orderings of design as politics put forward in practice. First, I will describe orderings inscribed in the Femtedim design involving both the design of the interface and of practices as they were at the beginning of the project, and secondly, I look at how the politics of design worked in two practices in which they were put forward.

## The Femtedim design

As I have already mentioned, the aim of the project was to create an open-ended design for the informal after-school educational setting of 5th Dimension. This already suggests a specific politics of the design, namely that it was supposed to contribute to establishing an ordering which allowed children to – or even constituted children as – acting in a variety of different ways.

### *The fluidity of the design*

The interface design of the Femtedim virtual world was minimal. Corresponding to the frame story, the virtual world should be quite empty due to its current process of vanishing. We built five platforms in Femtedim: An entrance platform, where the characters involved, the avatars, would arrive when entering the world, and four other platforms for the different groups of children to build villages on. Apart from the platforms, the 3D virtual world Femtedim was graphically empty.

Together with the frame story this graphic design provided a minimum of resources for the practice. Given this relatively blank visual and narrative background, the task

11 For a discussion of the term entanglement, see the introductory chapter of Callon (1998).

set for the children was to build up the Femtedim world. A very open space for acting was thus designed for the children and hence it was *they* themselves – rather than the design – who were expected to provide the resources in terms of ideas, skills, creativity etc. to build up the villages of Femtedim. Hetherington and Lee (2000) have drawn attention to what they call the 'blank space'. They give the example of the Solitaire board game. This game consists of a board with 33 holes. 33 sticks are ordered in the holes in one sets of three rows of seven sticks crossing another set of three rows of seven sticks in an arrangement that makes the nine central sticks be part of two crossing lines. Before starting the game the central stick has to be removed leaving an empty hole in the board. The game proceeds by moving one stick over another and into the central empty hole. The stick that has been jumped over can be removed leaving another empty hole. The next move allows the player to move another stick into any of the two empty holes. While social scientists usually focus on the actors and how 'filled' spaces (like the sticks) move, they systematically neglect blank spaces, Hetherington and Lee draw attention to the agency of the empty holes in the Solitaire game, to their decisive contribution to the proceeding of the game. This is an interesting observation, which in describing Femtedim lets us focus on the graphically and narratively empty space. Indeed, the children, the researchers and Avafar also contributed to setting the Femtedim activity in motion, but this should not draw our attention away from contribution of the blankness to the forming the design.

There are however different forms of blankness. The exercise books, which I saw repeatedly during my classroom studies (Sørensen 2006a) often had the structure of blank lines for children to fill in with numbers as elements of pre-written sums, with verb endings in pre-written sentences etc. These blank lines were however only *apparently* blank, because the nature of their supposed 'filling' was already defined, and hence rather *absent* than blank. The blankness of the Femtedim design did not refer to absent solutions, but to non-existing elements to be produced.

Akrich (1992) suggests the notion of *inscription* to designate the hypotheses implicit in a design about the environment into which the design is supposed to be inserted. Adapted to the vocabulary of this chapter, I will talk about inscriptions in terms of the *orderings* the design presupposes and puts forward in the practice it is going to be part of and take part in. The ordering of the Femtedim design as described in this section was that of a relatively empty space, which children were supposed to fill in. Filling in the blankness of the graphics and the frame story meant building up the villages using the same building objects and functions as available to the world owners[12] described above. Compared to the design of exercise books which set a *fixed* standard for how to fill in the lines, the norms for how to fill in the blankness of the Femtedim design were *fluid*.

Among their topological metaphors, Law and Mol define *fluidity* as an ordering of *invariant gradual transformation constituted of optional and exchangeable entities* (Mol & Law 1994; Law & Mol 2001; Laet & Mol 2000). This description fits well

12 World owners distribute and restrict rights to built in the virtual environment.

with the ordering inscribed in the Femtedim design requiring of the children to fill out the blanks of the Femtedim design in non-predefined ways, involving varying entities in terms of building objects, technological solutions, ways of collaborating etc.

Here we see part of the politics of the Femtedim design. It presents an ordering of the way the interplay of the children and the design (among other things) was going to take place. Not in a fixed, standardised way, but varying and transforming. The blankness provided a demand and a space to be filled in somehow, and the children should provide ideas, initiative, creativity and skills, together establishing a fluid ordering transforming with exchangeable entities. This corresponds to the second of the different aspects of the politics of artefacts identified by Winner, in which design suggests a certain social order as a prerequisite for the working of the design. If the children for instance were not to comply with the hypothesis inscribed in the design, but instead met the design with passive blankness looking dully into the computer screen, the design simply would not work.

*The regionality of the Femtedim design*

As I have explained, the graphic layout defined an entrance platform and four villages, where the children were supposed to build up the Femtedim world. Each platform was given a different name: 'Bahilah', 'Nisub', 'Itnom' and 'Akul'. It was hence inscribed into the design that children were to be divided into four groups. Privileges were assigned to each group. Only members of the group were allowed to build on the platform. The inhabitants of each platform were identified by names and privileges, and thus constituted a homogeneous population. While homogeneity ruled within the platforms, differences lay between them. Just as much as each inhabitant was similar to the inhabitants of his own platform, they were different from those of the other platforms in terms of identity defined by name and privileges.

Law and Mol (Law & Mol 2001; Mol & Law 1994; Law 2002) characterise this kind of arrangement as *regional*. It describes a container in which objects are located. Regions are homogeneous fields divided by boundaries within each of which one norm and one ontology rules. The extension of a region is limited by its boundaries. This politics of design is clearly different from the fluid described above. It sets a standard and fixed structure that is quite different from a transforming ordering with exchangeable entities described above. The politics of the graphic layout of the design was that of fixing children and platforms in four separate regions.

The description of Femtedim as regional is clearly different from the description of Femtedim as fluid. However, it is impossible to decide which of the two descriptions is more adequate. Just as much as the design is fluid is it regional: Femtedim put forward a fluid politics inviting children to be active and fill out the blanks with the effect that elements change along the way, while Femtedim at the same time put forward a regional politics that set a homogeneous stage with boundaries and a clear-cut arrangement of separate divisions of elements. There is no time involved in the regional Femtedim – it stays the same – whereas time is indeed a defining element of the fluid Femtedim.[13]

Such a double (or multiple) ontology or double (or multiple) politics of things is implicit in the logic of Law & Mol's symmetric descriptions of humans and things. While it is widely accepted that people may exercise different politics with one and the same thing, a thing itself is generally understood as singular, as only one. Turning to a symmetric approach that describes humans and things in the same terms makes it just as possible that things have a multiple politics as it is possible people do (Mol 2000; Law 2002). So yes, the politics of Femtedim was fluid *and* it was regional.

## The Femtedim Design in Practice

This section discusses two instances of how the design worked in practice in the design workshop, focusing on the ways in which the politics of design put forward by the blankness and the graphic layout of the design were continued in the interplay of design and practice.

### *Continuance and cohabitation of fluid and regional politics of design*

The field note summary below starts at the first day of the 5th Dimension project. Avafar had given the children assignments to go to other virtual worlds and describe for him what they saw:

> After the children had completed their assignments Avafar gave each child a citizenship of the world, and each group a platform, where they were supposed to build their villages. The four groups discussed separately how they wanted the layout of their villages. The Akul group wished to build a main road and construct the village around it. They discussed vividly whether the road should be of tarmac, stone or other, how the houses should adjoin etc. In the following months, they built up the platform village with houses next to each other on both sides of the road. A friend of the two girls in the group joined Akul after a few months, and assisted by ongoing negotiations a small neighbourhood was erected following a uniform style of glass walls and single colour furniture.

The Akul group was originally constituted by the graphics of the platform, assignment of privileges, and its separation from the other groups. Subsequently discussions of the layout of the village, the establishing of a plan and the building of a uniform style neighbourhood worked to consolidate their fixed and homogeneous identity as a region. Apart from continuing the regional ordering, however, the interplay of design and practice also contributed to continuing the fluid ordering put forward by the design, filling out the blankness of the Femtedim design, and indeed doing this in a non-prescribed way, involving new objects as well as children's ideas, initiatives, and skills.

---

13 For further discussion on the interrelation of time and materiality, see Sørensen (2006b).

Collaborating closely and sharing the codes of the building objects each of the Akul girls built up her own house with similar objects differing only in colours and combination. The procedure of building in Active Worlds involves first finding the object you would like to build in a printed list or in another world, secondly looking up the file name of this object, which I call the 'code' using the same term as the children, and thirdly writing the code into the 'properties' dialog box of an object in your virtual world. Subsequently, the colour of the object can be defined. Objects in Active Worlds are strictly related to individual users, which enables certain ways of collaborating. One way of collaborating is, as these girls did, to build with the same objects – even if they were all of different colours – since this allowed children to share part of the building procedure, namely that of finding the objects with which to build. While collaborating the two girls also worked in parallel, one for instance making herself busy in adding animated pictures and pictures taken of her own and the friend's avatar in the virtual environment, while the other was busy finding furniture as well as pictures from the Internet to decorate the walls of the houses. Soon after a new piece of furniture, animation or other was put into the house of one girl, it was copied to the other girl's house, which resulted in a long chain of interplay of new building objects, possibilities set by the structure of the Active Worlds building function, and the girls' managing and ideas about those possibilities and objects. Step by step, each newly developing building solution was adapted to the existing ones or the existing were transformed to make them fit to the new.

What was 'new' was sometimes an object that had to fit in terms of size, style and function. But it could also be an idea, like that of having a warehouse on the Akul platform, which quickly changed the existing logic, style and functions and changed the set up to fit in with the new idea. The same was the case for the third girl who entered the little team after a few months. She was quickly acquainted with the procedure and fit into the already existing buildings and procedures just as these were adjusted to make her fit into the platform. Soon a third house in similar style but of another colour was erected at the Akul platform and the procedure went on.

In this way, the politics of the design putting forward a fluid ordering of transforming with exchangeable entities through the blankness of the design continued in the interplay of design and practice. It continued not only as an interplay of the girls and blankness but also by involving other materialities such as the structure of the building function, animations and other objects, procedures, ideas etc. As an ongoing interplay of girls, design and building solutions etc. the fluid ordering was continued as a co-construction of design and practice.

This fluid ordering, however, in no way compromised the regional ordering put forward by the graphic layout. The regionality started the fluid process linking the core elements involved in the constitution of the fluid ordering, girls and building procedures. And apart from staying within the fixed region of the platform the fluid ordering also contributed to sustaining the homogeneity of the platform through the creation of houses of similar style with a homogeneous and stable identity. On the one hand the two orderings were each the result of the interplay of design and practice: the politics of design were put forward and continued through the interplay of design and practice as described, which in this case resulted in unchanged continuance of the politics of design. And on the other, the two orderings took part in a mutual interplay sustaining each other's maintenance, constituting harmonious cohabitation of fluid and regional orderings.

*Discontinuance and conflict of fluid and regional politics of design*

The coherent story of the Akuls suggests that the fluid ordering was limited by the regional ordering, keeping it from flooding beyond the boundaries of the platform, while this did not compromise the fluid functioning within the region. However, looking at what happened at the Itnom platform shows us a quite different picture of interplay of design and practice. Summarizing the fieldnotes about the Itnom platform creates the following description:

> One of the boys at the Itnom platform stayed in Femtedim while the other two scanned other virtual worlds in Eduverse to find nice building objects. When one of the 'scouts' found a new object they shouted the code across the computer lab to the boy who stayed back in Femtedim and who would subsequently build the object while the others went on searching for more building object codes. The boys quickly, eagerly and continuously built new things on their platform. But after only about a month it happened more and more often that they came to the design workshop and started a game of Warcraft or Quake on the computers instead of logging into Femtedim to continue their project. When asked about this change, one of the boys explained: 'we have all the coolest stuff, so what more is there to do'?

At the Itnom platform the interplay of the blankness of the design and the practice of the Itnom group and platform did indeed continue into an activity of 'filling in' in a non-predefined way. The division of labour of the Itnom boys divided the steps of the building procedure given by the structure of the Active Worlds building function among the involved actors as was done at Akul. Two of the Itnoms took care of the time consuming task of finding objects, and the last built the found objects at the Itnom platform. A crucial difference between the Itnom and the Akul arrangements was that the Akul resulted in individual houses within the platform, while the product resulting from the interplay of design and practice in the case of the Itnoms was one undivided layout of the platform.

This was clearly due to the division of labour, or rather to, what Law (1994) calls 'labour of division'. Compared to the Akul arrangement, the arrangement at the Itnom platform made clear divisions between the roles of each boy, making each entirely responsible and in charge of any decisions to be taken within his sub task, while there was no clear division between roles or tasks at the Akul platform. The girls performed the same roles, and shared the outcome. In the latter arrangement the girls worked in parallel on two products which required interplay and adjustment involving transformation with exchangeable entities and exchange between the two parallel 'lines of production' keeping up a uniform identity of the platform. Due to the sequential process of production no mutual interplay was necessary at the Itnom platform, but only a one-way delivery. Neither adjustment nor transformation with exchangeable entities relevant as long as each boy filled out his role in the sequence satisfactorily.

Thus, an important element of the fluid ordering was missing in the interplay of the design and practice in the case of the Itnom platform, namely that of ongoing transformation with exchangeable entities. The ordering of the interplay of design and practice at the Itnom platform is more reminiscent of what Law and Mol (Mol & Law 1994; Law 2002) drawing on Latour (Latour 1990; 1987) describe as a network ordering,[14] characterised by drawing and keeping things together and functioning as a running machinery, in which every part – technology as well as humans – play their specific role.

Out of the politics of design putting forward a fluid ordering came a network ordering. From transforming with exchangeable entities through blankness the design turned into an ordering of keeping things together, dynamic but unchanging. This transformation happened through the interplay of design, the platform, new building objects, the structure of the Active Worlds building function, and the allocation of each boy into one step in this sequential production process.

What about the politics of design that put forward a regional ordering through the graphics of the Femtedim design? This ordering was indeed continued in the interplay of design and practice: through the determined work directed towards the end of achieving the 'coolest stuff' the Itnom platform was consolidated as a region with its own identity. However, compared to the regional ordering of the Akul platform, which contained the ongoing development of the homogeneous identity of the platform *within* its boundaries, the regional ordering of the Itnom platform came in another version, very much dependent on relations *across* the boundaries of the platform, between the Itnom platform and the other platforms. I base this conclusion on the boy's comments that they had the 'coolest stuff', which set a comparison between the Itnom platform and other platforms, thereby creating a 'them-and-us' relationship, where the identity of 'us' is defined in relations to 'them'.[15] This 'them-and-us' relation involved the 'others' as specific dynamic partners in a competitive game. This regional ordering did not have the self-containing character of the Akul platform independent of what went on outside of the platform, but was on the contrary dependent on an interplay and contrast to the other platforms.

No other platforms, however, entered into a competition of getting the 'coolest stuff', but preserved the more self-containing version of the regional ordering, consolidating a stable identity. The continuance of a regional ordering at the Itnom

14 The network metaphor of actor-network theory is often criticised for neglecting the failing, temporary, and unstable (e.g. Lee and Brown 1994; Star 1991). Law and Mol (Law & Mol 2001; Mol & Law 1994) argue for the need for differentiated topological metaphors in order to be sensitive to the variety of orderings. In this step, they have narrowed the traditional and broader notion of network, generating more sensitivity to other orderings, and to distinguishing between orderings. The description of network in this chapter follows Law and Mol's notion, not Latour and Callon's.

15 Similar to the in-group out-group dynamics described by Sherif et al (1961).

platform with a stable and homogeneous identity was hence established once and for all at the moment the Itnom had achieved the 'coolest stuff'. As the boy explained, there was 'no more to do' in order to establish the regional ordering. Contrary to the Akul, where the achievement of a regional ordering was a *process* due to the fluid ordering intertwining with it, the regional ordering at the Itnom platform was constituted as a *product* quickly achieved once and for all. In this logic, there would, as implicit in the boy's explanation, only be 'more to do' if another platform would challenge their established regional ordering of having the 'coolest stuff'.

In this case, the politics of design continued in the interplay of design and practice. The regional ordering put forward through the graphic layout was continued in the design workshop. Not through a direct reproduction, however, but by linking the regional politics of design to the network ordering which gave rise to the 'coolest stuff' as a regional end product. The regional ordering was maintained even without the boys' active contribution. As long as no other platforms had 'cooler stuff' the regional ordering would be upheld at the Itnom platform. Contrary to this, the Akul girls' active attendance was required continuously in order to maintain their regional ordering, according to the logic of the intertwining of the fluid ordering and the self-contained version of the regional ordering.

## Conclusion

I have described two politics of the Femtedim design: the blankness putting forward a fluid ordering, and the graphic layout putting forward a regional ordering. And I have shown through two examples how these politics were continued, changed and unchanged in the interplay of design and practice in a design workshop for children. By describing the design in terms of politics of design put forward in practice, it has become clear that the fluid and regional orderings were not simply *there* as already settled, stabilised products when the blankness and graphic layout were set. They were not effortlessly inserted into practice. The design had to be realised, maintained, and continued in practice. The orderings inscribed in the design had to change in practice in order to continue as 'the same'. The continuity of the design was dependent on involving other elements such as new objects, children's ideas, discussions, divisions of labour etc. Hence, rather than describing design as a fixed structure, my analyses have revealed it as a process of politics of design put forward, picked up and continued, changed or unchanged.

When a teacher designs a lesson, the artefacts involved are usually understood as tools that teachers simply use without changing the design. However, by the vocabulary put forward in this chapter, I argue that a teacher does indeed design artefacts. He or she involves artefacts in specific practices, which as a result of the interplay of design and practice constitute specific orderings. Thereby, it is not simply a teacher inserting a finished design into practice. Among many possible directions she is contributing to continuing, and thereby constituting, the design in one specific way (with help, of course, from the children and the other participants involved).

The aim of creating an open-ended design for our specific research project could have been realised in many different ways. I have spent more space on describing design and practice than on the aims and intentions of designers in for instance pedagogical terms. This is because the way design and practice is realised concretely proves to be more subtle and complex than the designers' intentions. A narrow focus on designers' intentions may lead us to overlook aspects of concrete materiality and practice, and hence of politics of design that are not formulated as explicit pedagogical intentions. Had I focused on designers' intentions to create open-ended design, the fluidity of the design would have been highlighted, while a standard and fixed regional ordering like that of the graphics might have been overlooked. Referring to the designers' intentions, we could see the regional politics of the design as a failure, as an inability to live up to the pedagogical ideas. I prefer, however, to see it as a practical solution, which turned out to not even be contrary to the ideas of fluidity implied by the intentions of creating an open-ended design. While the blankness of the Femtedim contributed to establishing a fluid ordering, the regionality of the graphics contributed in the Akul case to keeping the activity gathered as *one*. Mulcahy (1998) distinguishes between prescriptions and framework. The latter involves multi-strategic work allowing for both homogeneity and heterogeneity, while prescriptions tend to silence heterogeneity. Instead of seeing these two strategies as opposites we can understand the graphics as securing the smooth working of the Femtedim activity, which allows the fluid activity to flow heterogeneously with the blankness of the design. In order to sustain the fluid ordering by avoiding it flowing in all directions and thereby undermining itself, regional standardising and fixing forces had to be involved. We could even say that the regionality inscribed in the design turned out to be insufficiently fixed or bounded to maintain fluidity. In the Itnom case, it flooded the boundaries of the region involving 'other platforms' as a constitutive element of its ordering, transforming the ever changing and adjusting fluid ordering into a functioning machinery of a network ordering, keeping the elements in place. But only until the 'coolest stuff' was achieved and regionality produced rendering the boys' involvement redundant.

Returning to my initial question about whether a fixed and standardised design results in rigid practice and whether open design brings about flexible activities, I have to conclude that there is no golden rule. A fixed and standardised design may result in flexible practices like the regionality sustained fluidity, whereas an open design may give rise to rigid practice, as when the blankness gave rise to an inflexible network ordering just focussed on achieving the 'coolest stuff'. By approaching design in terms of politics of design putting forward orderings in practice, we realize that design is an achievement of the interplay between inscriptions and practice. It also means that when we discuss design apart from practice then we miss the procedural aspect of design and we come to depict only a brief stage of the procedural life of design.

**References**


Akrich, M. (1992). The De-Scription of technical objects', in Wiebe Bijker & John Law (Eds.), *Shaping technology/building society: Studies in sociotechnical change* (pp. 205–224). Cambridge MA: MIT Press.

Callon, M. (1998). Introduction: the embeddedness of economic markets in economics. In Michel Callon (Ed.), *The laws of the markets* (pp. 1–57). Oxford: Blackwell Publishers.

Cole, M. (1996). *Cultural psychology: A once and future discipline*. Cambridge MA: Belknap Press,

Dreier, O. (1993). *Psykosocial Behandling, en teori om et praksisområde* [Psychosocial treatment – a theory of a field of practice]. Copenhagen: Dansk Psykologisk Forlag.

Dreier, O. (1999). Personal trajectories of participation across contexts of social practice. *Outlines: Critical Social Studies, 1*, 5–32.

Grint, K. & Woolgar, S. (1997). *The machine at work*. Oxford: Blackwell.

Haraway, D. (1991). Situated knowledges: The science question in feminism and the privilege of partial perspective. In Donna Haraway, *Simians, cyborgs, and women* (pp. 183–202). New York: Routledge.

Hetherington, J. & Lee, N. (2000). Social order and the blank figure. *Environment and Planning D: Society and Space*, *18*(2), 169–184.

Laet, M. de & Mol, A. (2000). The Zimbabwe bush pump: Mechanics of a fluid technology. *Social Studies of Science, 30,* 225-263.

Latour, B. (1987). *Science in action*. Cambridge, MA: Harvard University Press.

Latour, B. (1990). Drawing things together. In M. Lynch & S. Woolgar (Eds.), *Representation in scientific practice* (pp. 19–68). Cambridge, MA: MIT Press,

Law, J. (1994). *Organizing modernity*. Oxford: Blackwell Publishers.

Law, J. (2002). Objects and spaces. *Theory, Culture and Society, 19*(5/6), 91–105.

Law, J. & Mol, A. (2001). Situating technoscience: An inquiry into spatiality. *Environment and Planning D: Society and Space, 19(5),* 609–621.

Lee, N. (2001). *Childhood and society*. Buckingham, UK: Open University Press.

Lee, N. & Brown, S.D. (1994). Otherness and actor-network: The undiscovered continent. *American Behavioral Scientist, 37(*6), 772–790.

Mehan, H. (1993). Beneath the skin and between the ears: A case study in the politics of representation. In S. Chaiklin. & J. Lave (Eds.), *Understanding practice: Perspectives on activity and context* (pp. 241–268). Cambridge: Cambridge University Press.

Mol, A. & Law, J. (1994). Regions, networks and fluids: Anaemia and social topology. *Social Studies of Science*, *24*, 641–671.

Mulcahy, M.D. (1998). Designing the user/Using the design: The shifting relations of a curriculum technology change. *Social Studies of Science*, *28*, 5–37.

Pickering, A. (1995). *The Mangle of practice: Time, agency, and science*. Chicago: University of Chicago Press.

Sherif, M., Harvey, O.J., White, B.J., Hood, W.R. & Sherif, C.W. (1961). *Intergroup conflict and cooperation: The robbers cave experiment.* Norman, OK: University of Oaklahoma Book Exchange.

Sørensen, E. (2006a). *STS goes to school: Spatial imaginaries of technology, knowledge and presence.* Ph.d. Dissertation, University of Copenhagen

Sørensen, E. (2006b). The time of materiality. *Forum Qualitative Social Research*, 7(4).

Star, S.L. (1991). Power, technologies and the phenomenology of standards: On being allergic to onions. In J. Law (Ed.), *A sociology of monsters? Power, technology and the modern world* (pp. 27–57). Sociological Review Monograph, no. 38. Oxford: Basil Blackwell.

Suchman, L. (1987). *Plans and situated actions.* Cambridge: Cambridge University Press.

Winner, L. (1995). Do artifacts have politics? In D. MacKenzie & J. Wajcman (Eds.), *The social shaping of technology* (pp. 28–40). Buckingham: Open University Press.

# PART IV
# Organisation and Things

Chapter 9

# Working with Material Things: From Essentialism to Material–Semiotic Analysis of Sociotechnical Practice

Finn Olesen and Randi Markussen

> One can start from the idea that the world is filled, not in the first instance, with facts and observations, but with agency. The world, I want to say, is continually doing things, things that bear upon us not as observation statements upon disembodied intellectuals but as forces upon material beings. – Andrew Pickering, *The Mangle of Practice*

In the last few decades, a fruitful body of boundary-crossing research has developed in cracks in the walls between traditional science and technology institutions. Representatives from various disciplines, like anthropology, history, sociology, philosophy and psychology, feminist studies, cultural studies, information studies, etc. now investigate science and technology as cultural expressions rather than timeless, rational activity. There are several reasons why this turn to Science and Technology Studies, STS, has come about, as has been narrated in various publications (e.g. Pickering 1992; Callebaut 1993; Biagioli 1999).

In this chapter, however, we will only emphasise one aspect of the STS approach. It has to do with the way we study things around us as part of learning about human practice. One may study things as if they are somehow pre-given objects with definitely known properties, or they may be studied as if they are dynamic elements in a continuous flow of activities. We will follow the latter route and investigate the relationship between things we (can) say about material things, and the stance from where we are able to say such things. Essential to our argument is a field study we conducted at a medical ward at a large Danish hospital in the fall of 2000. During a five-month period we studied the incorporation of an electronic medication module (EMM) into daily work at the ward. Our field study was centred on how medicine, staff and writing were translated and transformed in order for the EMM to become a usable part of the ward's work routines (Markussen & Olesen 2002, 2003). In this chapter we will emphasise only one aspect of our study: The situated practices of dealing with medications after the introduction of an electronic medication system.

Prior to entering the details of the study, we wish to ponder on some philosophical and theoretical issues regarding material things and their doings in order not to take too much for granted in our understanding of medication as a situated practice. After a brief, overall introduction to our field study, we will discuss some philosophical peculiarities tied to the concept of material things, to show that certain influential ideas abut things depend on contingent presumptions rather than timeless facts about things; then, based on the writings of the STS scholar, Donna Haraway, we will challenge a number of conventional notions of materiality to establish a malleable concept of material things; finally we will tie this understanding to some core findings from our field study. The basic claim throughout the paper is that if the researcher only takes a confined approach to concrete reality, the actual workings of material things will remain hidden.

## Doing Electronic Medication

In the autumn of 2000, the two authors concluded a field study at a plastic surgery ward at a large Danish Hospital. Through a number of weekly visits we studied the successful incorporation of an EMM into daily work routines in the ward. The module is part of an electronic patient record, Medicare, already used by various professionals, individually and in groups, at the ward. From the very beginning the intended purpose of the EMM was to simplify a number of basic procedures related to medication. A sketch of the context of medication at the ward will help to understand the intentions.

Before October 2nd, 2000, the doctors at the ward prescribed medicine using a dictaphone, and typists wrote the prescription into the electronic patient record, e.g. 'Rp T Cipramil 10 mg x 2 daily'. The transcription was done on the first floor of the tower block hospital, and the resulting prescription text was sent to the 10th and 12th floor, to the patient unit, either on a loose sheet of paper for the physical version of the journal, or as electronic text. In the patient unit the nurses would either read from one of the two available computer monitors, or from the paper-based prescription sheet, what drugs the particular patient is to have, and in which dose.

The nurses on duty would copy the prescriptions for the particular patients assigned to them with a ball pen[1] to the medication form. This was then inserted in the *cardex*, which is the nurses' version of a patient record. They also wrote down the same details on a small paper label to be placed at the bottom of the medicine tray, and on a control form to be attached to the wall in the medicine room. Often they would write on yet another sheet of paper, the nurses' report, to be placed in the cardex after duty. All in all the nurses and other staff members had to copy the prescriptions to different kinds of paper forms to be placed at four or five locations.

1 The ink of the ball pen was significant in itself, as the colour signals on what shift the text was written. During the day shift the nurses would use blue or black ink, in the evening they would use green ink and the night shift nurses would use red. This material manifestation of daily rhythms appears to be a widespread convention, as we have learned from comments by nurses and other health professionals in various countries.

It is no wonder if they occasionally felt uncertain whether the right medicine was administered to the right patient in the right dose in the right form at the right time.

In the early months of 2000 four nurses and a consulting surgeon, making up the prescription group at the ward, decided to implement the EMM from October 2nd. – At this point one should note that before this date, the nurses clearly had a right to write down medicine as an integrated part of their work. Seen from the outside they gave away this right as they began to incorporate the EMM in their work. Meanwhile, the doctors, who did not do much writing apart from making notes for their own use, took over a right they had never asked for. We will elaborate further on this transformation in a later section. For now it is sufficient to note that in terms of doing things with things, some basic daily work practices were about to change.

It was the doctor, who previously made the (oral) prescription, who now had instead to write down the prescription in the EMM. At the same time the nurses were to refrain from repeating medication and instead use the doctor's prescription on printed lists as the basis for their drug administering. Furthermore, *the writing space* had been altered. Writing medicine was no longer about a nurse using a ball pen or a pencil to write down the name, dose etc. of a drug on a piece of paper. Instead, it was about a medical doctor using a computer keyboard to type into a module in the electronic patient record what drugs she has prescribed to a particular patient.

From a modernist perspective one may be tempted to claim that the hand and mouth of the doctor has been harmonized in an input activity, while the nurses and other professional groups have been aligned to mediate the output to the patient. The new situation would then appear to underpin the modern, dominant idea of technologically driven progress and autonomous, rational subjects. In our opinion, however, writing down and printing out medicine is far more complicated than can be expressed through this unilinear perspective on change. Writing and printing involves a number of complex coordinations of existing competencies and agencies, which defy the outcome of any such perspective (Markussen & Olesen 2003).

To support our argument it is necessary to investigate, and possibly subvert, certain images of social interaction and materiality. As we have just outlined, the staff use pens, keyboards, forms, etc. to engage in a delicate, but necessary work practice. From a modernist perspective these are straight-forward examples of how to do things with things, i.e. how rational human agents master work-tools. From our alternative perspective within STS, however, there is more to the case than autonomous subjects operating standardised tools in intentional actions. Both things and people are transformed during processes of change. It is precisely *the dynamic, interdependent evolving* of things and humans which makes it possible to stabilise particular relations between them over time. It raises the question, how such restrained changes can be studied? By what means can the co-evolving entities be dragged out from behind modern dichotomies of free human beings and determined things?

In the above example, writing is at stake as a specific mode of health care practice, that has to be transformed in order for medication to become safer and more efficient. In STS terms this raises the question: *What is writing* if it is not just a simple tool-using human practice? Let us try to hint at an answer as a first step to describing our approach to the study of material things and the merging of humans and things.

*Doing writing*

First a strategic claim. Writing at the ward, or in similar work situations, is not a neutral, instrumental skill. On the contrary, it is part of a constant microsocial stabilising of numerous sociotechnical relations, which in effect will transgress paper, databases, pens, keyboards, graphic interfaces and words. Why do we say that?

Historically, writing has always been a powerful means of social control and principle of organization (Ong 1982, Heim 1987, Martin 1988). That goes not least for our own time, in which communication has become a cultural beacon carried forward by the effects of internet use and other social interactions involving microprocessors. Also historically speaking, one can point out strong idealist traditions in Western cultures to separate language from its material contexts and machines, whether those are slate pencils, a printing press, or some other tools for lettering. Materiality represents simple work, while thoughts and language represent our privileged human form as *animal rationale* (Masten et al., 1997).

It follows that we have inherited a somewhat contradictory relationship with writing. At a modern hi-tech hospital it is evident that writing (as well as reading) is an extremely important mode of ensuring stability in daily work routines. Here one also finds the ambiguous relationship to writing where, on the one hand, materialized textuality and documentation, e.g. test results, measurement values, codes, are *sine qua non*, but, on the other hand, many agents aim at a paper-free reorganization of work processes supported by the computer. If decision makers are not aware of the materiality of the textual production, or the textuality of the material tools, they will often be tempted to aim at technological simplifications of delicate work processes, without considering *the situated microprocesses* that are involved. Consequently, intended improvements may be distorted by unintended changes.

The above reflections embed some fundamental presumptions about things and materiality which to a high degree determine the convictions and choices made, or not made, regarding our dealings with things. Some of them are *philosophical questions*, but not in a highbrow sense of intricate, scholarly debate. Rather, they involve a more mundane kind of philosophy. They are basic questions we could ask, but seldom do, with regard to our everyday practices. Most of the time we do not need to reflect on our work, we just do it![2] But sometimes the situation involves a breakdown, or an alteration, and we may then begin to reflect on what is going on. On a few occasions the reflections will raise doubt about foundational elements

2 See for instance Garfinkel (1967) for a classic portrayal of *ethnomethodology* as one important line of approach to studying non-reflexive, everyday routines.

of the everyday situation. And this, indeed, is a risky kind of endeavour, as it may literally undermine one's everyday conceptions of ... things.

Nonetheless, we claim that such philosophical assumptions make up a vigorous part of everyday life, and we might as well pay attention to this domain. In the following sections we will do exactly that. We begin the investigation into mundane philosophy of things by a conceptual analysis of this most ordinary word 'thing'. To be economical we will only look at how *material* things may be understood.

**Parts and Properties**

The term 'thing' is arguably one of the most indispensable, linguistic devices in any language, but what does it mean, do and represent? One line of initial questioning could be: Is there more to a thing than the sum of its parts or properties? Does it have an essence? One reason to assume this is that we apparently use one kind of concepts to describe the parts and properties of things, and another kind of concepts to describe, or refer to a thing in itself. It seems that we individuate things all the time in various ways, so what are we actually able to say about them? Two issues come to the fore.

First, is a thing, say a car, the sum of its parts, and if so, when will it lose its unitary status? Is the car a wheeled vehicle? Is it still a car when the wheels are removed, and are the wheels not now new things in their own right? Hence, before there was the original unified thing, the car, but now there are five independent things with their own, unique properties. The problem turns into a puzzle: When do we talk about a thing, and when do we talk about a context? Does, for example, the teapot act as context for the teapot lid? Is the tea tray context for various comestible things. – The puzzle has obviously to do with *classifications*, and one may wonder if there is an infinite number of things in the world, so that no classification scheme whatsoever may be able to exhaust the essence of a thing (Mary Douglas, 1994, Hacking, 1991).

Second, if we disregard the puzzles about the possibility of an infinite number of things in the world – and all those questions following from that, regarding classification as such and the risk of making arbitrary separations – we may return to the speculations about a thing as the sum of its parts. This, however, raises another and just as important, philosophical question about *the relations between a thing, and the properties we assign to it*. A car may be identical with the totality of its parts, but that does not account for the relation between the car and its properties, such as colour, shape, weight, and size. At the manufacturing plant the individual car is built by combining parts in a certain, planned fashion, but it is not possible to build a car in that material sense by combining its properties. So what is the *ontological difference* between the properties and the parts of a thing? (Quinton, 1973). Is it perhaps the context that yields properties to the thing? The situatedness?

Seen in this light there seems to be good reason to claim that 'there is more to a thing than its properties', simply because properties are not *immanent* to a thing, rather they *transcend* it. The same properties can apply to indefinitely many individual things, because to ascribe some properties to a thing is to classify it and compare it with other things that resemble it in certain ways due to some shared properties. While the car has the property 'red' in common with a lot of other things, it has the property 'car-shaped' in common with a number of things, which are only partly compatible with red things. Also, the colour and weight properties of a car will relate it to a lot of other things, as there will be a number of additional overlaps between other properties of these things. The actual properties of a car will limit the number of properties it has in common with other things, because there are fewer things in the world that have both red colour, car shape, car weight and car size in common, than things, which have only some of these properties in common.

It follows, then, that it can only be *contingently* true that the sum of properties of a thing is sufficient to individuate this thing from other things. There will be numerous other things that also have these properties as well. It will thus be extremely difficult, if not impossible, to produce a complete specification of the properties of a thing. Neither is it feasible to claim that any particular list of specifications is final. So we are back at the opening questions: How do we individuate things, so that we may claim that this thing is what it is because it has these properties, and that these properties are uniquely belonging to it? It is in this entanglement that *the problem of individuation* lies: The total amount of properties ascribed to a particular thing does not guarantee that this thing necessarily has been individualised. If the total amount of properties belonging to a thing is indefinite, it follows that the presumed qualitative identity between two things is *inductive*, and – as we have learned from David Hume long ago – empirically accumulated knowledge about the world may be refuted in the light of tomorrow's findings. In short, the unique, individual core of a thing must be something else than its properties. But what could it be, then?

We have so far been speaking about parts and properties of things, but what about *functions*? Not least, material things seem to be characterised by having functions for use, so what about them? Roughly formulated, a functional definition would assert that a thing is what it is due to the function(s) it has in a system or a structure. A car may thus be defined as a road-based carrier of people and things, that is its function! As such it is comparable with other means of transport, and one can start to list its advantages and disadvantages, like it is motorised, it is fast, it is reliable, it makes noise, it pollutes, it is expensive, etc. But functionality is both too broad and too narrow as a means to identify things. First, functional stances tend to be too liberal. Functionalists generally consider themselves uncommitted to ontology, hence it is legitimate to overlook the materiality of things. Whether a carburettor is made from e.g. clay, wood or steel it may serve exactly the same function in a petrol-driven engine – but intuitively these differences are significant to our understanding of the thing. Second, functional analysis seems to presume a privileged design purpose built into things, that warrants a particular kind of result from using them. Functionalism, thus, advocates a *teleology* in things, but that reminds us of the point made above, that it is difficult, if not impossible, to establish what are the immanent properties of a thing. The proper purpose of a thing does not appear to be any more immanent than properties. Hence, the assumed functional economy of a thing is only contingently true (and not guaranteed by its designers, as will be evident below). If nothing else, this suggests that functions somehow resemble the general category of properties, at least with regard to material things.

It was hinted earlier on that the researcher can benefit from studying the *context of things*. 'Context' is a somewhat over-worked term which in recent years has been applied by numerous groups of researchers, not least to characterise the joint social fabric. It does seem safe, though, to make a minimalistic claim that certain things occasionally serve as context for other things. But talk about a context implies talk about people, too, in the sense that 'context' suggests *linguistic relationships* between various entities. 'Context' literally means 'with text' or 'text-based relationship'. Relationships are established by people as an ongoing practice of linking things and people in this or that fashion to bring order into their life. This points to another feature mentioned above, that classifications do much work to constitute things and to place them in relations to each other and to people.[3] Not least is classification an ever present imperative at a hospital, and it may seem obvious that an EMM, or in broader terms, an electronic patient record, EPR, constitutes an especially efficient classification machine that can ensure order in many corners of the health systems. But is the EPR a thing after all, and if so, what can we say about it?

*Is the electronic patient record a thing?*

Let us begin with the puzzle about a thing as more than its parts. In recent years, there has been a struggle in Denmark between various players for the right to define the EPR. The National Board of Health, politicians, computer companies, several counties, singular hospitals and wards, appear to have overlapping, but different ideas about what is required for something to be an EPR.[4] How is that possible? One reason is that, unlike cars, most candidates to be an EPR do not (yet) exist in a stable, globally recognised clinical setting. That is, there may be national visions about EPRs, locally applied EPR-like systems, Beta-test versions of EPRs, etc. But there is no single classification scheme available to unify these candidates, to exhaust what is an EPR, and, as we saw regarding things as the sum of their parts, such a scheme might not be possible. It is not unreasonable to suggest that the struggle for definition rights is often politically motivated – 'political' being understood in a broad sense. Winning the right to define what an EPR is, is also winning the right to classify what is the right context for its use, and what parts are necessary for its proper working. So far, the struggle goes on.

What about EPR candidates and their properties, then? It looks like it can only be contingently true that the sum of properties of a thing is sufficient to individuate it from other things. Other things, too, have these properties. It will thus be next to

3 See Star & Bowker 1999 for more on the doings of classification systems. See also Olesen 1995 regarding the foundation of modern, technoscientific order.

4 See EPJ-observatoriets reports, e.g. 2002, 2003.

impossible to produce a complete specification of the properties of a thing. Neither is it meaningful to deem any particular list of specifications final. To speak about the 'right' or the 'complete' EPR is to individuate it based on a particular list of specifications of properties. Whether we talk about a unique EPR, or a class of identical EPRs, the problem with the contingencies of property lists will arise. If we accept this analysis, the struggle to define the Danish EPR appears to be an *ascriptionist* war, in which properties like 'effective', 'rational', 'economical', 'safer', 'easier' are ascribed or not ascribed to various EPR candidates. No system *has* these properties in the ontological sense mentioned before. It appears that e.g. 'efficiency' is not an immanent part of any EPR, and cannot belong to it in the same sense that a printer port or a database belongs. Again, political and other motivations to tie certian properties to specific EPRs must be considered alongside concerns for design and contexts of application.

So the EPR is difficult to make out as a thing on its own. Rather we must look at certain properties tied to the thing in a context. This is where writing suggests itself as a promising point of departure. Proponents of EPRs and EMMs assure us that work will be more orderly for the health professionals, and treatments safer for the patients, if these computerised things are applied. As we have already pointed out, writing is basic to tightly organised ordering practices in a hospital. In accordance with our approach it is not just a physical representation of mental operations to write things down. Instead, *it is a situated practice* that includes enfolded textual and material variations and shifts. Hence, we need to develop different conceptions of writing to understand it as a practice. To follow up on this lead, the next sections will investigate some consequential ideas about the relationship between people and things. The focus will be on the *material fabric of the world and things*. On the face of it, it would seem that the material world is the most stable point of departure if one wishes to learn about things and their contexts. As will be evident, however, we may well have to develop new ideas about the materiality of things in order to talk about their practical, but slippery nature. In this paper we choose to accompany the much debated science student and feminist scholar Donna Haraway. The main reason is that she has introduced an exciting new vocabulary to talk about people and things which avoids unproductive separations and dichotomies. Hence, Haraway invites us to take a stance, from where we can say something different about things and our relations with them.

## Situating the Material World

In the beginning of her book, *Modest_Witness@Second_Millennium. FemaleMan© Meets_OncoMouse™ – Feminism and Technoscience,* Donna Haraway claims the following: 'Challenging the material-semiotic practices of technoscience is in the interest of a deeper, broader, and more open scientific literacy, which this book will call situated knowledge' (Haraway, 1997: 11). Below we wish to pursue her challenge to traditional conceptions of science and technology in order to get a fresh perspective on how to investigate the doings of people and things. It is fruitful to zoom in on her important concept of a *material-semiotic* systems (or fields, worlds, practices, bodies, knots, etc.). As will be evident in later sections on our ethnographic findings, this provocative coalition of terms is very productive, if one wishes to confront hidden philosophical assumptions in everyday practices. 'To write' a prescription, say, is not just about mindful agents putting premeditated words to the paper in deliberate actions, but about performing and being performed in a situated, interdependent network of entities.

To do the elaboration, we move somewhat deeper into the details of some influential ideas about the concepts involved, i.e. 'material' and 'semiotic'. That will make it possible to relate to the kinds of understanding of being and knowledge production Haraway wishes to transcend. It will be evident that her understanding of material-semiotic things entails a challenge to established philosophical ideas which have been built into well-working, modern scientific narratives about 'objective' reality.

### *Taking a materialist stance*

Let us continue by trying to answer a straight-forward, solid question: What is materiality and materialism? First materiality. – The concept is rooted in the latin *materia*, meaning 'matter or substance'. The latin word is derived from the Greek *hyle*, meaning 'wood', but not wood in general, though, only that kind of wood used by the carpenter to build things. It follows, that matter is related to *form* from the very beginning; it is the carved wood that is implied in the concept of hyle. Matter and form are tied together in our conceptions and our experience (Flussel, 2000).

If one conceives of matter as *the stuff things are made from,* it follows that things are assigned certain properties, e.g. spatial and temporal extension, mass, mobility, divisibility, measurability. Often these are labelled 'quantitative properties', because they have to do with size and weight. Aristotle, who lived some 2300 years ago, saw raw matter as form-less or undetermined, while the form of a thing is that which actualises its potentiality and make it real. To him, properties were to be found in the individual thing. If we take a leap in time to the natural philosophers of the 17th century, we can see how matter begins to be conferred many of the basic meanings familiar to us moderns, not least through the development of experimental science. Most claims produced by natural science prove immensely powerful, which has to do with the unique possibilities of scientific institutions to make controlled measurements of material processes. Their results can be circulated and compared with data from other scientific institutions to develop stable determinations of natural behaviour, i.e. natural laws.[5] As will be evident below, later conceptions of reality

5 See Cantor (1989) for some interesting reflections on the growing needs to circulate objective knowledge following the development of new scientific institutions in the 17th and 18th century.

have criticized this understanding for being fallacious, not providing a fair picture of the complexity of the world.

What about materialism, then? If by 'materialism' one points to a stance from where the world is seen as the sum of physical matter, we are immediately led back to an understanding developed by 17th century empiricism and taken over by enlightenment philosophers. The basics of this understanding had been expressed in the theory of atoms by the Greek philosopher, Democritus, some 2400 years ago: *Materia* is what is given in knowledge about nature; there is no basic power or spirit intervening in the processes of nature. What exists is the extended, material reality, and it can be measured. Knowledge about the natural world is limited to what can be experienced through the senses – without interference from speculative phenomena and concepts. But even if there is no intention in the spiritless, material nature, things do not happen by accident. On the contrary, everything follows the clear laws of nature.

Also, mental processes and states can be reduced to material reality due to the atomic structure and material fabric of all things. Already Democritus had talked about the soul as made out of especially smooth and round 'soul atoms'. In the mechanical philosophy, introduced by the British empiricists in the 17th century and further developed in the 18th century by materialist philosophers, the interior of the soul was precisely investigated on experimental-material grounds. In the same period, inventors, such as Baron von Kempelen and Vaucanson, produced mechanical dolls that were not just expressions of mechanical enthusiasm and skills. These *automatons* also symbolised a basic mechanical-material conception of reality: We do not need the Cartesian 'double-ontology' that not only contains calculable matter, but also slippery soul substance of a very speculative nature! In this firm rejection of body-mind dualism one finds, however, an important recognition of the soul stuff or mentality as the distinct *other* in contrast to the material reality. As we well know today, this rigid contrast between mind and matter did not stay uncontested in philosophical discourse.

In the middle of the 19th century, materialism got a different meaning, very much in conflict with the mechanical materialism. The 'material' was interpreted *dialectically* by Karl Marx and Friedrich Engels, who sought the developmental principles behind the empirical, sensual world. It is no coincidence that the young Marx wrote his academic dissertation on Democritus and Epicurus, arguably the two foremost materialists of antiquity. As Witt-Hansen (1973) has been pointed, Marx never offered a straightforward answer to the question: What is your kind of a philosophical materialism? He would talk about materialism and idealism through aphorisms or in peripheral remarks in his social analyses. He does say, in opposition to Hegel, that the ideal is nothing but a mental transformation and translation of the material. This act of transformation and translation is what Marx calls spiritual *production*. By emphasizing human productivity Marx distances himself from Feuerbach and other materialists. In the first thesis on Feuerbach he criticizes him for ignoring the role played by human sensuous activity in practice, i.e. in history, politics and economy. Instead, Feuerbach stays satisfied with a contemplative materialism that yields a passive, observing role to human beings. The distinctive mark of Marx's materialism is that, while he buys into the claim made by contemporary materialists that people are products of their material conditions, he adds that because we are productive beings we also *actively* change our material and spiritual environments. His philosophical anthropology is thus much more generous to our participation in the world.

The materialism advanced by Marx and Engels, *historical materialism*, would reject mechanical materialism, or 'vulgar materialism', of the kind described above, because of its basic claim that only physical bodies in motion exist as the basic building blocks in the universe. For Marx and Engels, on the contrary, it is necessary to investigate reality on separate ontological levels, where each level has its own reality in accordance with dialectic laws of historic development. This assumption makes it very sensible to talk about historical materialism. While historical materialism does not presume reality to be just extended matter, it presupposes that reality is developing, or built, on top of a material foundation. But in the same way that a building is not reducable to its foundation, so is reality not just extended matter. The world also comprises social, political, cultural, aesthetic phenomena. The concepts of 'basis' and 'superstructure' made it possible for Marx and Engels to point out dialectic tensions between the material and the socio-cultural levels of any society. They thereby offered a different, much more dynamic, conception of materiality and materialism.[6]

The strong political dimension, central to historical materialism, has set its mark on a large number of subsequent positions, trying to come to grips with our practical, shared existence, either as endorsements, or as attempted refutations of this dynamic mode of materialism. Marx and Engels' materialistic, political arguments and philosophical anthropology will consequently also be found in those positions. This observation allows us to move several steps further to Haraway's stance on material reality. As will be evident, she attempts to dissolve a number of strong tensions between philosophical anthropology and contemporary, sociotechnical reality in which not everything is what it seems to be.

### *Material-semiotic stuff*

Donna Haraway has acknowledged that she is '... something of an unreconstructed and dogged Marxist', who remains '... very interested in how social relationships get congealed into and taken for decontextualized things' (Haraway 1997:8). Like Marx,

6 It is true that higher levels of reality depend on lower levels, i.e. the social superstructure depends on the basic material and economical conditions. At the same time one should not aim at reducing the moral, religious, or philosophical institutions to some basic material structures. Furthermore, there are constant interchanges between the various levels. When reality is thus parted into several ontological levels, each with its own kind of existence, the physical reduction presupposed by mechanical materialism is totally misleading. Reality is much too complex for such an understanding to be final.

she rejects simple, scientific attempts to reduce social reality to 'congealed' objects in a mechanical-material grid. She rejects any straightforward, Cartesian contrast between subject and object reality. Rather, she prefers to study sociotechnical alliances and relations, which she takes to be preconditions for scientists and philosophers, who mistakenly substitute frozen images for social life.

Haraway willingly subscribes to Marx's determination to demonstrate how objects and nature are full of social process and work – '... even if many current science scholars have forgotten his priority here' (Haraway 1997: 43). At the same time she disagrees with his basic assumption about the given, human nature and its privileged role, or rather, she disagrees with seeing work and practice as exclusive *human* characteristics. Marx has expressed such views in relation to the anthropocentric interpretation of technical change through history. To him, the technico-scientific development represents a progressive, dialectic process in which human beings have emancipated themselves from nature's constraints in attempts to realise their own nature.

The history of science and technology has in other words served as an argument to demonstrate the human desire for emancipation, i.e. the progressive humanisation. This makes it sensible to claim that Marx's thinking was based on a positive view of technological development for the good of humanity where technoscience would eventually contribute to the eventual emancipation of man (Siggaard & Skovsmose 1986). Similar anthropocentric conceptions are found in influential Marxist readings from the 20th century. It is evident in Adorno and Horkheimer's historico-philosophical social research and in Habermas's subsequent social philosophy, not least expressed through the well-known term 'technical knowledge interests'. Other Marx-inspired traditions like activity theory and critical psychology seem to presuppose this principal, ontological separation between human agency and non-human things and phenomena.

This is where Haraway distances herself from the Marxist tradition, or perhaps better, tries to carry over the tradition to let it become a *post-humanist* social theory in accordance with contemporary social life:

> But unlike Marx, and allied with a few prominent and deliberately crazy scholars in science studies, with armies of very powerful and paradigmatically sane scientists and engineers, and with a motley band of off-the-wall ecofeminists and science-fiction enthusiasts, I insist that social relationships include nonhumans as well as humans as *socially* (or, what is the same thing for this odd congeries, sociotechnically) active partners. All that is unhuman is not un-kind, outside kinship, outside the orders of signification, excluded from trading in signs and wonders (Haraway 1997: 8).

It follows that, while Haraway buys in on his broad conception of material reality, she asks us to bend Marx in two significant ways. First, historical materialism fails to consider non-humans as actors besides humans; and second, as indicated at the end of the quote, their status as actors must include the handling of signs and other non-material work. That leads to the weaving of the material and *semiotic* dimensions of Haraway's conception of reality.[7]

*Figuring things out*

As we argued in the section on writing, Western cultures seem to act from a basic idealist conception of words as something hovering over the paper. Just think of Plato's philosophy of the real world of ideas, or the magic role of the word in the Judeo-Christian tradition. In these cultures, there is a gulf between the practices of putting letters, words, and sentences to paper or on hard disk, and the metaphysical understanding of words as transcending their material context. Gradually, with, for example, the replacement of hand-written books by mass-produced, printed type volumes in the renaissance, and with the hermeneutic-humanist interest of modernity in trying to grasp the meanings hidden in our texts, there has come to be a culturally accepted separation between the *materiality* of the written word and its *meaning*. A separation between things and signs.

Words are often taken to be representations of the essence of human being, that is, reason; and language has in paradoxical ways gained status as our connection to eternity, not least through religious and cultural practices. Whether language represents God or Nature, it points beyond the specific, social and material context in which it was first expressed. That seems to be a special property of language: the ability to free itself from its original context, from its own history. It is largely because of this cultural imagery that we tend to dismiss the possibility of significant bonds between words and their contexts of production. Western cultures have, more precisely, gotten into the habit of making deep, meticulous analysis of the numerous, symbolic representations of our unique, mental essence, *and* of the emancipating and/or alienating effects of materiality on our life. Typically, we presuppose a boundary between these two reality domains, whether it is a Cartesian sign-thing ontology, or it is a more advanced understanding of reality, as in Marx and Engels. In a sociotechnical culture it may not be enough, however, to see nuances through the lenses of dialectic materialism. They have not, so to speak, been ground to show the continuous transitions from the material to the semiotic dimensions of reality and back again. We need to find a different stance from where to investigate the relationship between humans and things. Not a radically different one, as should be obvious by now, but one that is able to overcome the culturally-born dichotomies between humans and things, and between signs and matter.

Donna Haraway, together with the French sociologist Bruno Latour (1988, 1993) and other STS scholars, has demonstrated the merits of trying to dissolve absolute ontological boundaries between material and symbolic dimensions of sociotechnical practices. She has identified figures and figurations as explicit expressions of '... the tropic quality of all material-semiotic processes, especially in technoscience'

7 In Haraway's writings 'semiotic' should be taken in a broad sense to express the textual and symbolic dimensions of the world as they are woven into fields of practice.

(Haraway 1997: 11). By that she wishes to point out that a *figuration* is not just a figurative ornamentation of literal speech. Nor are figurative utterances 'just' images or symbolic expressions of literal meaning. Rather, we live with and through such figurations. Figurations are *performative images* that one may dwell in. The famous *cyborg*-figure is arguably a special sign of a sociotechnical culture's transgression of any subject-object dichotomy, of any fixed material-mental boundary-work (Haraway 1991). But there are, Haraway insists, many other such figurations (Lykke, Markussen & Olesen 2000).[8]

In Haraway's use of images, literal and figurative modes are always intertwined (Bartsch et al. 2001), and this entails that rhetorical practices are also in effect political practices. This goes for technoscientific practices too. To talk about the conquering of extended, lifeless nature in the 17th century, or historically developing, material world divided into manifest levels of reality in the late 19th century, are two examples of political practices. Both bring to life a number of figurations that are embodied and thus able to perform sociotechnical work as such on top of human, verbal practice.

This brings us back to the initial Haraway quote: 'Challenging the material-semiotic practices of technoscience is in the interest of a deeper, broader, and more open scientific literacy, which this book will call situated knowledge.' With her concept of material-semiotic reality Haraway makes it possible to challenge a number of 'hard' facts about nature's eternal, invariant atomic structures. Her conception also invites us to point out those rhetorical devices by which material and semiotic reality apparently is ordered in mutually fixed, static arrangements, not just within scientific institutions, but also, for instance, in health care contexts. Let us just mention two such figurations.

'Modest Witness' is a figure that was formulated in the 17th century by the famous British natural philosopher Robert Boyle in an environment of experimental physics, still in its infancy. His intention was to create a neutral, direct connection between the scientific matter of fact and Nature without intervention of human intermediaries (Shapin & Shaffer 1985, Olesen 1995). The experimental scientist is precisely a modest, almost invisible figure, and due to this arrangement the scientist also becomes a political figuration. First, the modest witness is more or less equal to a British gentleman with special moral obligations and standings, i.e. women or poor people cannot be in a position to become modest witnesses to the basic processes of

8 Haraway assumes that all language is figurative, and even if they are not mentioned specifically in *Modest Witness*, she is aligned with the two writers on metaphor, Georg Lakoff and Mark Johnson, on this view of language. In a number of books, the latter describe how we practically live through metaphors (Johnson & Lakoff, 1980; Lakoff,1987, Johnson, 1987). Our social life is characterised by projections from basic, *experiential* knowledge into abstract conceptions of the world. For instance, our personal, physical experiences of learning how to stay in an upright position may be projected into abstract ideas about how difficult it is to live a balanced life in society. A discussion may be seen as a fight, or the memory as a container, etc.

nature. Second, Boyle and other experimentalists succeeded in establishing a unique moral order, which is still considered exemplary to scientific and non-scientific social practice. Basically, this order demands of its members that they are morally committed to endorse the outcome of any experiment they have witnessed – of their own free will – in the laboratory. Third, nature and human society are arranged in a strong dichotomy, and natural scientists are, in a sense, commissioned as administrators to determine possible relations. Finally, the modest witness stands as the figure who deals with context-free, non-situated knowledge – not least due to his unique moral position. For all these reasons, the modest witness is a political figure, who influences the way we live. Not least, Haraway wants to show how the idea of the scientist as a modest, neutral observer of natural processes is a translation of ideas about masculine identity, which excludes the feminine gender from culturally significant interaction with nature. She is able to demonstrate such political issues by dissolving rhetorically founded, and very solid walls put up by modernists between material and semiotic reality.

If we take Haraway's insight to our own case, it becomes possible to look at 'the electronic patient record' as another political figuration in a Danish context, stretched out in material-semiotic systems of reality. As a figuration its presence is evident in campaigns to rationalise and improve the Danish health care systems, not least in press coverages, professional journals and political debates.[9] As such 'the electronic patient record' (or just the EPR) is made up of fictions, facts and situated materiality. If *the* EPR was just a physical machine to be used by rational professionals in health care work, its alleged advantages would not be discussed, negotiated and defined as much as is the case. At the moment the political debates are still undecided about its effects and identity, but certain features are discernible: The EPR acts as an agitator for the responsible management of patients. It warrants better political and economic control with health care spendings. Not unlike the modest witness, the EPR stands as a figure who deals with health care knowledge in reliable, unbiased ways. Furthermore, improved social order is spoken through the figuration in the sense that it gives all citizens equal access to their own health data, which, by the way, will not be forgotten somewhere by a tired doctor. Hence, the EPR is a dedicated champion of democratic rights and orderly behaviour. Another figuration, the 'electronic medication module', or the EMM, has begun to stand up as a close *aide de camp* to the EPR. Competent, safe handling of medicine will save lives and counteract fears of human mistakes, and the EMM is there to take on that role. At the moment the EMM seems to work very well as a political figuration to promote the national Danish EPR precisely due to its lifesaving abilities.

Now, this reading of certain material things may seem exorbitant to some readers, but it does make it possible to disclose some of the rhetorical devices by which material and semiotic reality is ordered in mutually fixed, static arrangements, in science and in health politics alike. The modernist image of intentional humans and

9 It has e.g. been named the 'catalyst that is changing the Danish Health Care system' (Rapport fra Elektronisk PatientJournal, Sygehus Fyn, maj 1998).

their technological devices may thus be opened up for discussion. By appointing figurations, like the modest witness or the electronic patient record, as representatives of a category or a species, one creates a setting in which to disclose some features that may demonstrate, in a post-Marxian fashion, the political dimensions behind prominent human practices. Also, such a setting shows the socio-material embeddedness of the figure and what it represents. The material aspects of reality are never 'just material' as has been argued. Materiality, too, embeds fictional constructions.

At this point we leave the discourse about the embedded, situated material-semiotic arrangements of knowledge and things with a sharpened awareness of the dynamic mingling of things and humans, signs and materiality. Let us return to some of the empirical findings from the plastic surgical ward to discuss them in the light of these ideas.

## Working with Medication Lists

By focusing on the ward as a dynamic and situated, material-semiotic space of multiple practices we attempt to demonstrate how the successful incorporation of the EMM can be seen as an effect of numerous work processes entailing many reconfigurations of humans, things, and meanings. We will also look at the EMM as a material-semiotic figuration that appears to play a steady role in the successful improvement of handling medicine, much like modernist conceptions of technology. This focus will hopefully demonstrate the price to pay for rationalising medication in terms of transformed material-semiotic agencies.

Let us take a closer look at the most obvious result of the new writing-reading practice at the ward after the introduction of the EMM: The printed paper list with the doctor's prescriptions bearing the headline: 'Medicine list – current'. This list makes up a very important stage in the dynamic process from verbal prescription by a doctor to physical absorption by a patient.

On the (modernist) surface, it is a piece of paper partly covered with black laser-printed text. When we begin to scratch the surface, however, it becomes clear why perceiving the list as a material-semiotic system is productive, because it reveals the intertwined materiality and linguistics of the 'Medicine list current'. Here we will linger on a particular set of properties of the system, which concerns the reconfigurations of doctors, nurses and medicine lists.[10] As will be evident, the core of the new reconfigurations is to be found in 1) the creation of *a stable column* in the medicine list, and 2) the politics of *daily rhythms*. To justify these odd bedfellows, it will be beneficial to look at an example of a 'Medicine list – current', slightly modified to fit into this paper (Figure 9.1). It was created on the first day of the EMM's introduction into the ward, and printed for use on that same day. In other

10 We will touch only on a few points of the subject in this paper, but will make it the main theme of a forthcoming book on health care informatics and STS.

MEDICINE LIST - CURRENT

Social security noxxxxxx
Name: xxxx xxxxxxx

| Prescribed | Change/disc | Form/Strength | Name/Dosage |
|---|---|---|---|
| Fixed | | | |
| 09-20-2000 | 26-09-2000 | Effervescent pills<br>300 mg | Zantac<br>1 pill at bedtime |
| 09-20-2000 | | Injection liquid<br>100 mg/ml | Klexane<br>20 mg subcutaneous daily |
| Periodic | | | |
| 10-02-2000 | | Pills<br>20 mg | Diural<br>1 pill daily |
| p.n. | | | |
| 09-20-2000 | | Pills<br>15 mg | Serepax<br>1 pill twice daily |

**Figure 9.1 A reproduction of one of the very first Medicine lists of the EMM to be used for measuring out medicine at the ward**

words, the list shows a still unsettled material-semiotic system, trembling on the borderline between the banal and the exotic.

In this reproduction of the list, originally written in Danish, we have attempted to retain the headline, fonts, and font sizes along with the horizontal lines, in order to give a fairly precise idea of what a list looks like when it is printed to be used by a nurse for measuring out medicine. The reader should imagine that the list covers the top half of a standard (A4) sheet of paper. At the bottom of the sheet is a line of text, stating the date and time and the initials of the person who logged in to Medicare.[11]

At the time of production the fields in the prescription module were filled out partly based on the doctor's entering data, on system designers and programmers ideas with regard to adequate set-ups for data, and on the software's suitability for creating such fields. At this early stage of entering data into the EMM, the doctor primarily filled out the blanks based on her requirements and ideas of meaningful information as a medical doctor. For instance, the doctors consider '1 pill at bedtime' to be a clear, unambiguous message. It is a message that is communicated daily between health care professionals in the verbal form preferred by most doctors as basic mode of communication. But this conception of unambiguity does not take

11 The initials of the person who logged onto Medicare in the morning would almost always be put at the bottom of that day's subsequent medicine lists. The individual health professional at the ward rarely felt any need to log off Medicare after use. The local working collectives, especially those including nurses, had in other words no need to act out differentiated identities in regard of password formalism.

into consideration *the column as a material tool* for the nurses to ensure greater precision in the task of measuring medicine at the correct time. One doctor stated directly to us that he found the 1+1+1+1 code 'idiotic and a nuisance'. To him there was no connection between this notation and the daily rhythm of individual patients. Most people take their medicine during the main meals, i.e. 3 times a day, hence, the four times daily built into in the formalism do not fit: 'You could say that the patient is forced to adjust to the hospital's rhythm, as defined by the four times', he stated. It is necessary to go into this subject more deeply in order to understand why the nurses' and Medicare's need for a new material-semiotic configuration very much depends on a shift in the doctors' writing practice.

Previously, it was the nurses themselves who filled out pre-printed lists distinguished by grids, rows and columns, and designed for the tasks involved in measuring out medicine. But the prescription module is not (yet) designed for such tasks![12] When the nurse, responsible for the patient in question, has printed the medicine list, she puts it in a plastic folder at the front of the cardex made for the individual patient. The cardex is a thin, dark blue dossier containing various forms in a specified order, and placed along with the other patients' cardex on a shelf in the ward office. When the next normal time to administer medicine is approaching, i.e. 8 a.m., 12 noon, 6 or 10 p.m., the medicine list is retrieved from the cardex and taken together with the other medicine lists into the medicine room next door. The lists are laid beside the medicine closet, and the nurse then begins to measure medicine into small plastic cups based on the information she extracts from reading the lists, one by one. During our field study we gradually became aware how closely the process of measuring out medicine was connected to the material-semiotic conditions of writing.

The nurse will measure out medicine by following a column with her eyes and perhaps a finger. But it is evident in Figure 9.1, that there is a total lack of vertical lines for support in the 'Medicine list – current'! The table does fulfil its function in the light of the physicians' and programmers' requirements. On the other hand, the health professionals, who wanted the new list to prevent misreadings, have lost the stabilizing effect of vertical lines on the up-and-down movements of the eyes, when compared with their pre-electronic charts and forms. The column 'Name/Dosage' is meant to show whether the patient should be given medicine at this time, e.g. in the evening. Even though it says '1 pill at bedtime', that is not in accordance with the concrete needs in the medicine room, when the nurse measures out the products. Does it mean '6 p.m.', 'in the course of the evening', or 'when the light goes out'?

12 It is important to stress that, to us, the effective design process is not caused by 'designers'. Like 'scientists' and 'technologists', designers only become 'freestanding' agents with causal powers as a result of delegations at the end of a number of heterogeneous social processes. The continued design of the EMM is evolving thanks to situated, micro-social processes of translation and transformation. See also Latour (1987) for more on this stance to design and technology.

Previously, the text in the columns of the medicine list was well assimilated into the process of measuring out medicine, thus helping to maintain a high degree of certitude in this procedure. But the computer-assisted 'Medicine list – current' is not compatible with the former process, as we now can see. The new situation was therefore awkward for the nurses. It may well be that they no longer need to write down the medical products themselves, a task now left to the prescribing doctor and an electronic database system. At the same time, however, a shift in the balance between text and materiality had happened in this crucial phase of the medicine's transformation from verbal prescription to physical consumption. The very concrete measurement phase was, so to speak, marked by a weak, vertical materiality, and something had to be done to the unstable things at hand.

An unplanned, new kind of practice started to evolve around the writing of medicine prescriptions. Hence, some of the nurses gradually took on the task of pushing the doctors to write correctly and on time – if not with enthusiasm, at least straightforwardly. A nurse expressed the sentiment:

> We can't be bothered to be nursemaids for the doctors. They must remember to write the prescriptions themselves. Of course, they differ; some just write them, while others have to be reminded. It's probably a question of the generation gap, where we younger nurses refuse to do the doctors' remembering for them. … So it's a conflict that, on the one hand, we leave it to the doctors, and on the other hand, we are dependent on being able to print out the medicine list!

In other words, a new kind of dependency to be handled in the complex, collective arrangements at the ward had arisen. The material-semiotic and the sociotechnical dimensions clearly intersect. At the same time the new situation illustrates the ambiguity of the work needed to incorporate the EMM. A clearcut initial sharing of work tasks in connection with the incorporation is not simply transmitted to the relevant participants, as a modernist diffusion model of technological circulation would have it (Latour 1987). Instead, the incorporation prompts a number of pragmatic transformations of roles, needs and agencies. One senior intern did see herself as complying to the new demands – but in accordance with her medical logic. At one point she entered a prescription and wrote down the dosage as '0+0+1'. When asked, she had no doubt that any nurse would make out from the text that the patient is having this product in the evening, but not in the morning or at midday. On the other hand, she did not find it necessary to write the 4th digit to tell that the patient is not having this product at night time: 'The nurses know that!' she stated confidently. This is an example of a partial connection between some of the involved actors, where shared knowledge, daily rhythms, and ink-based columns on a sheet of paper are colliding in the attempts to make a new formalism work.[13]

In the local context, the medicine list must provide some kind of columns, which the nurses can use for measuring out medicine. This can be illustrated by another

13 See Strathern (1991) for a detailed unfolding of the concept.

# MEDICINE LIST - CURRENT

Social security no: xxxxxx-xx
Name: xx

| Prescribed | Change/Dis. | Form/strength | Name/Dosage |
|---|---|---|---|
| **Fixed** | | | |
| 09-20-2000 | | Pills<br>500 mg | Panodil<br>2+2+2+2 |
| 10-02-2000 | | Pills<br>20 mg | Diural<br>1+0+0+0 |
| 09-20-2000 | | Pills<br>100 mg | Persantin<br>2+0+2+0 |

**Figure 9.2 A medicine list in harmony with the situated needs of the nurses**

medicine list, produced about a month later, and correctly completed – in the nurses' eyes.

We have added the vertical lines to the above list to illustrate the nurses' requirements. Note, that it is a question of training the eye and finger to check whether this patient is to have a specific product at this time. For instance, the patient is to have two 500-mg Panodil pills, but no Diural. If readings from the list were to be relatively stable, the doctors had to learn to write according to the 1+1+1+1 code, and not 'four times daily'. It is a compromise, where the nurses will add vertical lines – with ink, graphite or thoughts – if doctors, the computers and the printer will only live up to a disciplined writing practice, where morning, noon, evening and night are translated into digits. We see shifts across well-established borders between professional groups, humans and non-humans, and between textualities and materialities. The involved doctors, nurses, the EMM, the medicine lists, all had to perform and be performed differently, for the new system to be 'more reliable'.

The material-semiotic transformations developed further according to the needs arising in the course of the Fall 2000. Even though it was banned, several nurses began writing on the printed medicine lists, because they need to write as part of their medicine-related practice. It appeared that, for some, the writing acted as *a marker* signaling uncertainty as to the correctness of the medicine list. In the sociotechnical arrangement of the EMM there had been no allowance made for this alliance with paper as a mnemotechnical tool. The reconfigured writing practice was expressed in various ways, from pencilled question marks by the name of a product, corrections written over the dosage text, to pencilled vertical lines, or the crossing out of discontinued medicine. Often the nurses reflected on medications in concrete work situations. For instance, a nurse looked at an item in a medicine list that stated that a patient was to be given morphine for severe pain. She knew from experience that morphine often causes patients to be constipated. Consequently this patient, too, might well need something for that condition. She therefore chose to write her thoughts down on the medicine list to discuss the issue with others later.

'Medicine list – current' contains a column headed 'Change/Disc'. It is intended to show when a product may have changed dosage or been discontinued, i.e. treatment has been completed or interrupted for a period. Some nurses had mentioned the discrepancy between the title's claim to be a 'current' medicine list and the reference to products not currently being given. A nurse described how she had measured out medicine for a patient who, from his bed told her that he was no longer to have this product according to the doctor. She had not noticed the discrepancy during the measuring in the medicine room, where her eyes were literally fixed on the Name/Dosage column. Again, we see that an ideal simplification demands a good deal of work by the actors involved, in this case even a patient. The nurse further stated that she had begun crossing the discontinued medicine out with a pencil before going to the medicine room, so as not to measure it out by mistake. Another nurse showed us a list she had written on because she was not sure of the dosage shown for a certain product. Her eyes had stopped at a surprising dosage in the text, making it necessary for her to put words on paper. That way she materialized her uncertainty, so that it was not forgotten but could be followed up by herself or other nurses. The uncertainty was kept alive and passed on through the paper. One begins to see the dawning need to reclaim the materiality of the medicine list. The rule against writing is in effect capable of running counter to the aimed-for simplicity in handling medicine, so it must be betrayed with a layer of graphite added by hand to the machine-printed layer of ink.

Our last example illustrates well the often sublime transition between the material and semiotic dimensions of medicine. It proved impossible to prescribe children's vitamins through the EMM, because the product was not found in the module's database. In consultation with a doctor, a nurse therefore wrote 'Multitabs Junior 1+0+0+0' with a ballpoint pen at the bottom of a 'Medicine list – current', so that her child patient could be given the necessary vitamins. When the patient's other medicine was altered and new medicine lists printed out, the handwritten prescription was cut off the original medicine list, put in a plastic pocket, and laid with subsequent lists. This mix of text and paper was in no way planned, but proved to be a necessary and practical local counter-program to the formal program of the medication module, which did not satisfy situated needs and interests.

The incorporation of the medicine list arose from rules that were intended to ensure a simpler, more reliable procedure, but it meant that the nurses lost a writing tool that was significant for their collective work form. In other words, for the first couple of months after October 2nd, 2000, the EMM was exclusively seen as a set of *rules*, and not as *tools* for the nurses and other health professionals.[14] This pair of concepts expresses quite well what was put at risk on the ward. There was a continual transformation of the rules laid down, so that they were not obstructing gradually recognized needs by (transformed) nurses for tools with which to make note of their deliberations. Halfway through the planned period of incorporating the module, the prescription group allowed the nurses to write on the 'Medicine list

14 This play on words occurs in Engeström (1990, pp. 171f).

– current' (but only in the right margin!). With this, both map and landscape, module and medicine handling, were significantly altered in ways that were not planned prior to the inauguration of the system. For a time, at least, the EMM had become a stable actor in the hypercomplex, sociotechnical arrangements at the ward.[15]

## Conclusion

In this contribution we have explored some relationships between the things we (can) say about things and some theoretical stances from where we can say specific things about things. It has also been emphasized, that the way we study things around us is inherent to what we may learn about human beings in a situated practice. In other words, the philosophical conceptions of the materiality of things we have presented here, entail a view of humans and things as intertwined in heterogeneous sociotechnical arrangements. One may study things as if they are somehow *pre-given objects* with certain known qualities; but they can also be studied as if they are *dynamic elements* in a continuous flow of activities.

A conceptual analysis of the term 'thing' showed that detached, essentialist notions of parts and properties are rather futile. Following this, we argued that attempts to define a national electronic patient record based on a fixed list of properties cannot rely on singular classifications. There is no single classification scheme to exhaust what an EPR is, and it may never come about. To speak about the 'right' or the 'complete' EPR is to individuate it based on a particular list of specifications of properties. Whether we talk about a unique EPR, or a class of identical EPRs, the problem with the contingencies of a property list will arise. We suggested that political motives will be a prominent part of the arguments to favour one list over others. Giving up the attempts at essentialist definitions of the EPR, we went on to investigate things in meaningful contexts of material practice. Two established notions of materiality and human practice – mechanical materialism and historical materialism – were discussed. We ended up in support of the material-semiotic, post-Marxian stance proposed by Donna Haraway, not least because she questions the basic philosophical anthropologies of the former stances. Her notion of material-semiotic figurations offers a different, politically motivated understanding of social practice, allowing for a rather broad understanding of human-things relationships. This allowed us to see the EPR and the EMM as figurations with moral and political bearings, and thus opening up the human-thing dichotomy for closer inspection.

15 About a year after the introduction, we learned that the EMM did not fulfil its roles so well anymore. The consulting surgeon had left the ward. Hence, the doctors were not encouraged by an eager colleague to fulfil their roles in the local incorporation of the system, and they were left with struggles between medical and collaborative logics. Several nurses had begun to write too extensively on the 'Medicine list – current', 'so we will probably have to do something to straighten up the discipline on the use of the list' as a member of the group said. In any case, the situated sociotechnical practices are clearly dynamic and new stabilities will (have to) replace older ones.

In the last section we tried out this understanding on findings from our own field study. The aim was to demonstrate that a dynamic sense of the material-textual reality will disclose – often in surprising ways – the effectual doings of things. By looking at the 'medicine list – current' as a representative of a category or a domain, it became possible to exhibit some situated, micro-political entanglements of sociotechnical practices, in which humans and things are intricately woven into one another. Material things are never 'just material', as we have argued. Materiality also comprises fictional constructions.

Based on our analysis and study we find it misleading to motivate the introduction of a new sociotechnical system by pointing to its successful use in other sociotechnical arrangements, or by claiming that the system carries certain inherent qualities guaranteeing some specific ends through its (correct) use. Instead, we suggest that a successful incorporation of technological devices in a work practice can be seen as an effect of multiple undertakings, performed within a gradually expanded chain of situated, partially connected processes.[16] Both actors and processes will undergo some alterations due to the work.

As we have tried to make evident, the field of STS, and Haraway's work in particular, can be used to perform playful, politically motivated excavation of the field of dynamic tensions between what is material and figurative in things. But the tensions will remain hidden for those who do not look for the semiotic work in material reality, and who overlook the material agency of semiotic figurations.

## References

Bartsch, I., DiPalma, C. & Sells, L. (2001). Witnessing the postmodern Jeremiad: (Mis)understanding Donna Haraway's method of inquiry. *Configurations*, *9*(1), 127–164.

Biagioli, M. (Ed.) (1999). *The science studies reader*. New York: Routledge.

Callebaut, W. (Ed.) (1993). *Taking the naturalistic turn – Or how real philosophy of science is done*. Chicago: University of Chicago Press.

Cantor, G. (1989). The rhetoric of experiment. In D. Gooding, T. Pinch, & S. Schaffer (Eds.), *The uses of experiment: Studies in the natural sciences* (pp. 159–80). Cambridge: Cambridge University Press.

Douglas, M. (1994). The genuine article. In S. H. Riggins (Ed.), *The socialness of things – Essays on the socio-semiotics of objects*. Berlin: Mouton de Gruyter.

Engeström, Y. (1990). *Learning, working and imagining -Twelve studies in activity theory*. Helsinki: Orienta-Konsultit Oy.

Flusser, V. (1999). *The shape of things: A philosophy of design*. London: Reaktion Books.

Garfinkel, H. (1967). *Studies in ethnomethodology*. Englewood Cliffs, New York: Prentice-Hall.

16 See Strathern (1991) for a detailed unfolding of the concept of partial connection.

Hacking, I. (1991). A tradition of natural kinds. *Philosophical Studies*, *61*, 109–126.

Haraway, D. (1991). *Simians, cyborgs, and women – The reinvention of nature*. New York: Routledge.

Haraway, D. (1997). *Modest_Witness@Second_Millennium. Female Man© _Meets_ OncoMouse™: Feminism and techno science.* New York: Routledge.

Heim, M. (1987). *Electric language – A philosophical study of word processing*. New Haven: Yale University Press.

Johnson, M. & Lakoff, G. (1980). *Metaphors we live by*. Chicago: The University of Chicago Press.

Johnson, M. (1987). *The body in the mind – The bodily basis of meaning, imagination, and reason.* Chicago: The University of Chicago Press.

Latour, B. (1987). *Science in action*. Cambridge, MA: Harvard University Press.

Latour, B. (1988). *The Pasteurization of France (Part one: 'War and peace of microbes'; Part two: 'Irreductions')*. Cambridge, MA: Harvard University Press.

Latour, B. (1993). *We have never been modern*. New York: Harvester-Wheatsheaf.

Lakoff, G. (1987). *Women, fire, and dangerous things – What categories reveal about the mind*. Chicago: The University of Chicago Press.

Lykke, N., Markussen, R. & Olesen, F. (2000). 'There are always more things going on than you thought!' – Methodologies as thinking technologies. Interview with Donna Haraway, part two'. *Kvinder, Køn og Forskning*, *9*(4), 52–60.

Lykke, N., Markussen, R. & Olesen, F. (2003). 'Interview with Donna Haraway.' In Don Ihde and Evan Selinger (Eds.), *Chasing technoscience: Matrix for materiality*. Indiana: Indiana University Press.

Markussen, R. & Olesen, F. (2001). Information technology and politics of incorporation – The electronic trading zone as coordination of beliefs and actions. *Outline*, *3*, October, 35–47.

Markussen, R. & Olesen, F. (2002). Kyborger på arbejde – Elektronisk medicinordination. *NIKK Magasin*, *2*( 2), 20–22.

Markussen, R. & Olesen, F. (2003). Reconfigured medication – Writing medicine in a sociotechnical practice.' *Configurations*, *11*, 351–381.

Martin, H.-J. (1988). *The history and power of writing*. Chicago: The University of Chicago Press.

Masten, J., Stallybrass, P. & Vickers, N. (Eds.) (1997). *Language machines – Technologies of literary and cultural production*. London: Routledge.

Olesen, F. (1995). Kendsgerningernes verden og orden. *Philosophia*, *24*(1–2), 43–70.

Ong, W. (1982). *Orality and literacy*. London: Routledge.

Pickering, A. (Ed.). (1992). *Science as practice and culture*. Chicago: University of Chicago Press.

Quinton, A. (1973). *The nature of things*. London: Routledge and Kegan Paul.

Shapin, S. & Shaffer, S. (1985). *Leviathan and the air-pump – Hobbes, Boyle, and the experimental life*. Princeton: Princeton University Press.

Siggaard Jensen, H. & Skovsmose, O. (1986). *Teknologikritik*. Copenhagen: Systime.

Star, S.L. & Bowker, G. (1999). *Sorting things out – Classification and its consequences*. Boston, MA: MIT Press.

Strathern, M. (1991). *Partial connections*. Savage, Maryland: Rowman & Littlefield Publishers.

Witt-Hansen, J. (1973). *Historisk materialisme* [Historical Materialism]. Copenhagen: Berlingske Leksikonbibliotek.

Chapter 10

# Words and Things: Discursive and Non-Discursive Ordering in a Networked Organisation

Steven D. Brown and David Middleton

We wish to consider what is done with a kind of artefact that has become ubiquitous in the practices of any organisation – archives of email messages. The ordering and use of these archives bring into the focus the relationships between words and things, and sociality and things within unfolding organisational practices. In particular, the ways in which archives of messages are configured and used in organisational settings collapses any distinction between sociality and materiality. We aim to demonstrate, using an analytic approach derived from discursive psychology, how archives configure interdependencies between persons and things within organisational practices. In so doing, we challenge the conventional assumptions concerning the role of computer-mediated communication in organisational settings where 'the social' is taken as the gold standard against which communicative effectiveness is judged. Rather, we need to understand how archival practices of computer-mediated communications are devices that order the socialities of organisational practice.

Computer mediated communication (CMC) clearly allows organisational members to realise collectively relevant plans and goals. It might also be taken as making a workgroup or organisation more effective by either democratising relations between colleagues or by empowering particular people. Alternatively, CMC by its very nature makes users orient to emergent group norms when communicating with fellow users. These kinds of issues are at the heart of classic studies of CMC carried out within a social psychological framework (e.g. Hiltz & Turoff, 1978; Sproull & Kiesler, 1998). If these diverse studies have something in common, it is that they all take 'the social' as the standard against which communication is to be judged. Or to be more precise, that specific instances of interactions between users can be understood with reference to a version of an ideal form of sociality. A given CMC practice can then be evaluated in terms of how far it realises this ideal form or approximates to it in its actual application. In such a view, people are taken as offering information to one another in face-to-face settings with all manner of additional information gleaned from observing non-verbal stimuli and other features of the immediate setting (Kiesler et al, 1984; Sproull & Kiesler, 1986). In other words, people are treated as isolated information processors, who exercise permanent vigilance in an attempt to glean whatever information they can from the immediate moment.

Now that is an interesting model of the person, one which seems perfectly reasonable for understanding certain sorts of interactions. But not perhaps a model that can serve as a default description of everyday social life. For example, how can we understand the emergence of shared meanings in a given interaction when such meanings are clearly not a property of the information exchanged? At a more fundamental level how does meaning arise at all from information processing? That is, how does the 'signal' encode not only the information to be exchanged but the grounds upon which it should be understood, contextualised and potentially enacted? (Dreyfus & Dreyfus, 1986; Winograd & Flores, 1986). Models of the social based on information processing are clearly problematic.

So maybe what we need is a better model of the social? Perhaps one like that contained in Hutchins' distributed cognition approach? This does at first appear to move us forward. Hutchins & Klausen's (1996) description of the communication of representational states in a simulated airline cockpit, for example, is able to empirically identify instances of shared tacit knowledge amongst flight personnel who have just met. But whilst at an empirical level this is to be welcomed, another set of problems is brought into focus. How is this tacit knowledge derived (see for example Leudar, 1991)? How can we account for its use? In order to do so, Hutchins and Klausen claim that we must posit a shared 'intersubjectivity' at work. Intersubjectivity refers to a shared understanding of the matter at hand which underpins a given interaction. It is this prior intersubjectivity alone which, they claim, enables us to make sense of the following:

| | | |
|---|---|---|
| 0254 | OAK24L | NASA nine hundred … roger contact Oakland center one thirty two point eight.<br>[F/O pulls his hand back from the altitude alert knob when ATC says 'contact Oakland center.' 2.5 seconds after the end of ATC transmission, F/O looks at Capt.]<br>[Capt looks at F/O.] |
| 0300 | F/O | Thirty two eight. |
| | Capt | Thirty two eight? |
| | F/O | Yeah. |
| | Capt | OK |

(Hutchins & Klausen, 1996, p. 16)

This extract is a small piece of interaction recorded with a commercial airline crew training in a flight simulator. There is an awful lot of detail contained in even such a small extract. The extract opens with the crew being given an unexpected instruction by the local air traffic control centre. The crew are at a moment in their flight where they expect to receive confirmation to move to a higher altitude. Control of the flight is instead passed to a new centre (Oakland). What fascinates Hutchins & Klausen, however, is the significance of the two looks exchanged between the First Officer (F/O) and the Captain (Capt.) and the short verbal exchange which follows. Immediately after the radio message, the Captain is responsible for tuning the flight radio into the new frequency used by the Oakland control centre. The Captain conspicuously fails to do so, and this failure occasions the First Officer's look. The Captain returns a blank look, displaying to the First Officer that he is aware of the nature of the problem which has occasioned the look. The First Officer then volunteers the radio frequency of the Oakland control centre, to which the flight is being passed. The Captain then seeks confirmation of the frequency from the Flight Officer before the interaction terminates.

Now the analysis of the interaction supplied by Hutchins and Klausen is certainly detailed, and it allows us to see that the kind of social interaction which goes on around the complex technological routines of commercial air flights is subtle and nuanced. However, we would want ask to what extent we must invoke a notion of 'intersubjectivity' in order to understand the extract. Drawing on discursive psychology – an approach to talk-in-interaction developed in social psychology (see Edwards & Potter, 1992; Edwards, 1997) and the application of conversation analysis to work place studies (e.g., Drew and Heritage, 1992) – we can in principle analyse this kind of interaction by looking at the discursive formulation of each turn in the sequence. The Flight Officer's look, for example, constitutes a fairly obvious prompt to the Captain, who replies in kind. We do not need the concept of intersubjectivity to explain this, nor do we need any special model of the social. It is enough to say that the kind of things the Flight Officer and Captain engage in are fairly routine question-answer sequences, where each turn – whether verbal or non-verbal – affords the next in a more or less direct manner.

So our first substantive point is that it is not necessary to have a model of the social in place before analysing interaction. Indeed, if a model of the social is at work, then we would treat this as an analytic matter. That is, we would want to show how speakers display an orientation to a particular model of the social and the way in which such an orientation is worked up in the interaction itself. And this leads to the second substantive point. If models of the social are things that participants use and thus things to be analysed and explained, rather than things we draw upon to make sense of interaction, it follows that the role and use of CMC in organisational settings are up for re-negotiation. All of which brings us to our third and crucial point. If we assume that speakers in CMC interactions have a problem with 'things', that managing joint attention to objects or artefacts is a problem, then such an assumption implies that ordinarily in face-to-face interaction we do not have this problem. Again, we would want to treat this as an empirical matter rather than a theoretical assumption. This is precisely what we will be doing in this chapter. The approach to things in discursive psychology and the analysis of work place communication looks not at the artefacts or objects themselves, but rather to an analysis of how they are formulated and described by speakers. For example, Charles and Marjorie Goodwin's (1996) discussion of seeing as a situated activity provides numerous examples of how objects, (in this case aircraft) are 'an ongoing contingent accomplishment within a particular community of practice' (op cit p. 87). Things, then, can be viewed in terms of the kinds of descriptive practices which speakers bring to bear upon them. The mutual orientation of speakers to things is a discursive accomplishment, which can be studied as such. Go back for a moment to the flight crew in Hutchins and Klausen's work. They clearly formulate a variety of objects in their utterances to one another. The significance of the Oakland control centre, for example, is worked up in the interaction between the First Office and Captain. But Hutchins and Klausen make an interesting further point. They claim that in order to understand the interaction, one must recognise that there is something about the nature of the technology involved in commercial airflight which has an effect on the interaction. They describe this as a matter of the durability of a medium for retaining a given representational state.

Now that presents an interesting challenge to discursive psychology, and we would put it like this: if there seems to be a kind of stability or a form of restriction placed on a discursive interaction, how is this to be accounted for? In order to address this issue we will introduce the idea of the 'non-discursive'. What we mean by this is the production of order through a means which is not primarily linguistic. In using this term, we will develop Hutchins & Klausen's point that the technology has a kind of grounding effect on interaction and places limits on the kinds of descriptions and explanations speakers can trade with one another. But, as we hope to show, this does not mean that one has to assume a given object-world in advance of a piece of interaction. Quite the contrary, the object world is as put together, as constructed, and hence as amenable to empirical study. So what we are ultimately trying to do is to show how the discursive and the non-discursive serve as two interdependent means of producing order and regularity.

## Case Study: Oilsite and CMC

We will make our argument by discussing some case study materials. These are drawn from a project which examined groupware supported activities in two multi-site organisations (see Brown & Lightfoot, 2002). We will be drawing upon materials from one organisation in particular, which we have given the pseudonym 'Oilsite'.

Oilsite designs and builds infrastructure for the oil industry. They put together petroleum refineries across the world. Wherever there is crude oil to be pumped out of the ground, Oilsite have an interest. The company is owned through a holding operation based in the US and Japan. In the foyer of their main UK office, there are three large clocks, showing the time in Dallas, Yokohama and London. Oilsite has a great many problems trying to co-ordinate these three centres. It sends personnel round the globe from one site to another. Co-ordination is important not only because of geographical distance. Schedule is the sovereign measure at Oilsite. They order activities in time. Plants must be up and running by exact deadlines. Failure to follow and meet schedules involves a complex and costly series of financial penalties. Schedule is then back-flushed through all of Oilsite's activities, as are penalties. Suppliers who fail to deliver to Oilsite on time, or who supply materials which fail to meet quality requirements, are contractually obliged to cede to a shifting scale of 'backcharges'.

Here's the first problem then: how to co-ordinate a mass of personnel, materials and activities which spreads around the globe? Schedule is one answer. However schedules are more than the adherence to a particular set of deadlines. Deadlines set up sequences of complex practices across time and space (Abbott, 2001; Dreier, 1999). They make everyone, including suppliers, irrespective of where they are or what time it is, adhere to the same strict programme of events. It is also necessary to put into place technologies which ensure that all sites and departments can communicate continuously with one another: phones, faxes, video conferencing facilities. Furthermore there is significant use of email.

Scheduling sequencing is almost but not quite a 'virtual' technology. It exists initially as a series of inscriptions – tables and charts. These inscriptions are distributed via a cascade of meetings. But in the course of this, they are transformed, giving rise to different kinds of sub-scheduling sequences and deadlines. Scheduling sequences become more virtual, less localised in a core set of materials, as they proliferate throughout the organisation. Which means that the problem then shifts to ensuring that this mass of inscriptions in which scheduled sequences are embedded are themselves co-ordinated and interlocked.

This task is tackled in a novel way by Oilsite. The kind of massive refineries in which they specialise are built in modular form. They are designed as separate bits with standardised connections that ensure that the bits all eventually fit together into the finished product. Oilsite has translated this modular format to organise its own systems of reporting. Modularisation of the organisation and associated artefacts is also an answer to the problems arising from a multi-site company producing a complex range of petro-chemical products. There is a core group who deal with the day to day running of the company (e.g. finance, IT, personnel) and then a number of distinct project groups. Project Definition, for example, is separated from Project Engineering. The different parts of the company, then, purportedly fit together in much the same way that the different modules of the refinery do – thus linking differences in space and time. Which means that the key task of scheduling sequences is to ensure that the work of each modular part of the organisation comes together at the right moment. Conversely, it means that the failure of a given modularised part of the organisation to reach its own particular deadline can be detached from the overall schedule. A replacement can be attached in its place.

There are many examples of this process of detaching and reattaching modules. A gas conversion unit falls off the barge used to transport it. Equipment from a particular supplier fails to pass quality checks. Relationships between personnel in two different departments become strained. In each case, Oilsite responds in a similar way: it sends out messengers. Troubleshooters are 'parachuted' into field sites or seconded to recalcitrant departments. They open out new lines of communication between modules, make decisions on whether the module itself can be salvaged or else dispensed with. Scheduling a sequence is therefore time critical but in an interesting way. Modularisation ensures that the overall sequencing of production is not tied to a linear arrangement of modules. Each module can set up its own scheduling sequence in relation to local constraints such as the availability of material and staff. Overall scheduling of sequences consists in the detachment and reattachment of modular events.

Within Oilsite, then, a version of sociality, of how social relations might best be structured within the organisation, is formulated in terms of engineering practice – from the materials themselves. Modularity becomes the form around which the 'human side' of the business is managed. It is also the means by which scheduling sequences are driven down through the narrowest capillaries of the organisation. But this particular version of sociality also requires rapid and generalised communication. Materials must flow. People must co-ordinate their actions both in time and space in terms of scheduling sequences in relation to the detachment and reattachment of modules. This is why information communication technologies gain overarching importance for Oilsite. Modularity ensures that the schedule is not threatened by the failure of a component part. But it also creates hidden spaces in which potentially disruptive practices and activities may be developing. It is therefore not enough just to ensure that the modules are all connected one to another. There must also be methods put in place for producing transparency, for guaranteeing visibility between modules and the ongoing accomplishment of scheduling sequences.

Computer-mediated communication, in particular email, is the major tool for engineering this visibility. All employees routinely use email, contribute to electronic discussion lists, refer to information held on the intranet pages and so on. Moving upwards, the diaries of senior managers are often accessible through the electronic network, as are strategy-related documents. The residue of this computer mediated communication remains available in a variety of ways. The storing of things like emails, systematic or otherwise is a focus of concerted effort by many members of the organisation. Elsewhere (Brown, Middleton & Lightfoot, 2001) we describe this at some length. However, here we can see in the following brief example drawn from a corpus of interviews with Oilsite managers that archiving the products of CMC can be a key concern and resource in organisational engagement and accountabilities. The following extract opens with a question about the storage of email messages:

**Interviewer**: Do you take them and store them?

**OilSite Manager Engineering Computation**: Far, far too many. But I put them into categories and then I actually try and archive them all onto CD, as I have access to a CD writer, so I archive them again. I do sometimes go back to them but I do store. Putting them into the categories of the folders is what takes the time and that is why there is always a bit of a back log. But I do try and do that as you never actually know, it is amazing how often I do have to go back and look up one of these things.

**I**: What sort of things do you go back to then?

**M**: Well, it is if somebody comes up and says or somebody sends a message and says that I want to do so and so. And you think that we have already dealt with that. So we go back and it has been dealt with and perhaps that person will find it from that sort of thing. But there isn't a lot of protectionism; generally speaking we do not write the sort of memos which absolve, where they absolve ourselves for more blame for any future reference. But

> there is not a lot of that that goes on. So I do not spend a lot of time going back there and looking for get out clauses. But quite often things come up again and you think that I know I've looked at that and I don't want to look at that again. Or maybe just to find out who was interested before so you can pass information on and that sort of thing.

In the first part of the extract it becomes clear that not only does the manager store the emails he receives but also that this practice of storing is attended to as a problematic issue ('far, far too many'). The manager then goes on to point to a tension that exists between the laborious routine of organising and storing electronic archives against the potential benefits of doing so when it proves necessary to recall something from the archive ('it's amazing'). The occasions which necessitate such activity are then presented as instances of colleagues making requests that the manager would like to deflect through offering up archived material as evidence that the issues have already occurred and been addressed in the past ('and you think that we've already dealt with that'). In this way the manager attends to the past as both an issue that is continually re-invoked in the daily activities of the organisation, and as a practical resource which can be mobilised to perform rhetorical work of establishing and maintaining order in the present of ongoing and complex processes across time and places.

So what occurs here is a discursive deployment of the past in the course of communicative action. This deployment is quite complex. As the extract progresses, the manager begins to attend to a dilemma raised by his earlier comments, namely that he may be seen to be producing 'interested' or tailored versions of the past in order to simply avoid having to comply with other requests. His way of managing this dilemma is to emphasise that what is stored in the archives is not itself partial. He is not seeking 'get out clauses', nor is there any tendency to 'write memos which absolve'. By describing the contents of the archive as pure information, which may be usefully passed on occasionally to others, the manager attempts to frame his own remembering as an activity which simply serves to benefit the organisation by recalling its own history to itself in a way which strategically informs its future directions. Indeed this is often the way that electronic archives are described by their advocates. They present information communication technologies as the means of actively storing up the past in a way that bears dividends in the future (Khoshafian & Buckiewicz, 1995). The past is routinely equated with information, which is presumed a value free commodity. Information cannot be 'interested' or 'biased', it can only be partial or corrupted in some way. These shortcomings can be addressed by 'an intelligent organization' (*op cit* p.42).

Now in order to describe an electronic archive in this way, the archive itself must be organised in such a manner as to afford this kind of logic. That is, a work of ordering needs to be performed on the constituent pieces of equipment whose relations come to define what the archive is. We can see this already in the first extract, where the manager describes the electronic archive in terms of a system of folders which are duplicated across a number of different materials (e.g. a central system and then CD's). This work of ordering the archive, which is driven by the current projects of the organisation, goes on alongside the discursive work of remembering, and acts as an essential support and buttress to it. Without the non-discursive labour of forging relations between components in the archive there is no possibility for playing out the evidencing strategies which dominate the manager's rhetorical performance of the past.

So the visibility which CMC produces within Oilsite does not come about through unlimited access to all, or through a liberating of information. It is not the fact of connection itself, or the circulation of new kinds of informational objects which makes modules visible to one another. It is instead through the creation of a highly public space for the performance of accountability. When everyone is connected, this places an obligation on each employee to display their own attention to that connection. Such obligations are about visibly making sure that all members and parts of the organisation attend to connection as part of the evolving ordering of production processes. This can take the form of replying to requests delivered over the email such that others can see one's activities. Or ensuring that one contributes to debates on discussion lists, even if this is confined to 'me too' types of responses. To be judged to be 'out of the loop' is a serious threat to personal accountability within Oilsite.

Two problems then emerge. First of all, there is an awful lot of email traffic within Oilsite which is considered to be wasteful, non-productive. These messages are written in a mode of sociability or 'phatic' mode. Their sole purpose is to remind others of the fact of the connection of the sender – 'I'm here'. Second, there is a tendency for copying messages to multiple addresses. This is a proliferation of the phatic. Ensuring that one's presence is noted by as many people as possible. But it also reflects something else 'at work'. Something which is cutting across the modularity impressed upon sociality by the material design of Oilsite.

Looking at the kinds of extracts like the above, we may be tempted to conclude that people at Oilsite spend all their time in conversation, passing the time, doing work, exchanging gossip, fixing a schedule. And we might then go on to conclude that it is the interactional structure of such conversation that holds them all together, that binds them as co-workers. But that is not what we are suggesting here. Already, it seems to us, that there is something to be explained in the way that managers at Oilsite spend so much time worrying about the archiving of email messages. This is not, we argue, a purely discursive matter. This displays an orientation to something else, something that cannot be explained by looking at the discursive formulation of objects. Email archives are a peculiar species of objects. They are powerful, certainly, but they gain this power through their ability to lodge themselves in everyday interaction. They are objects inasmuch as one can point to them, describe them, evaluate them and so on. But because they are so important for interaction, they become in effect a kind of subject. That is, something to be negotiated and taken into account in a given interaction. Objects are therefore not external to social relations, but in them, both being parts of unfolding activities and practices. We can illustrate this point if we examine the multiple ways in which email archives are at Oilsite. Computer mediated communication readily affords the creation of multiple email archives. Electronic archives are far more than the storing up of the past, either actively or passively of an organisational record. Electronic archives are subject to a continual ordering and reordering. Non-discursive work of ordering must be performed on the chards of electronic traffic. Such ordering affords relations that define what the archive is and make possible further forms of communicative action that also orders *sociality and equipmental relation* in organisational practice. The archive is ordered as the third party in CMC, as a quasi object (Serres, 1980; 1995).

Managers in Oilsite complained about the number of emails they received and the practical problems this created in terms of the time spent archiving. We may read this complaint in two ways. On the one hand it is a complaint about the literal problem of spending time ensuring that messages can be archived in the right folder, and that this archiving maintains the integrity and utility of the archive as a whole (i.e. archiving by project may prove less successful than archiving by month). That is, the effort involved in non-discursive ordering. At the same time we should also understand this non-discursive labour as about tying in senders to projects, recruiting alliances, and control at a distance (see Brown, Middleton & Lightfoot, 2001). Too many messages simply undermine the ability of the managers to achieve this kind of order effectively. Viewed as a discursive problematic, time spent on archiving exposes managers to claims on their own accountability – namely that their time would be better spent elsewhere. We may then hear in formulations of the problems of archiving a dual struggle with establishing order amongst both discursive and non-discursive elements. In other words, the archives are introduced in the ongoing activity to establish and maintain order in complex ongoing activities. In addition, this very means of doing so introduces new relations and dynamics into that activity which resolves some problems of maintaining order in ongoing complex activities but creates others.

## Distributive Archives

How is this dual problematic addressed? One common method is to tackle the problem by introducing novel elements into the archive. In the following extract the manager in question describes how she informally enrols members of her section as *de facto* archivists by ensuring that they have access to messages which she is aware that they will find 'interesting' and feel compelled to keep:

> **Interviewer:** The ones that you do tend to keep – what kind of general category are those things?
> **Oilsite Personnel Manager:** Erm, things that are still ongoing. I design the on-the spot-bonuses and rather than everytime I get one deal with it and then there it goes into a file and so that gets kept. I run the management employee communication team which is the consultative care-team, it works with council and I keep the back notes to that. So it is things that I might read in the future, like if I don't really think I am going to or I think that somebody else is keeping them. Like I say filing is not my forte. Having done my building I am not wanting to evaluate it at all. You can guarantee that those people absolutely drive me potty. (Laughter) Have you got it now?

**I:** They are quite useful to have around?
**M:** Yes they are very useful to have around. They keep the filing for you. You want those people to be doing the filing for you. You don't want to be doing it yourself.

The extract begins with the manager pointing to different messages that she would tend to store in electronic archives, but then an interesting hedge is introduced. Messages that she does not 'really think I am going to have to' keep or those that she suspects may be held by others can be safely discounted. The clear implication here is that as a manager, section members can be mobilised as informal archivists. One can establish the likelihood that an archive may be maintained by others which can be accessed at some later date without having the trouble of maintaining a complete archive oneself. This is a non-discursive solution to the problem. In other words, perceived inadequacies in the upkeep of the archive are resolved by adding new and novel elements into what is to be counted as the archive – that is, colleagues and subordinates. This is in effect a means of binding external others into the archive by informally mobilising more proximal others as archivists. It is as though she were building a pathway towards the senders who are tied into the archive by using fellow workers as material extensions of the archive itself ('You want those people to be doing the filing for you'). The archive is the third party which makes the communication possible and to which Oilsite members appeal as a guarantor of deeds and words. It is an object through which organisational players establish identities in terms of their relationship to the archive. It is an object defined by transformational orderings and the effects these produce and have on those who engage and are engaged with it. Clearly this is a delicate issue to discursively negotiate, and hence some of the peculiarities of the manager's replies ('Have you got it now?'). This is more than a matter of the archive as a distributed network of the discursive and non discursive that can be used in settling issues of past accountability, what might or might not have been done in the past. As the manager points out, it is also about 'things that are still ongoing'. The distributed archive is crucial in maintaining the order, or re-ordering of complex activity across times and places in the scheduling of sequences.

Another way of negotiating the same issue is for a manager to claim that they are similarly mobilised by their fellow managers:

**Interviewer:** Would you ever resend stuff from archives or as the basis of one of those conversations?
**Oilsite Manager Design Engineering:** Oh yes, often managers who do not archive will ring me and say do you remember back in May and have you still got (laughter).

Managers come to rely upon distributed archival practices within their own organisation to buttress their own archives as a feature of maintaining order in their ongoing activities. But at the same time they also attend to the possibility that these archives may be used against them, as in the following extract. The extract begins with a question about how users write emails which attempt to promote a favourable version of themselves to senior managers:

**Interviewer:** How would that kind of thing, say that people ... the way in which people say it is almost like they're being helpful but they are sticking the knife in at the same time? How would that type of thing be done?
**Oilsite Personnel Manager:** I don't know of any good examples I have had recently. It is the sort of thing that you know someone is dealing with something and then you write a memo copying their four senior people. Written sort of you are the one that has picked this up and what a good person you are to have done this and to have found it out and it does actually then ... say that the person that you are also including on the mail message that you are actually already doing something about it. It's sort of a subtle 'I am a good boy,' but you are only giving them half of the story.
**I:** I thought that I would just let you know?
**M:** Actually I can remember a good one, I did have a good one it was something to do with the wiring not being done and we had asked to, I would ask ISB to do the plan for the building and then a month later they sent us a message saying further to our letter of a month ago. It came into us saying why have we not done the wiring yet on 1E and copying their boss and turning it by saying that we now need to do this because we have been asked to have it done by Friday or the following Monday or something, and fortunately both myself and the facilities manager have got a copy of the message asking them for the plan. Which in spite of the fact that all the other messages were on this email it was forwarded to the boss the last one wasn't and boy was he furious when I forwarded him the final message that he had not been copied on. They had shaved off the top lesson, they had just come back to a point before my message was actually on it and said look that Facilities had dropped the ball again and we had already agreed on what we were going to do was to do.

In the first part of the extract the manager describes how personal accountability is often at stake in email interactions and how users can strategically exploit this through practices of copying in superiors (see Brown & Lightfoot, 2002). In the second part, this is described by recounting an episode where her own section was involved in a dispute with another. At the heart of this problem was the doctoring of an email communication by the other section, since email interactions are routinely copied by the system into the body of successive messages. What this means is that a sender can tailor how the complete interaction is recorded in a current email simply by editing out chunks of the words that have been copied over to a new mail in the interaction. Luckily the manager describes how she was able to expose this tailoring of the past by forwarding a complete copy of the interaction extracted from her own archives. As a technology of ordering the archives are introduced to deal with conflicts between parts of the company (customers, local authorities and others) over such issues. Nonetheless, precisely because these conflicts do exist, the archives too can become subjected as technologies for those struggles. Again, the archives do not make conflicts disappear but affects their dynamics and modes of performance by being a technology that can be enrolled in them.

What this extract points to is a wider problem with distributed archiving. It is notable that such kinds of disputes were typically settled in face-to-face meeting (the irony here of course is that in Oilsite the introduction of CMC was meant to eliminate the need for precisely these kinds of meetings). Settlements are typically arrived at when speakers can display another form of evidence – such as a written copy of an email. We would argue that at such moments CMC stops becoming a solely discursive activity and becomes also a non-discursive activity. That is, a matter of ordering bits of paper, stored messages, print-outs and so on as well as managing the demands of immediate interaction.

## The Non-discursive and Organisation Structure

So where we have arrived at is the idea that there are always two sets of ongoing activities: the discursive moves made in interactions and the non-discursive ordering of things (e.g. emails, archives, materials). So to ask how we talk about things is to focus on one activity alone. We might equally ask 'how are things moved around and ordered in such a way that they become fit objects about which to speak?' The email archive, as we have shown, is a particularly intriguing instance of this. It is something which is worked upon, ordered and continually shaped by ongoing organisational activities. Yet it is also something which we can display as something continually oriented to in the talk of Oilsite personnel. In effect, the email archive is integral in social relations.

Let us try to contextualise this by asking one final question: where does an organisation actually remember? How are the present-future functions of the archive deployed as part of the ongoing organisational practice of scheduling sequences. One thing we can be sure of is that the place where archiving occurs is not the same place where any demands for accountability and free flowing coordinated production are initiated. Or more crudely, that archiving occurs in spaces that are entirely distinct from where the major decisions occur, from where the aura of power and central executive discretion emanates. We can show this empirically. In the following long extract a senior manager is questioned about differences in record keeping at various levels in the organisation:

> **Interviewer:** The impression that we seem to be getting is that a lot of the strategy type meetings are being done very informally, even since there are not a huge lot of formal minutes being taken at the meetings?
> **Oilsite Manager Executive Development:** I don't think that that happens anyway. We always take formal minutes when you have got a third party there. So if you have got a meeting with a client, erm, and on project task forces and stuff you will take internal meetings. That is part of the project discipline. But our side of the project meetings, the meetings I go to very rarely are they minuted, very rarely. And that is ok as well, to me it would not be appropriate. We had one meeting a few days ago where we did record it because it was a project action and I actually just sent around that meeting note today formally, but that is quite unusual actually for myself. But in the job that I am doing now it does not come up.
> **I:** We have got the picture especially with the OMG, perhaps they meet ten times a week, but no one is thinking papers are wrong?
> **M:** That is an internal, that is a fairly informal grouping, yes it is. It is informal but it is basically four operations managers, you have to bear in mind ... But no there are never ...

no secretary's there. There are four or five managers working together on issues around the table progressing some issues. I would tend to get some stuff done to work out because most of the resources of the company are represented by the people in that meeting. But no we never record minutes. Absolutely unnecessary. It is not that sort of a meeting and that is typical of the meetings that go on. There are very few internal meetings of projects that get recorded formally, in my opinion. Some disciplines might do it differently.
**I:** It is an intriguing ... as that is entirely where the big decisions are made ... in meetings ... therefore you would record them in the minutes? It seems that, you are OMG and must be making decisions all the time though, and they are not recorded?
**M:** Yes. You know you are basically colleagues together. There is not any, you do not want to leave that meeting having to defend what you have decided at the meeting against others. If there was something that came up at OMG which was divisive, there was not an agreement or there was something like that it would go to another level. I have never been to one of those meetings. It tends to be a consensus pretty well. And very often actions won't be decided on the day it will go forward to another day and it will be progressed over a period of weeks, and that is ok as well as it is the nature of the beast.

What emerges in the course of the extract is that very senior meetings, the places where big decisions are made, are rarely minuted. This is felt to be 'absolutely unnecessary'. The reasons for this as they are mobilised by the manager in question are interesting. At that level 'you are basically colleagues together', which is to say that matters of routine accountability are on a very different footing. One is not expected to have to mobilise extensive evidence to defend one's position. As such there is no need for the present to be continually consigned to the archive through a supplementary mechanism in the form of minutes. The joint recall of these 'colleagues together' suffices. So it is the introduction of diverse parties, customers, diverse sections with diverse tasks, responsibilities, interests – and therefore pending conflict – that minutes are archived. The bosses not taking minutes is not a matter of their being bosses, he says. If he is right, other meetings of a small group of regularly meeting equal colleagues would not be archived either – lest they had to take care that they might be held accountable by others, say, higher up.

What we are presented with here is the space prior to the place of archiving, the space from which archiving is itself commanded, but which stands outside of the archive. This is a space that is not bound by the usual rules of audit. Managers here keep no formal records, save a few notes in their own personal workbooks which are never entered into the organisation's wider archives. Why should this be the case? Because entering such records into the archive would make them subject to the usual rules of truth. Records of senior meetings would then become part of the play of correctness and its strategic undermining which constitutes the usual activity which goes on around electronic archiving. By refusing to allow any supplement to their own highly fallible human memories senior managers take themselves out of the economy of correctness.

But in staying out of this economy, managers do not reject truth altogether. In fact they make available to themselves a more potent form of truth. Occupying an unauditable space allows senior managers to challenge archiving practices without themselves being challenged in return. Since their own past is not captured in any archive maintained by the organisation, senior managers are able to claim that these archives are merely supplementary, that they do not capture the real essence of the business – that they fail to express the guiding vision or project of the organisation. But – and this is crucial – such a claim can only be launched if managers simultaneously have complete access to the organisation's archives. Because it is only by coming to terms with the established practices of correctness, with the authorised version of the past, that they are able to mobilise a radically different version of the organisation's past, one which, they are able to claim, is more fundamental and more 'truthful' than any existing version. Since it alone is based on a vital and proximal memory rather than a supplementary, technical and external practice of archiving.

## Conclusion

All of which is another way of saying that our focus on how things are talked about can be reversed. Things make us talk in particular ways. They make us communicate in particular ways, they make us manage in particular ways. Now this is not to say that things are 'just there', that they can serve as the *a priori* grounds upon which interaction can be understood. To argue that would be just as bad as arguing from an *a priori* description of the social. No, things are ordered, put together and made sense of in precisely the same way that words are. But these are two different activities which we must draw upon different sets of resources to understand. This we then take to be the immediate analytic task – to develop a vocabulary for talking about how things afford talk, for how things are ordered in such a way that they become fitting topics for talk. And, of course, also how talk gets things *done*, because clearly this company is not just in the business of moving messages around, and having meetings.

Overall then this chapter offers a conceptual re-orientation to how we think about the relationship of subjects and objects and how ordering and so forth are part of getting things done. We examined how objects are formulated and disputed in CMC, paying particular attention to the kinds of discursive resources brought to bear by users. The role of electronic archives in resourcing disputes arising from contested formulations shows how the maintenance of electronic archives requires the enrolling of other subjects, and the sustaining of networks of artefacts. In addition the 'non-discursive' work of archiving and the discursive formulation of artefacts are accomplished simultaneously. Finally we concluded that attending to the non-discursive enriches our understanding of how conversation is managed within CMC settings. Such management of CMC is shown to be more than establishing some bridge over to the object world that is not to hand by means of communicative devices that substitute for gesture, gaze (deixis) etc., in thc interactional generation of shared context. The process is better understood as one whereby objects are brought between speakers. That is, the way objects configure dialogue and at the same time are ordered as topics in such communicative action. This is not to argue that things serve as some given but, rather, that things are also ordered in precisely the same way that words are. Organisational practice emerges in the way the material resources of the archives order such practices within interdependent orderings of the discursive and the non-discursive – of words and things.

**Aknowledgements**

Thanks to Ole Dreier and Alan Costall for their most helpful comments on this chapter.

**References**

Abbott, A. (2001). *Time matters: On theory and method.* Chicago: University of Chicago Press.

Brown, S.D. & Lightfoot, G.M. (1998). Insistent emplacement: Heidegger on the technologies of informing. *Information Technology & People*, *11*(4), 290–304.

Brown, S.D. & Lightfoot, G.M. (2002). Presence, absence and acccountability: Email and the mediation of organisational life. In S. Woolgar (Ed.), *Virtual society? Get real!*. Buckingham: Open University Press.

Brown, S.D., Middleton, D. & Lightfoot, G.M. (2001). Performing the past in electronic archive: Interdependencies in the discursive and non-discursive organisation of remembering. *Culture & Psychology*, *7*(2), 124–144.

Dreier, Ole (1999). Personal trajectories of participation across contexts of social Practice. *Outlines*, *1*(1), 5–32.

Dreyfus, H. & Dreyfus, S. (1986). *Mind over machine*. New York: Macmillan.

Drew, P. & Heritage, J. (1992). *Talk at work: Interaction in institutional settings*. Cambridge: Cambridge University Press.

Edwards, D. & Potter, J. (1992). *Discursive psychology*. London: Sage.

Edwards, D. (1997). *Discourse and cognition*. London: Sage.

Goodwin, C. & Goodwin, M.H. (1996) Seeing as a situated activity: Formulating planes. In Y. Engeström & D. Middleton (Eds.), *Cognition and communication at* work. Cambridge: Cambridge University Press. (pp. 61–95).

Hiltz, S. R. & Turoff, M. (1978). *The network nation: Human communication via computer.* Cambridge, MA: The MIT Press.

Hutchins, E. & Klausen, T. (1996). Distributed cognition in an airline cockpit. In Y. Engeström & D. Middleton (Eds.), *Cognition and communication at work* (pp. 15–34). Cambridge: Cambridge University Press.

Kiesler, S., Siegel, J. & McGuire, T. (1984). Social psychological aspects of computer-mediated communication. *American Psychologist*, *38*, 1123–1134.

Khoshafian, S. & Buckiewicz, M. (1995). *Introduction to groupware, workflow, and workgroup computing.* New York: Wiley.

Leudar, I. (1991) Sociogenesis, coordination and mutualism. *Journal for the Theory of Social Behaviour*, *21*(2), 197–220.

Rice, R. & Love, G. (1987). Electronic emotion: Socioemotional content in a computer-mediated communication network. *Communication Research*, *14*(1), 85–108.

Serres, M. (1980). *The parasite*. Baltimore: Johns Hopkins Press.

Serres, M. (1995). *Angels: A modern myth*. Paris: Flammarion.

Sproull, L. & Kiesler, S. (1986). Reducing social context cues: Electronic mail in organizational communication. *Management science*, *32*(11), 1492–1513.

Sproull, L. & Kiesler, S. (1998). *Connections: New ways of working in the networked organization.* (6th ed.) Cambridge, MA: The MIT Press.

Winograd, T. & Flores, F. (1986). *Understanding computers and cognition*. Norwood, NJ, USA: Ablex Publishing Corp.

# Chapter 11

# Learning to Do Things with Things: Apprenticeship in Bakery as Economy and Social Practice

Klaus Nielsen

## Introduction

Today the concept of learning is everywhere. Learning labs, learning centres, courses on self-reflexive learning, etc., just to mention a few areas in which the concept of learning has disclosed itself in the last couple of years. The concept of learning has become a major 'buzz' word in academic discourses in Denmark. However, when listening to the interview tapes with apprentices, as part of analysing qualitative data in the research project 'Learning in Modern Danish Vocational Training', I realized that they did not address issues of learning as much as notions of economy when they discussed education. I began to notice this discrepancy and started to wonder why I, and many other people, with a profound interest in learning never relate to issues of economy in discussions about learning. Instead, we seem to neglect the economic influence on learning entirely.

First of all, this article presents a further development of the general problem of the neglected economic aspects in discourses of learning, starting with a research project of how apprentices learn their trade. It seems that comprehension of learning in practice becomes much more transparent when we include aspects of economy, rather than merely basing our understanding on epistemological perspectives of learning. In this connection I will define an epistemological perspective as a specific approach to learning in which matters of knowing the world is central. Below, I will elaborate on the various definitions used in the article.

The arguments in this article are primarily based on empirical material from a study of how baker apprentices learn their trade, and subsequently, the methodological design is described. Examples from the empirical material are laid out and discussed in two paragraphs. The first section describes how the economic and educational discourses in the bakery are interwoven. In the second empirical section, examples are given of how the baker apprentices try to mediate learning the trade of baking, as well as the economic aspects of this practice. Finally, in the discussion, the consequences of including the economic aspects of people's everyday existence are considered in relation to issues of learning generally.

*The general neglect of economy*

In academic discussions of learning in practice the dualism between learning in schools and learning in a workplace has been dominant. It has been a discussion based on the assumption that the main difference between the two settings was one of knowledge. It became a discussion apparently about the different kinds of knowledge, which are supposedly embedded in the different social arrangements of schools and workplaces (see e.g. Nyeri, 1988).

The baker apprentices attended a trade school as part of their training in order to become bakers. However, according to the baker apprentices the primary difference between learning at the trade school and learning in the bakery was that all perspectives related to economy were neglected in the trade school. One of the apprentices describes the difference between trade school and bakery like this:

> [In trade school] we can take as long as we like to make a perfect Danish pastry, the teacher does not say anything. You can't take that back to real life, there you need to produce, and that you only learn by producing, getting better and better, until you figure out what a Danish should be like, instead of measuring its diameter – it is way too old fashioned. I believe the school should apply the production method. Here we make rolls by hand, I mean, where do they do that today? If the machine breaks down, we just get hold of a new dough machine (Kasper).

According to the apprentice, it is a matter of producing large quantities in the bakery with the aid of different kinds of machines. At the trade school apprentices work with small quantities of dough and they do not encounter any hysterical masters who shout at them because they have made a mistake, or are too slow. Rather, the teacher does not say anything. Furthermore, there is time pressure in the bakery, which is not present in the school context; there the apprentices have all the time they need in order to work on the details. Looking at the physical arrangements in a bakery and the bakery at the trade school, it is hard to detect any differences. In both settings there are ovens, large tables, mixers, etc. Even though it is not said directly, it is clear in the quotation that aspects of economy and production play a crucial role in the bakery.

Returning to the discussion mentioned above, the baker apprentices shared an important insight. According to the bakers, the primary difference between learning at school and at the workplace is not a matter of different kinds of knowledge, but first and foremost a matter of how schools neglect the economic aspects of practice. Or using the reverse argument, economic aspects play a crucial role when addressing issues of learning in the bakery, but not at school. In the following I will explore these issues more thoroughly. The following is a closer look at how we understand learning from an epistemological perspective and an introduction to an economic perspective in relation to learning.

*Learning and epistemology*

One of the many reasons why the notion of economy is excluded from discussions of learning has to do with the way we relate learning to epistemology. A paradigmatic understanding of epistemology is found in Descartes' thinking. According to Descartes our knowledge of the world becomes more certain if we follow a systematic method where we first analyze/divide the problem we are facing into its smallest recognizable parts. Secondly, we synthesize/reconstruct the parts by following strict logical rules to a more complex recognition of the subject matter at hand (Descartes, 1996). The dialectic of the process of analyzing and synthesizing is what Descartes prescribes as the method, which provides us with a certain knowledge of the world. This systematic way of knowing the world has a great impact on what we consider to be science, and consequently, also on how education should be organized. It is the latter, which is of interest in this article. Descartes' understanding of epistemology has a bearing on how educational situations are arranged. Educational curricula are often organized on the principles of confronting the student with the most simple and basic element of a subject matter and then moving into the next element (Woolfolk, 2001). This way of thinking is influenced by Descartes' conception of knowledge. The same applies to the way problem solving is represented in textbooks of educational psychology; one solves a problem by identifying the basic elements and then moving onto the more complex elements (Woolfolk, 2001). Behind these institutional patterns of arranging education we find the Cartesian conception of epistemology and knowing the world/learning about the world. In the epistemological perspective, learning is a question of learning about the world.

The main problem with this understanding of learning is that the process of knowing the world divides our recognition of the world into small parts, and thereby divides the issues we want to know about into discrete unites. Consequently, the problems we face and analyze are removed from their context in the process of reducing complexity. From this it follows that matters concerning emotions, desire, morality, power and economics are excluded from the process of learning/knowing the world since these issues address complex qualities in our being in the world. However, it does not make sense to reduce these issues to the smallest recognizable units. Reading through the index of mainstream textbooks on learning, or in educational psychology, none of these matters are described to any large extent. In this article it is especially issues of economy that will be pursued further since, in my opinion, they have the greatest implications for learning.

*Learning and economy.*

By addressing economy, I am taking the stand that humans maintain, express and understand themselves through the use of material goods and services. My argument in the following is that aspects of economy and learning support each other. Issues of economy are central and inseparable when addressing issues of learning in practice. Additionally, I will argue that by paying attention to the interaction between economy and the organization of a practice, a better comprehension of learning can be reached, than merely by taking an epistemological approach to learning. The perspective on learning laid out in this article is inspired by theories of learning as socially situated (see Lave & Wenger, 1991; Lave, 1997; Dreier, 1999). In this perspective, learning concerns how participants in an ongoing social practice change their participation. By including this perspective on learning, issues of economy become important in order to understand changes in ongoing social practices, and in that connection also issues of learning.

The term economy comes from ancient Greek and is defined as somebody who manages a household (oikonomia: household manager). Furthermore, it is a concept relating to the production, distribution and consumption of goods and services (Merriam Webster Dictionary, 1999, p. 365). In economic anthropology, this double connotation of the term economy is preserved and differentiated in terms of community economy and market economy (Gudeman & Rivera, 1990). It is a helpful distinction for this article so I will shortly define the two concepts. The notion of community economics describes how smaller groups locally produce in order to support their independence. Sharing is central to community economics. Land, material resources, knowledge is what a community shares and the source of its maintenance. Market economy is based upon competition among buyers and sellers who exchange goods and services. The goal of participation in the marked is to secure a money profit, which is private property.

In everyday life both these perspectives on economy exist. However, whether it is aspects of the dominant community economy in the bakery or aspects of a market economy make a big difference to issues of learning, so I will maintain the distinction between the two understandings of economy.

If we merely perceive learning from an epistemological perspective then only learning, which takes place in institutions where the economic aspects of practice are not accessible for the students, can be considered real learning. Learning in work places or in families where issues of economy play a crucial role is a contaminated kind of learning, a reproductive and second-rate kind of learning. The critique of apprenticeship has often had this character.

The following is a more concrete elaboration on the relationship between learning and economy. It is an example of how economy develops the trade and influences what the apprentices need to learn and how.

## The Socially Situated Bakeries

Bakeries have a long tradition in Denmark and Northern Europe in general, going back at least a thousand years as an organized trade. The baking trade was protected in the Middle Ages in the market towns by the guilds, and the dominant way of learning the trade was through apprenticeship. As the names of thc cakes and the bread indicate (e.g. French bread, Sarah Bernhardt cakes, Viennese pastry, brown sugar pastry, etc.), the baking trade has always been internationally orientated towards Europe by developing new products, finding new recipes in order to please the customers. One could argue that aspects of economy have always been part of developing the trade. The following is a peculiar illustration of this. The famous Danish pastry was developed in Denmark in 1850 when conflicts about wages in a strange way led to the introduction and advance of Danish pastry. During a strike the journeymen in Copenhagen demanded higher wages. However, the masters used lockout against the journeymen, and invited journeymen from Vienna to work instead. As the Viennese journeymen could not read the Danish recipes, they introduced their own cakes instead, where especially the 'Plundergebäck', a cake made of yeast dough became very popular with the customers. After the strike Plundergebäck was transformed by the Danish journeymen into what we today know as Danish pastry. A very concrete example of how economy and learning/developing the trade is part of the same process.

However, today the bakeries are in an economically difficult situation. The concept of 'bake off' is putting the bakeries under economic pressure. 'Bake off' is a concept used by gas stations and kiosks. They have a small oven where they can 'bake off' the prefabricated bread and cakes and sell them freshly baked to customers. Consequently, within the last ten years the number of bakeries has dropped from 1800 in Denmark to about 1300 bakeries today. The confrontation between the trade embedded in old craft traditions and the economic demands is very visible and significant in the everyday working life in the bakeries.

### *Methodological considerations*

In the following I will shortly address some of the methodological considerations on which the present article is based. Learning in practice is a field that has only been examined to a limited extent. Thus, the purpose of the study is exploratory which means that interesting statements and considerations that occur in the course of it generate new hypotheses to be pursued and examined. This requires that the design of the study has a certain openness and flexibility to make it possible to generate new hypotheses without reformulating the entire study.

Two methodological approaches were applied, participant observation and semi-structured interviews. The process of observation is dynamically built around the interview as the center of rotation. The reason why the interviews are at the center of rotation is partly that it is through them that the participants in the context can express themselves and the significance of being a baker becomes visible. Partly because the material from the interviews is by far the most extensive, comprising about two hundred and fifty transcribed pages. However, the interviews cannot stand alone, as they do not represent the context of which the interviewees are a part. To use several different methodical approaches is to regard the process of research as a dynamic process, where construction of knowledge is the essence and where a dynamic interaction between observation and interviews is possible. Social reality is, indeed, in many ways immense and it requires several complementary perspectives to be able to form a complete picture of it.

*Participant observations*
By observing what actually happens in a community of practice, it is possible to gain insights into how it operates. Furthermore, through the observations it was possible to create a fertile background for the interviews. The method of observation in this study is seen as a systematic attempt to select, produce and report on those parts of behavior and surroundings related to individuals' interaction 'there and then', and which are in accordance with the purpose of the study. In this study, I have worked as a first-day apprentice in three different bakeries. One bakery was located in a small supermarket in Aarhus with a master and two journeymen. Another one was located in Ry (a small town 45 kilometers from Aarhus) where one master and two journeymen worked. Finally, I worked for a day in a bakery in a larger supermarket, where there was a master, ten journeymen and two apprentices. The latter supermarket was very close to being a bread factory.

*Semi-structured single interviews and group interviews*
Seven individual interviews with six men and one woman were carried out for this study. Four of the interviewees were baker apprentices; two were journeymen and one a master. Furthermore, three group interviews were conducted with three groups of baker apprentices with four apprentices in each group. Six men and six women were interviewed in these groups. The criteria for participant selection included willingness to participate in tape-recorded interviews, and the ability to articulate experiences of learning as working bakers. The participants were volunteers and were not paid for any part of their involvement. The interviews were designed as semi-structured interviews centered around particular themes, but with the option of exploring specific themes in greater depth (Kvale, 1996). The quotations used in this article are the ones which best illustrate the points of research interest and all names mentioned are pseudonyms.

## Empirical Examples: Economy and Learning

Economy and learning are highly intertwined in the discourse of education in apprenticeship. This is both a historical fact (Coy, 1989), but also a central facet of today's discourse about how apprentices learn in the workplace. In the following I will argue that the economic aspects play a crucial role both when it comes to the structure of the education in the bakery, and how it also influences the contents of what is taught. Furthermore, I will argue that issues of learning are inseparable from issues of economy when we focus on the bakery. However, I will try to show that issues of economy are not seen as something that prevents learning from taking place, rather to gain insights it is important to understand how economy and social practice in the bakery are related to issues of learning.

*The structure of the education*

The economic discourse plays a crucial and visible role in the structure of the apprentice's education in the bakery. It is certainly a central topic in the bakeries. One of the interviews with a master provided us with a good example of how the aspects of learning and economy are interwoven. This particular bakery is relatively small and employs a master, two journeymen and two apprentices. The bakery is primarily organized according to principles of a community economy.

After having listed all the things the apprentice needed to learn, the master went further into the rationality as to why he had chosen this sequence of what was taught first, second and so on:

> Well, I need to teach him so he knows it, and he will know it. It may be an advantage that it is a small bakery, the more he knows, the more help he will be, right. It will be easier for us, gradually. The first year with an apprentice, right, it is hard, isn't it, that is also why he is sent over to make bread because he is of most use there now. But when he is moved away from there, he will also get to do all the other things (Ole).

As seen in the master's description, the rationality of the educational sequence in the bakery is also embedded in a kind of thinking, which includes economic aspects of practice. However, as the quotation from the interview with the master shows, the notion of economic thinking is not something that prevents learning. The master underlines that the more the apprentice knows the greater the benefit for the bakery. According to the master the apprentice is also an investment, which costs the master and the bakery a lot of work in the beginning, that is, the first year or so. However, if the apprentice is well trained, he will become a profitable investment for the bakery. The apprentice begins in the bread section of the bakery because this is where most help is needed, and this is where he can be of most use initially.

The social arrangements surrounding the apprentice are also organized from a perspective which includes economical thinking. The first year or so, the apprentice works next to a journeyman who keeps an eye on the apprentice. As stated again by the master, the rationality behind the arrangement is: *there is still someone [the journeyman] to keep an eye on him [the new apprentice], so he does not make any major mistakes* (Ole). Again the social arrangement with the journeyman who constantly supervises the apprentice is found in economic thinking because it is too expensive to let the apprentice make too many or too grave mistakes which could prevent the production flow. However, as the apprentices express themselves, working together with a skilled journeyman is the crucial way of learning the trade because the journeyman functions also as a role model of how to do things in the bakery, somebody who supports the apprentice, helps him or her in difficult situations and somebody who sets the standards of the trade. One of the apprentices describes how the journeyman whom he works right next to supports his learning process:

> Yes, first he shows you how to do it, and he shows it very fast, it just passes by. You don't see much. Then afterwards he shows it slowly and explains a bit why you do so and so. I believe that is the most practical way.
>
> *Interviewer:* And then you try it afterwards?
>
> Then I try it afterwards, yes. That is the way it is, and then if you have any questions, he shows you how you shouldn't do it. That is fine, I think (Anders).

As this quotation shows, it is often the journeymen who provide the practical instruction and keep an eye on the apprentice in the beginning of their practical education in the bakery. However, if the apprentices in the beginning of their practical education in the bakery are able to make quality products, then supervision from the journeymen will be less intense, and the apprentices will have the opportunity to work more independently.

The whole social arrangement of the apprentice's education is aimed at enabling the apprentice to work independently of the master and the other journeymen. Again there are both considerations about learning and economy involved in the reasoning behind this arrangement. The master nicely described it like this:

> Because then he [the apprentice] can do many things when he has become good at it, right, when he can work on his own, and the rest of us can do something else. Because there are days when there are only two of us because of holidays or days off…then he will have to be able to work very independently in the course of another couple of months, when he will be working on his own with a lot of things. And must be able to do it. And…and then the biggest help will be that he can make bread. And…that is why we have done it that way (Ole).

The overall aim of the practical education in the bakery is to provide opportunities for the apprentices to work independently because that is what the apprentices should be able to do when they end their education and start working as journeymen. However, there are more reasons why the aim of the apprenticeship education in the bakery is to make the apprentice work more independently. Firstly, master and journeymen are able to attend fully to other assignments in the bakery by not constantly keeping an eye on the apprentice. Secondly, if the apprentice is able to work on his own, he is also able to replace staff; he would be able to work during holidays or when the other staff members are ill, etc. The aim of independence in the apprenticeship education is not, however, to enhance individual autonomy for its own sake: the emphasis upon autonomy is embedded in the economical thinking.

However, the apprentices in the bakery appreciate the opportunities to work independently of the journeymen and master. They feel a sense of responsibility. One of the apprentices describes the situation where he has just been given the responsibility for part of the daily production in the bakery, and finds it a significant learning experience:

> Lately while I have been in the section of cakes and confectionary, I have started to get used to checking what needs to be discarded, what is old, what is dry, where we need to fill up, doing it independently, filling up the shelves, whipping cream, figuring out what needs to be done, what we are short of. Sometimes I consult the senior journeyman by saying: we need this and that. And he says: then you do some of that. And then I will fill up. Sometimes he shouts, if there is something that needs to be filled up, or that I should have been more attentive – but otherwise it is my responsibility. You learn a lot that way – positively (Poul-Erik).

In the apprentice's description, it is clear that he is no longer just supervised by a journeyman or merely doing what he is told by a journeyman or master. He is responsible for part of the production in the bakery, and he has to maintain some kind of overview and fill up what is lacking, etc. Furthermore, the journeyman is no longer supervising the apprentice; rather the apprentice consults with the journeyman when there is something he needs to know. The above quotation is a fine example of how issues of learning and economy are not necessarily in opposition to each other.

Confronted directly with the notion of economic reasoning, or the academic notion of exploitation, the master states:

> Well, of course you are exploiting him slightly that way, it is cheap labor.... for the 3 years you have them, 3½ years I believe, the first year you don't make a lot on them, so to speak, because they make so many mistakes and don't manage to do what they are supposed to. But the last 2½ it is still good, cheap labor. Of course it depends on what you mean by exploitation, right, because they have to learn it, don't they, and, really I don't think that we exploit them (Ole).

It is clear from the quotation that the organization of the apprentices' education is planned from the criteria of what is economically profitable. The apprentice is an investment, who is expensive in the first year, but becomes profitable in the last couple of years when he or she works like a journeyman, but is paid like an apprentice. It should be added that this notion of exploitation is no secret to either the other journeymen, or the apprentices. When confronted with these issues in the bakery, the master called out to the apprentice first to find out what his wage was at the moment, then to the journeyman about what his wage was, and then he subtracted the wages and came up with how much he saved by having an apprentice. The apprentices find it important that they are people that are being invested in, and receiving a paycheck for their efforts every month is of crucial importance to them.

However, it should be noted in connection with the quotation above, that the master added that he himself did not feel that he exploited the apprentices. He stressed in the interview that he made sure the apprentices learnt the trade of baking, that he made sure the apprentices went through all the different aspects of the baking trade, and that he tried to give the apprentices meaningful assignments right from the beginning of their time in the bakery.

The point is that the economic aspects are important, and often decisive when we want to understand issues of learning. However, in the course of planning and executing the apprentice education, the master, and also the journeymen, mediate aspects of learning and economy without any problems. One could argue that insights into aspects of economy provides one with a better understanding of the learning processes in the bakery, rather than consulting learning theories developed on an epistemological basis.

*The customer's perspective*

When we take a close look at a specific instruction situation in the bakery in which a master instructs an apprentice, we find a complex interwoven pattern of economic and learning perspectives in that same situation. It is unnecessary for the master to break the task at hand into discrete elements, as suggested by the epistemological perspective mentioned above.

When the apprentice learns to make certain products, he or she also needs to include the perspective of the customer. To learn to see the products from the perspective of the imaginary customer is an important part of what the apprentices need to learn. The look of the product has a higher priority than how it tastes. It is important for the apprentices to learn to make cakes that look delicious.

The master gives a concrete example of how he shows the apprentice to make cakes:

> The first times he does it, I take part in it. First, I do it while he stands next to me and observes, I may be decorating with chocolate and nuts on top and stuff like that.
>
> *Interviewer:* Decorating?
>
> Yes, decorating. A cream cake, for example, has in most cases some decoration. It may be a grape or a piece of tangerine, some chocolate or a chocolate coating. He decorates it and makes sure the cake looks nice. He will begin with that. He will get the cake, and then he will have to finish it by decorating it. Sometimes I will say: try to figure out your own way of decorating it. Then he will have to think and try to decorate it so it looks nice. And we can talk about it afterwards. After he has done that some times, then you can allow him to make it from the start. He has to start by making raspberry jam and then put cream on and the different things that need to go in it and stuff like that (Ole).

As this shows, the aspect of decoration plays a crucial role when it comes to making cakes. The decoration is the pivotal point in the processes. As stressed in other interviews, this should be seen in the perspective of how the apprentice needs to learn that cakes and bread that look delicious sell. Bread or cakes with funny shapes are thrown out.

Furthermore, in this quotation it is clear that the learning processes start backwards in relation to the production processes. The overall aim of the learning process is introduced first to the apprentice and then the master and apprentice work their way backwards in the instruction process compared to the production process. The apprentice is introduced to the nearly finished product that only needs a little decorating. After the apprentice has learned to decorate, he will have the opportunity to make the cake from the beginning. In this perspective, it is the social arrangement which is important rather than the method suggested by Descartes and the epistemological perspective. If we imagined how the process would be arranged from an epistemological perspective, it would begin with the smallest recognizable elements. In this case it would be the ingredients for the cake, the raspberry jam, the cream, the chocolate, and the tangerine. The second step would be to synthesize the different ingredients into a cake, something that would probably mean a lot of waste, while the perspective of the costumer would easily would be lost.

*The threat of technology*

In the previous paragraphs in this article the dominant economic perspective has been what was initially termed community economics. This was linked to observations and interviews in smaller bakeries. However, turning to observations and interviews from a larger bakery with one master, ten journeymen and two apprentices, the market economic perspective becomes more obvious. It is a bakery, which is very close to being an industrial bakery, where advanced technology plays a dominant role in taking over the skilled work of the participants in the bakery.

So far, I have argued that issues of economy are closely related to issues of learning. However, the examples given have been positive in the sense that they have shown that taking economic aspects into account does not exclude the apprentices from finding the bakery a resourceful place to learn. However, in the following I will argue that the introduction of a specific kind of new technology in the bakeries can lead to a disqualification of the apprentices. A disqualification in the sense that it prevents the apprentices from participating in other contextual settings – the bakeries – in a qualified manner. It becomes obvious how vulnerable the bakeries are to the development of the market economy.

One of the journeymen described how new technology influences what it means to be a baker, because it is not necessary for the apprentices to learn to make white bread, rolls, etc. He said this:

> We have two bread maker machines, we don't have to make bread anymore – it all rolls out, we just have to put the loaves into moulds. And with rye bread, we throw the dough into a funnel, and then they come out with the same weight and all, ready to be dipped in some poppy seeds and then put into a mould too (yes). They [the apprentices] don't weigh them themselves, mix them or anything. Our roll machine – they don't do the morning rolls themselves or learn to shape them by hand – the roll machine does it all, puts them on a baking tray – it does everything for them. They just have to turn them over in poppy seeds and then stuff dough in the other end. They don't really learn the trade, they don't, I don't think so (Carsten).

The journeyman describes how the technology of making white bread makes many skills superfluous. Furthermore, a lot of the cakes are prefabricated in a factory, and all the apprentices and journeymen need to do is to take them out of the refrigerators, place them on trays and put them in ovens. These are activities which disqualify the apprentices, and which makes it difficult for them to pass the journeyman examination. The alternative, according to the journeyman, is to let the apprentices work and learn in smaller bakeries which cannot afford new technology nor to employ many journeymen. It is in these bakeries that apprentices will become responsible, and consequently learn from taking part in the everyday practice in the bakeries. It is worth noticing that several of the apprentices and journeymen stressed that less technology in the bakeries would provide the apprentices with better opportunities to learn the trade of baking. Furthermore, in the interviews it was emphasised that the prefabricated cakes were of a lower quality than the handmade ones. According to bakers and apprentices, the prefabricated cakes contained more artificial sugar and were much dryer than handmade cakes because they had been frozen and were supposed to last for longer periods of time.

The positive aspects of introducing new technology were also outlined. The amount of work was less, and it was possible for journeymen and apprentices to have a more flexible work schedule, as they were able to produce more and faster. Obviously, it is easier to take out cakes from refrigerators and put them on trays, than actually bake the Danish pastry itself. On the other hand, the reduction in the workload was only temporary, within the last year five journeymen had been made redundant in the bakery.

However, it is crucial to stress that to understand the learning processes of the apprentices, it is important to focus on issues of economy, rather than merely addressing issues of epistemology. One has to examine closely the relationship between the bakery (the context) and the market in order to understand how different skills are developed or extinct, and how this influences the lives of the bakers.

To sum up briefly, I have given three different examples of how the economic discourses influence the learning process of the apprentices both directly and indirectly. First, by the way aspects of economy influenced the organisation of the assignments in which the apprentices take part. Secondly, by working on products they need to sell, and finally, by focusing on how new technology disqualifies the skills of the baking trade.

My conclusion for the first section of the article is that the economic aspects are a crucial part of what the apprentices learn. As mentioned in the beginning of the article, traditional concepts of learning do not include issues of economy. However, in the following I will try to introduce another way of addressing issues of learning, which includes aspects of economy.

## Empirical Examples of Different Kinds of Orientation

In the following I will argue that we need to take another stand on how we approach issues of learning in which aspects of economy are included rather than excluded. Inspired by a situated perspective to learning, my focus will be on how matters of identity are a pivotal phenomenon when approaching learning in practice. As a consequence of how aspects of economy and learning were inseparable, the baker apprentices developed different kinds of orientation to being-in-the-world-as-bakers. A central concept in this connection is the concept of orientation. Before outlining the specific kinds of orientation central to the bakers, I will say a few words about the concept of orientation.

One way of conceptualizing issues of economy in relation to learning is to focus on the different kinds of trajectories of participation, which are arranged in the various bakeries for how the apprentices can participate and, consequently, what is relevant to learn. Following this line of thinking, it is important to conceptualize how the personal trajectories in the bakeries which the apprentices themselves arrange, and the different kinds of orientations develop in relation to the various trajectories of participation. The concept of orientation tries to capture how apprentices develop different ways of living with the different contradictions and conflicts in the bakery, often related to issues of economy. Aspects of economy are not just something which happens to the apprentices. By using the concept of orientation it is stressed that this is about how the apprentices live their lives in general, and it also relates to how the apprentices act in and across other contexts as well (e.g. in their spare time, how they organize their family life, etc.). A similar concept that could have been used is the concept of strategies, which, however, often becomes associated with only cognitive processes. Furthermore, the concept of orientation indicates that the subjects are aiming at realizing certain goals, though not always completely clear about what these goals are. Working towards and trying to realize these goals in their everyday lives is what constitutes the meaning of the 'here-and-now' activities in which the subjects are involved. Finally, the concept of orientation has a social basis as they are related to the activities in other contextual settings.

This section outlines the three different and most dominant kinds of orientation found in the material. However, at the present moment the analysis of the material is not concluded, so other kinds of orientation may be disclosed. The three kinds of orientation are the craft-dominated orientation; the social/materialistic orientation, and, finally, the educational orientation (inspired by Wilbrandt, 2002; Tanggaard, 2003). Even though, these orientations are outlined very categorically, they do not exist in the 'pure' fashion developed below. Fortunately, real life is more complex.

### *The craft dominated orientation*

The craft dominated stand is orientated towards the traditional virtues of being a baker. There are actually different versions of this orientation. The primary orientation is directed at becoming a master oneself one day. We found this implicitly stated in different ways in the interviews with the apprentices, however, it was most clearly formulated by a journeyman. The journeyman had been working in several different bakeries, one of the reasons being that he wanted to expand his skills as a baker with the explicit aim of owning a bakery himself. He said:

> You become increasingly more skilled everywhere you go (...) and it is because I have this dream of having my own bakery that I have to see as many things as possible (Thomas).

The journeyman had developed a strategy of working in a bakery for a year or so and would then leave the place in favour of another. In order to advance his skills, and consequently obtain his own shop, in the end he had to work his way through a lot of bakeries. The journeyman gave us an example of how he himself actively organized his learning process in relation to the practice he was part of with regards to a future participation. This way of learning the skills to become a master in one's own bakery is learnt by 'going waltzing' (to change learning places), which is the traditional model for learning a craft. Within this orientation we find a clear scepticism in relation to learning something at trade schools. According to this orientation, the only way to learn is by being an apprentice or journeyman in different kinds of bakeries. The craft dominated stand is broadly orientated toward the trade in general, and those who hold this view are ready to move to other bakeries in order to learn more.

*The social/materialistic orientation*

The social/materialistic stand is orientated towards the wage, the need for good colleagues and good working hours. Paradoxically, the transformation of the bakeries into larger units of production with significantly more use of technology gives way to the social/materialistic orientation. The larger industrialized bakeries have more employees, which offers the possibility of meeting more colleagues. Furthermore, within the larger and technologically advanced bakeries it is no longer necessary for bakers and apprentices to start very early in the morning to begin production. Much of the bread and cakes are prefabricated, and it is only necessary to take them out of boxes, place them on trays and roll them into ovens, which automatically switch on in the morning before anybody begins work. This orientation is more dominated by other considerations than the actual craft. This stand is orientated towards having a successful private and family life and living a normal social life, where one does not sleep when other family members are awake and engaged in social activities. The social/materialistic orientation comes closer to regarding work as industrial work. However, there is a tendency to accept that maintaining the craft is the duty of the trade schools, and something that cannot be done in the bakeries, so some resign when it comes to upholding the standards of the craft in the local environment. Those who share the social/materialistic stand are orientated towards other bakeries if they provide better opportunities for a higher wage, better working hours, etc.

*The educational orientation*

The educational stand is orientated towards pursuing more education. For many bakery apprentices being a baker is not the ultimate goal. The education as a baker is merely a step on the way to another kind of education or profession. Several of the apprentices I spoke to would like to become chefs, however, they could not find a restaurant that would accept them as apprentices, so they chose the bakeries as the second best opportunity hoping to become chefs later on. Other apprentices regarded being a baker apprentice as the first step to becoming an engineer within the food area. One said about his future career:

> Well, yes, what if I don't want to be a baker, but would like to work in a bread factory or be a consultant or just not use the training practically, but would rather move on, then it is nice to know a little bit more about the material's characteristics and so on (Poul Erik)

As the quotation shows, this apprentice had another perspective on what it meant to be an apprentice in a bakery. He perceived it as a temporary process, providing him with interesting insights that could be useful in his own career. The educational stand is not involved in the local bakery, but has a more distanced perspective on what happens in a bakery. The trade school and courses are important because they potentially provide access to other types of education.

As argued so far in the examples from my study on learning in the bakery, the economic discourse plays a significant role regarding issues of learning. Taking aspects of economy into consideration when addressing issues of learning it becomes clear what was possible for the apprentices to learn. In this article I have primarily focused on what was possible for the apprentices to learn in relation to aspects of economy. Only one case described how market economy and new technology disqualified learning.

## Discussion

I will argue that it is not a coincidence that the economic aspects of human existence are neglected in discussions of learning. As shown in the discussion of the Cartesian influence on what we consider as learning, this frame of thinking provides us with limited space in order to comprehend issues like learning in practice.

The epistemological perspective on learning becomes an idealized version of human existence in which desires, emotions and interests are left out of the picture. This also leads to the assumption that learning and education are in themselves positive things, which nobody should question. To question and discuss learning in relation to power, economy and various interests is tantamount to blasphemy.

In this article focus has been on apprenticeship because it is so obvious that economy and learning are closely interwoven. Furthermore, it has been argued that aspects of economy are not merely something which determines what it is possible for the apprentices to learn. The apprentices integrate the economic conditions into their life in general. However, one could argue that learning and economy are closely interwoven in formal institutions like schools as well. Just to mention one example: To place twenty-five students in each class with one teacher is not motivated by learning theory, but by economic considerations. Only by addressing an economic perspective do we understand why and how such arrangement have been organised as the central mode for education in modern culture.

Another central feature when introducing issues of economy into discourses on learning is the notion of contradiction as a central dynamic for processes of learning. When approaching learning from a traditional perspective, all aspects of conflict seem to vanish since learning appears to be a process of acquiring the different kinds of knowledge embedded in the various contexts. However, once we introduce issues of economy, then different social interests become central and we see how contradictions become a key motivator for learning.

## References

Coy, M.W. (1989). *Apprenticeship*. New York: State University of New York.

Descartes, R. (1996) *Om metoden*. Copenhagen: Gyldendal.

Dreier, O. (1999). Læring som ændring af personlig deltagelse i sociale kontekster. In K. Nielsen & S. Kvale (Eds.), *Mesterlære – læring som social praksis*. Copenhagen: Hans Reitzels Forlag.

Gudeman, S. & Rivera, A. (1990). *Conversations in Colombia: The domestic economy in life and text*. Cambridge: Cambridge University Press.

Kvale, S. (1996). *InterViews – An introduction to qualitative research interviewing*. Thousand Oaks, CA: Sage.

Kvale, S. (1997). Research apprenticeship. *Nordisk Pedagogik*, *17*, 186–195.

Lave, J. & Wenger, E. (1991). *Situated learning: Legitimate peripheral participation*. Cambridge: Cambridge University Press.

Lave, J. (1997). Learning, apprenticeship, social practice. *Nordisk Pedagogik*, *17*, 140–152.

Nielsen, K. (1999). *Musical apprenticeship: Learning at the Academy of Music as socially situated*. Skriftserie for Psykologisk Institut, Århus Universitet.

Nyeri, J.C. (1988). Tradition and practical knowledge. In J.C. Nyeri & B. Smith (Eds.), *Practical knowledge: Outlines of a theory of traditions and skills*, London: Routledge and Kegan Paul.

Schön, D.A. (1987). *Educating the reflective practitioner – Toward a new design for teaching and learning in the professions*. London: Jossey Bass.

Tanggard Pedersen, L. (2002). *To læringsbaner ind i elektronikken*. (In press).

Tanggaard, L. (2003) Læringsbaner igennem elektronikken. In K. Nielsen & S. Kvale (Eds.), *Praktikkens læringslandskab* (pp. 161–173). Copenhagen: Akademisk Forlag.

*Webster's Third New International Dictionary*. (1968). Springfield, Massachusetts, USA.

Wilbrandt, J. (2002.) *Vekseluddannelse i håndværksuddannelser. Lærlinges oplæring, faglighed og identitet mellem skole og virksomhed*. Uddannelsesstyrelsens temahæfteserie, nr. 14.

Woolfolk, A. (2001). *Educational psychology*. Boston: Allyn and Bacon.

## Chapter 12

# Urban Makings and the Formalisation of Informal Settlements

Gustavo Ribeiro

This chapter looks into patterns of urbanisation that are marginal to formal[1] development undertaken by the public sector or by private developers. In doing so it identifies two types of urban making:

1. An urban making which is implemented through unplanned, collective intervention in the environment. This is effected by individuals performing intentional actions, like going to work, to the bus stop, or to the stream, gathering in public spaces, playing, etc. In the process of performing such actions, people are collectively contributing to the creation of networks of footpaths (beaten tracks) and urban spaces (Ribeiro, 1997). This form of urban making is a continuous event which stretches through months/years and transcends individual intentions. It is characteristic of shantytowns, which dodge the control of official agencies and which have basically to rely on the limited human and economic resources available within each settlement. But such process rarely occurs in isolation, without the influence of external actors. Even a shantytown entirely built with the effort of its inhabitants will be pressured to interrelate with its urban surroundings. This may occur through the action of authorities or private landowners and may lead to changes in the settlement and not rarely to evictions.
2. Processes of improving the conditions of shantytowns and of incorporating them into a broader pattern of urbanisation involve regulating and formalising such settlements to various degrees. The intervention of public institutions, foreign donors and Non Governmental Organisations (NGOs) introduces organisational structures and formal mechanisms for implementing projects, which affect people's interaction with their environment and the quality of urban spaces and of individual dwellings. Urban making through direct action

1 The term formal refers to urban development, which is planned, regulated or financed through conventional/authorised institutions/channels (such as central or local government, banks or credit institutions etc.). The term informal refers to developments outside those channels (see Drakakis-Smith, 1982 for a discussion of the terms formal and informal).

by individuals and the implementation of long term patterns of urbanisation as unplanned events are replaced by mediated urban making through the intervention of external actors and the introduction of formal planning procedures.

This chapter is based on a study of low-income settlements in Bangkok and Chiang Mai (Thailand) which have undergone formalisation, through the implementation of projects targeted at supporting people and improving their living conditions. Such projects are carefully designed to promote the participation of local inhabitants at all levels: from problem formulation, through project design and budgeting, to implementation.

These participatory mechanisms support processes which involve urban interventions, but which are primarily aimed at the education and empowerment of low-income communities. Still, besides visible impacts towards strengthening low-income groups and besides attempts at promoting community-led social changes, new urban conditions and patterns of interaction between inhabitants and settlements are emerging as a result of these processes.

The central argument of this paper is that processes of education and empowerment facilitated by a public organisation and a NGO cannot be seen in isolation from changes in the physical environment effected through daily social practices and through the very implementation of the above-mentioned processes.

Another important argument presented here is that formalisation in processes of urban production raises issues about the role of design and planning in relation to mechanisms of public participation. And to the extent that upgraded or resettled neighbourhoods are presented as improved alternatives to informal settlements, it becomes particularly relevant to draw comparisons between the two. This paper looks at unplanned, planned and hybrid forms of urbanism and the processes of making and design which they engender.

## Background

In 1996 the Danish Government, through its environment and international aid agency, The Danish Co-operation for Environment and Development (DANCED),[2] provided the Thai Government with a US$ 1.3 million grant for a project targeted at the improvement of environmental conditions in urban areas occupied by low-income communities. The Urban Communities Environmental Activities (UCEA) project

2 DANCED was established in 1984 with the objective of contributing to the greatest possible extent to the protection of the environment and nature in developing countries. With the ascension of Venstre (a right wing liberal party) to power in November 2001, international development aid by Denmark was severely cut down. In addition, the environmental concerns which figured very high on the political agenda of the Social Democratic Party, were relegated to a second plan. DANCED was done away with and its projects were placed under the Danish Development Aid (DANIDA).

(1996-2002) follows, as the name suggests, DANCED's overall policy of placing local communities at the centre of environmental programmes and giving them responsibilities for decision making, design and implementation. (Boonyabancha, 1999, p.103)

The public institution co-ordinating the implementation of UCEA in Thailand,[3] The Community Organisation Development Institute (CODI) has set up, since its inception in 1992, a programme which aims both at improving the living conditions of the urban poor communities and at strengthening their organisational capacity, through the promotion of community savings and credit groups[4] (UCDO, 2000, p.1).

In its role as a support mechanism CODI has stood as a catalyst in, and arguably as an initiator of, a process of social change. Such a process, which aims at promoting 'a large scale community-driven development movement,' places the decision making and managing responsibilities largely on community networks and community groups.[5]

In line with CODI's approach, the Urban Communities Environmental Activities (UCEA) project focuses on a process where environmental improvement is not an end in itself, but a means for promoting social change (Ribeiro et al, 2000). In addition, the environment is attributed a highly transitory role for two main reasons: (a) the focus of UCEA is on activities as tools for people's education and empowerment; (b) the low-income communities in question are under the threat of eviction by the local authorities.

The above outline places the environment of squatter settlements (dwellings, canals, public spaces) in a condition, which is not simply that of a setting for

---

3 On the 28th July 2000, the so called Urban Community Development Office (UCDO) was merged with the Rural Development Fund (RDF) and a new public institution was created, namely, the Community Organisation Development Institute (CODI).

4 In order to achieve that, CODI relies on a revolving fund which is made available to all urban poor groups who organise themselves to apply for loans for their development projects. According to a recent survey, by 2000 'over half Thailand's 2,000 urban poor communities in 50 provinces… linked together into 103 networks through a broad range of community development activities, including housing, income generation, environmental improvement, community enterprise and welfare' were members of CODI. (UCDO, 2000, p.1)

5 CODI relies on collective instances represented by community groups and increasingly by community networks to achieve a type of management and decision making which aim at representing the interests and wishes of socially and economically excluded groups. In that way, CODI aims at providing alternatives to decision-making initiated by authorities (local or central), by learned professionals (specialists, academics), by NGOs and by individuals with illegitimate power within communities (e.g. community leaders [called *Nakleng*] involved in criminal activities, such as drug traffic), (see for instance Phongpaichit and Piriyarangsan, 1994). CODI reports occurrences of misuse of power and funds within the sphere of its activities (UCDO, 2000, p.12), but has documentation to support the argument that community-lead processes are self-regulatory and that mismanagement and corrupt practices will be counteracted in time within community groups and networks. (UCDO Update, 2000)

activities neither that of a mere object of intervention. The environment appears first and foremost as a means for educating and organising people. *Making* in this context is not only production (e.g. the rebuilding of a canal embankment) but also and centrally the constitution of social processes (organisation, empowerment and education).

The present chapter investigates this multiple role of the environment in UCEA as means for social change, as object of intervention and as setting. It raises questions about the process of design involved in the implementation of environmental improvements in selected low-income settlements in Chiang Mai and about the role of such environmental improvements in future interactions between people and their environment.

## Squatter Settlements

> China is the weed in the human cabbage patch. … The weed is the Nemesis of human endeavour… Of all the imaginary existences we attribute to plant, beast and star the weed leads the most satisfactory life of all. True, the weed produces no lilies, no battleships, no Sermons of the Mount … . Eventually the weed gets the upper hand. Eventually things fall back into a state of China. This condition is usually referred to by historians as the Dark Age. Grass is the only way out … . The weed exists only to fill the waste spaces left by cultivated areas. *It grows between*, the poppy is maddening – but the weed is rank growth … : it points a moral. (Henry Miller quoted in Deleuze, 1999, p. 19)

Squatter settlements in Thailand, follow a pattern which is found elsewhere in the world, and normally occupy publicly owned land that has remained marginal to formal processes of urbanisation; that is, land with poor accessibility, marshy areas, flooded sites along canals, etc. The poor occupies such land, through strategies of survival, with minimal resources and means of construction, which may include recycled timber, plywood panels, bamboo mats, corrugated tin roofing sheets, amongst other materials, to create low-cost shelters.

Squatter settlements have an inherent power to change and adapt, for their investment is minimal in the creation of shelters – a power to fold and unfold in accordance to changing political conditions. These architectures and urbanisms of 'necessity' operate with extremely limited material conditions and challenge the involvement of professionals such as planners and architects in the provision of cheap, large scale housing: at the very moment the architect or planner steps into this process an increase in the costs of shelter production already occurs and their very involvement may rapidly become an unaffordable commodity!

Of special importance to this paper is the fact that the formation of squatter settlements involves, simultaneously with the creation of a physical environment, the constitution of social structures. The act of making the settlement consists not only of generating products: footpaths, streets and dwellings – as would be the case in the building of a new urban area. Making is in itself a social process, involving the interaction between people and the use of urban spaces. Appropriation of public spaces is therefore tightly related to their production.

The production of physical structures invites in turn a different approach to that of consolidated urban areas. Instead of investigating permanence and persistence of urban structures, we are presented with changes, instead of morphology, patterns of use.

## UCEA

'UCEA aims at changing interactions and power relationships between organisations, networks, groups and individual stakeholders in a complex setting,' through a focus on environmental management. (DANCED, 1999, p.9)

Public participation in environmental projects aims amongst other things to create ownership of interventions (sidewalks, bridges, etc.) by the community involved. By actively contributing to a project, from decision-making, through design, to implementation, the community will, thus, be in a better position to appropriate the project as its own and to look after its maintenance. UCEA could be seen as a radical example of that approach, through its focus on environmental *activities* instead of environmental *products*.

UCEA gives priority to the process of learning and to strengthening the organisational capacity of communities (Boonyabancha, 1999, p.102, Ribeiro et al, 2000, p.3). An example of that is the project for the restoration of the embankment of Mae Ka Canal in Chiang Mai where it crosses Kham Phang Ngam settlement.

Mae Ka Canal used to be very narrow at Kham Phang Ngam, causing floods during the rainy season. Access to and from the community was cut off and children were prevented from going to school. The community decided therefore to widen the canal in order to channel the excess of water. The community planned and executed the restoration of the embankments of Mae Ka canal, but it was destroyed by new floods. After a second restoration, the embankment was destroyed once more (Ribeiro et al, 2000, p.16).

The case of the reconstruction of the Mae Ka Canal embankment was taken up in an interview with the director of CODI and overall responsible for the implementation of UCEA, Ms. Soomsook Boonyabancha, and her point was that the priority in that as well as in other UCEA projects was the process of learning by the local people. The fact that the community identified a problem, provided a solution, implemented it and then learned from their mistakes was the most important thing. The actual physical result was of secondary importance. (Ribeiro et al, 2000, p.3)

That approach raises questions about how professionals such as architects may contribute to a participatory design process. It is clear from the above example that UCEA gives priority to activities, as heuristic, empowering gestures, over products. Making in the environment is an event whose main goal is to promote learning and social change in the long term.

Activities can be seen in the context of UCEA as methods for actualising the community, for the empowerment of people, for promoting participation, social networking and learning in the community. Such an approach reflects CODI's overall policy:

> CODI helps people to play a role in the development of their own areas. People see, people learn and they can believe they can do it. [CODI is interested in] the processes that will get the essence of the people out (Boonyabancha quoted in Ribeiro et al, 2000, p.4).

UCEA's focus on process rather than on physical products seems to highlight the dynamic and transitory nature of the informal settlements in question. Such settlements as physical structures are not likely to survive as such, rather, they may quite probably be removed to another site. The process of learning and the building up of self-confidence is something that the people will be able to take with them[6].

In Tung Pattana, a squatter settlement comprising 30 houses built on stilts along the Mae Ka Canal in Chiang Mai, UCEA has supported through a $2,500 grant, the implementation of a boardwalk designed and built by the community, without the assistance of architects or engineers (Asian Coalition for Housing Rights, 1998, p.29). Before its construction, residents had to negotiate their way to their dwellings by 'wading through the water or hopping along bamboo poles strung between the houses' (Asian Coalition for Housing Rights, 1998, p.29).

With its ingenious system of concrete posts and movable wooden panels which can be bolted at different levels according to the level of the water in the Mae Ka Canal, this boardwalk has become a point of reference for those involved with community development projects in Thailand as well as internationally. Compared with Tung Pattana's boardwalk the walkway in the community of Bang Na, made of bamboo reinforced-concrete resting on layers of compacted garbage, has been met with rather less enthusiasm by visitors (Asian Coalition for Housing Rights, 2000, p.11).

When drawing such a comparison, those supporting these projects draw our attention to the fact that we should look beyond the products themselves 'into the complicated circumstances which yielded these walkways, … [to] find a gold mine of learning material in *both* settlements: one devastated by AIDS, lack of jobs and basic services, and many-times displaced by eviction; the other facing environmental

6 Seen in the context of architectural design, such an approach has led to a conception of environments or buildings primarily as sites for social activities, as settings for action and not as finished compositions for aesthetic contemplation. That approach can be found in the architecture of Joao Filgueiras Lima (Ribeiro G *Sarah Network* in Arkitekten No 22 September 2001 pp 16-23; Latorraca G (2000) Joao Filgueiras Lima. Lisbon: Blau; Lima JF (1999) CTRS. Sao Paulo: Sarahletras.), who has developed flexible pre-fabricated complexes for the Sarah Network of Hospitals in Brazil and in the work of Lina Bo Bardi who based her architecture on a careful investigation of popular productions (Ribeiro G. *Lina Bo Bardi: Times of Rudeness* in Arkitekten No 4 February 2000 pp 2-9; Ferraz M (1993) Lina Bo Bardi. Milan: Charta).

**Figure 12.1 Tung Pattana Boardwalk (Photo: Jørgen Andreasen)**

**Figure 12.2 Tung Pattana Boardwalk (Photo: Jørgen Andreasen)**

hazards, flooding, eviction threats and hostile officials.' (Asian Coalition for Housing Rights, 2000, p.11) It is proposed that both 'projects are rich in lessons in making innovative, strategic investments in establishing the right way to stay, mobilising scant resources, knitting communities together, making decisions democratically, negotiating with hostile city administrations, managing money… doing *many, many things* beyond the act of simply upgrading access.' (Asian Coalition for Housing Rights, 2000, p.11)

Besides the importance of the process, which has led to the construction of the raised walkways in both settlements, it is undeniable that such interventions have radically changed the conditions of accessibility to individual dwellings. In addition, they have provided a new habitable surface and a social space, where before there was none. Seen in relation to the process that has led to their production, such boardwalks stand at the point of their conclusion, as a clearly defined goal and, one would be inclined to believe, as an element which plays a relevant role in the motivation of the members of the community in mobilising their efforts.

These boardwalks, as urban elements, as spaces which allow for uses such as accessibility and social interaction, can hardly be downplayed in their role as physical products. Their potentials to be maintained by the residents can be measured by the extent to which they support basic daily actions; actions which will wear them down, but which contain, at the same time, the key towards their sustainability.

Also relevant here is the fact that the designers and builders are local people with established social practices that involve the physical environment before and after the construction of the boardwalks. Their design is therefore invested with such social practices together with the limits and possibilities offered by physical structures.

If we shift for a moment to the case of a self-built shantytown on firm ground (like that of Vila Paranoa in Brasilia), the spatial elements which allow for access and for the performance of social activities are there from the start. The primary appropriation of the site is effected by creating beaten tracks on the overgrown field (Ribeiro 1997). Its maintenance as an urban site is effected through the very performance of activities. People vote with their feet, they walk, meet and play in certain places and on those spots the ground is cleared from vegetation.

In the case of Tung Pattana and Bang Na the site is not yet appropriated, periods of flood and draught prevail and impose therefore conditions of access to individual dwellings as well as the performance of activities between them. The project of raised walks in those communities can be seen as primary gestures of appropriation of the site, which perform a role in the transformation of urban spaces.

In that sense, a dissociation between processes and products and a promotion of the former over the latter may be seen as an *a posteriori* discourse which risks misrepresenting the role and performance of the walkways in Tung Pattana and Bang Na.

## Collective Action in the Environment

The aforementioned study of Vila Paranoa investigates how collective action in the environment led to patterns of urban change and to the generation of urban landscapes (Ribeiro 1990, Ribeiro 1996, Ribeiro 1997).

Such collective action occurred in the course of about three decades, from 1960s to early 1990s, in the case of the shantytown Vila Paranoa. It consisted of people moving between different places of interest (home – bus stop, home – lake, neighbour – market, etc.). That movement generated a beaten track on the ground and defined a network of footpaths. Such network of footpaths is at the source of the layout of urban spaces of Vila Paranoa (Ribeiro 1990, Ribeiro 1997).

Collective action in that case is the result of individual intentional action and will to perform particular tasks. It is therefore self-motivated and without the interference of external agents. The will and initiative to act by the members of the community is integrated with the performance of daily actions, such as going to work, washing clothes, visiting friends, shopping. It is therefore a self-supporting/sustainable system, which is at work in the creation and development of these types of squatter settlements. The intentional action of each individual will be superimposed in the course of time producing an urban landscape which is not the contribution of a single individual, but of a community.

The process outlined above has been described by some authors, in my view misleadingly, as spontaneous (e.g. Chifos & Yabes, 2000 or Epstein, 1973). But reference to unplanned urban growth as spontaneous masks the fact that such processes are motivated both at individual and collective levels. People's comings and goings and related impacts on the environment, such as the creation of footpaths, can, as argued elsewhere (Ribeiro 1997), be understood in the context of intentional actions – not the intention of creating urban spaces, but the intention of reaching the bus stop to catch the bus or the intention of going to the market to do the daily shopping of groceries. Merleau-Ponty refers to such intentions as practical intentions:

> … when I move towards a world I bury my perceptual and practical intentions in objects which ultimately appear prior to and external to those intentions, and which nevertheless exist for me only insofar as they arouse in me thoughts and volitions. (Merleau-Ponty, 1962, p.82)

The creation of urban spaces may be described as the overlapping of individual actions in time. But it is, in fact, more than the accumulated effect of individual actions, for each action creates a footprint in the environment and such footprints, or changes are incorporated in the new environment. Just as collective action can be understood as a dynamic process which unfolds in time, so can the environment itself. Such a dynamic conception of the environment has, for instance, been explored by McCabe and Balzano in their writings on event cognition (McCabe & Balzano, 1986).

The changed environment or the environment under continuous change plays a dynamic role in subsequent patterns of interactions with users (Ribeiro 1997, Ribeiro 1996). The more people walk along a footpath, the more they wear it down, the more consolidated it becomes as a track as opposed to the ground surfaces alongside the footpath.

Through that perspective, the concept of collective action is understood as the succession of individual actions which do not simply appear in isolation but which become related because they change the environment and because the changing environment plays a decisive role in the unfolding of future interactions and thus affect how further physical changes take place.

## Participation in Development Projects

When considering people's participation in development projects, as is the case of UCEA, we have a different state of affairs. The prime motor for collective action is not within the community, but outside it, it is namely the agencies that initiate development projects. This is inevitable as a project is conceived prior to action.

People's participation in such conditions, already presupposes the setting up of *a priori* frameworks which provide an environment for people's involvement in projects. Participation as a project event can be contrasted with patterns of usability (see Ribeiro 1990, and Ribeiro, 1997) which create the layout of squatter settlements as illustrated earlier.

Participation can be seen as project related, collective action. In that sense, collective action occurs within the framework of a project. Such a project precedes collective action, and by creating space for its implementation it is also imposing limits to how such an action may occur.

A project adopting a participatory approach is still faced with the crucial step of becoming self-sustainable (sustainability being one of the main goals of UCEA (Boonyabancha, 1999, p.109, URDI, 1998, p.4, CODI, 1998, p.16). Project co-ordinators talk about the importance of elaborating exit strategies, where facilitators ensure that the activities they have promoted are sustained by the communities when the project formally comes to a conclusion. In order for that to happen, the project needs to stop being an externally initiated event and turn into a self-motivated social practice based on the will and resources of a community as well as on the collaboration of local authorities.

Projects such as UCEA can be seen through the perspective of formalisation of processes of production and reproduction of urban settlements. The integration of such levels of formalisation into the daily life of people and into informal practices is, through this perspective, central for reaching sustainable development within such communities.

Although it is not the aim of this paper to assess the sustainability of UCEA,[7] it can be said that besides establishing partnerships with local authorities, its potential to become integrated in the daily practices of the community will be of crucial importance in the coming years, if the project is to fulfil one of its central aims.[8]

7 The reader is referred to UCEA evaluation reports (eg URDI, 1998).

8 This chapter discusses sustainability as a parameter introduced by UCEA. It does not deny the fact that sustainability is in itself a problematic concept, which needs to be

A focus on the process dimension of UCEA projects denotes a reference to the duration of the activity of production (from problem formulation, through design, to making) which may overlook the fact that use and maintenance are just as constitutive of the intervention as the process of production itself. In the case of self-built shantytowns, as pointed out earlier, such a distinction between product and process is challenged to the extent that use involves continuous production and reproduction, respectively through change and development of existing urban structures on the one hand, and through their maintenance on the other (Ribeiro, 1990; Ribeiro, 1997). In its turn, the consolidated environment is constantly promoting new uses.

CODI's discourse promoting processes over products has two notable consequences:

1. It downplays the role of environmental conditions (space layouts, building materials, landscape elements, etc.) in affecting patterns of use and appropriation. It can be argued that a built element (bridge, walkway, embankment) will acquire a particular role already to the extent that is has been constituted as an object of intervention in the context of a project; from problem formulation by a community (e.g. limited access) to the implementation of a design proposal (e.g. a walkway). Through collective action, a proposal will be reflected upon, discussed, designed and built. But as it stands as a realised product it becomes integrated in the development of future actions. Bourdieu makes the following comment about this constitutive gesture: 'in taking a point of view on the action, withdrawing from it in order to observe it from above and from as distance, … [the knowing subject] constitutes practical activity as *an object of observation and analysis, a representation*. (Bourdieu, 1977, p.2 emphasis on the original). Here, we see a marked contrast to spatial processes of production and reproduction in self-built shantytowns, which cuts across such a constitution of discrete objects, and which in my view are best described as the non-meditated perception of affordances as the basis for action (Gibson, 1979, Ribeiro, 1996).
2. In addition, CODI's conception seems to overlook the dimension of maintenance through use, that is, the incorporation of the physical intervention into the daily life of the community. It downplays, according to the argument presented here, an important dimension of the sustainability of a project.

UCEA, in its conception as a forum for learning, resists the accommodation of qualitative assessments of environmental improvements from a technical and functional points of view. This is clearly visible in the implementation of the Mae Ka Canal embankment reconstruction at Kham Phang Ngam.

Continuity and sustainability of environmental projects seems to be formulated in CODI primarily through a focus on participatory structures, educational/

critically examined. Such a critical discussion is presented by Peter Marcuse (1998) in his article entitled 'Sustainability is not enough'.

empowerment forums, networks, which come into being and are maintained precisely through the performance of organisational activities. Changes in organisational structure, networking and education rely on people's continuous commitment. In that way, continuity seems to be defined at an organisational level, overlooking the role of physical interventions/constructions and their uses. If, for instance, a particularly engaged community leader moves to another city, the whole community is affected by the absence of that individual. To be sure, community organisation and leadership play key roles in environmental sustainability, but so do daily social practices, which are closely integrated with physical structures, their production and reproduction.

## References


Angel, S., Archer, R.W., Tanphiphat, S. & Wegelin, E. A. (1983). *Land for housing the poor*. Bangkok: Select Books.

Angel, S. & Amtapunth, P. (1987). The low-cost rental market in Bangkok. In PADCO/NHA, The land and housing markets in Bangkok: strategies for public-sector participation. Vol. 3, Technical Report 6.

Asian Coalition for Housing Rights. (2000). Face to Face: notes from the network on community exchange, January 2000.

Asian Coalition for Housing Rights. (1999). Housing by People in Asia: Newsletter of the Asian Coalition for Housing Rights, No 12, April 1999.

Asian Coalition for Housing Rights. (1998). Housing by People in Asia: Newsletter of the Asian Coalition for Housing Rights, No 11, April 1998.

Boonyabancha, S. (1999). The urban communities environmental activities project and its environmental fund in Thailand. *Environment and Urbanization*, *11*(1), April 1999.

Bourdieu P (1977). *Outline of a theory of practice*. Cambridge: Cambridge University Press.

Chifos, C. & Yabes, R. (2000). *Southeast Asian urban environments: Structured and spontaneous*. Arizona: Arizona State University Press.

CODI (1998). Completion report: Urban Communities Environmental Activities (1996–1998). Unpublished Report.

DANCED (1999). Urban Community Environmental Activities (UCEA) Project, Thailand, Phase 1. DANCED Ref. No. M123-0057. Draft Evaluation Report.

DANCED (1998). Participation in environmental assistance: DANCED Reference Note.

Deleuze, G. (1999). *A thousand plateaus: capitalism and schizophrenia*. London: Athlone Press.

Epstein, D.G. (1973). *Brasilia, plan and reality: a study of planned and spontaneous urban develpment*. Berkeley: University of California Press.

Ferraz, M. (1993). *Lina Bo Bardi*. Milan: Charta.

Gibson, J.J. (1979). *The ecological approach to visual perception*. Boston: Houghton-Mifflin.

Latorraca, G. (2000). *Joao Filgueiras Lima*. Lisbon: Blau.

Laursen, J.H. (2001). *Miljø fra top til bund. Politiken 1 Section*, Sunday 11th February 2001.

Lima, J. F. (1999). *CTRS*. Sao Paulo: Sarahletras.

McCabe, V. & Balzano, G.J. (Eds.) (1986). *Event cognition: An ecological perspective*. Hillsdale, New Jersey: Lawrence Erlbaum.

Marcuse. P. (1998). Sustainability is not enough. *Environment and Urbanization*, *10*(2), October 1998, 103–111.

Merleau-Ponty, M. (1945). *Phenomenologie de la perception*. Paris: Gallimard.

Merleau-Ponty, M. (1962) Phenomenology of perception. [Colin Smith, trans.] London: Routledge.

Nørgaard, L. (2001). En mand med overblik. *Arkitekten*, No 8, April 2001.

Phongpaichit, P. & Piriyarangsan, S. (1994) Corruption and democracy in Thailand. Bangkok: The Political Economy Centre, Chulalongkorn University.

Ribeiro, G. (2001). G Sarah Network. *Arkitekten*, No 22 September 2001, 16–23.

Ribeiro, G., Diaw, K. & Andreasen, J. (eds.) Community development in Thailand: The case of Community Organisation Development Institute (CODI) and the DANCED supported UCEA project. Report on a visit to Bangkok and Chiang Mai in November 2000. Under ENRECA Project: Community Initiatives and Democratisation of Planning (unpublished manuscript).

Ribeiro, G. (2000). Lina Bo Bardi: Times of Rudeness. *Arkitekten*, No 4 February 2000, 2–9.

Ribeiro, G. (1997). An ecological approach to the study of urban spaces. *Journal of Architectural and Planning Research*, *14*(4), 289–300.

Ribeiro, G. (1996). Acting, dwelling and squatting: an ecological approach to the relation between person and urban environment. *Ecological Psychology*, *8*(2), 131–151.

Ribeiro, G. (1990) .Perception and design in the urban environment. PhD Dissertation, University of York.

UCDO. (2000). UCDO Update: A publication of the Urban Community Development Office in Thailand, October 2000, no 2.

URDI (1998). Summary report of the evaluation of Urban Community Environmental Activities Project.

Yap, K.S. (Ed.) (1992). Low-income housing in Bangkok: A review of some housing sub-markets. Bangkok: Division of Human Settlements Development, Asian Institute of Technology.

**Acronyms**

DANCED – Danish Co-operation for Environment and Development
UCEA – Urban Communities Environmental Activities
CODI – Community Organisation Development Institute
ACHR – Asian Coalition for Housing Rights

# Name Index


Agre, P., 114
Akrich, M. 147, 148, 154
Ariew, A. 18

Bærentsen, K. 114
Barker, R., 121
Baron-Cohen, S. 52, 62
Bourdieu, P. 88, 235
Bowker, G. 7, 173
Brown, S. 159, 196, 198, 201, 203
Bugrimenko, E. 70

Clark, A., 113, 119
Cole, M. 89, 93, 148
Costall, A. 4, 39, 51, 54, 68, 89, 90
Cummins, R. 17, 26

Davies, P. 18
Descartes, R. 178, 179, 211, 219, 223, 224
Dipert, R. 21-23, 31
Douglas, M. 171
Dreier, O. 7, 9, 132, 133, 152, 197
Dreyfus, H. 37, 194

Engeström, Y. 114, 187

Forchhammer, H. 6, 8, 31, 132, 134
Foucault, M. 134

Garfinkel, H. 170
Gibson, E. J. 68
Gibson, J. J. 4, 30, 45, 46, 68, 89, 90, 235
Goffman, E., 142
Goodwin, C. 195
Goodwin, M. 195

Hacking, I. 171
Haraway, D. 8, 152, 168, 174, 175, 177-181, 188, 189
Heft, H. 79, 82
Hegel, G. W. F. 176
Heidegger, M. 37
Holzkamp, K. 11, 132, 133
Houkes, W. 2, 3, 21, 24, 34, 41, 42
Hume, D. 172
Hutchins, E. 5, 52, 113, 114, 194-196

Ingold, T. 89

Jensen de Lopez, K. 4-6, 89-91, 96, 103-106
Joerges, B. 1, 51

Karpatschof, B. 1, 95
Keller, K., 134
Kendell-Scott, L. 4, 90
Kirsh, D. 113, 119, 120
Kitcher, P. 18
Kvale, S., 224

Lakoff, G. 95, 180
Latour, B. 159, 179, 184, 185
Lave, J. 9, 114, 212
Law, J. 7, 147, 151, 154-159
van Leeuwen, L. 68
Lemmonier, P. 130
de Léon, D. 5, 40, 114, 120
Leontiev, A. 53, 54, 132
Leslie, A. 52, 63, 67, 71, 83
Leudar, I. 39, 194
Lucy, J. 95, 104
Luria, A. R. 89

Markussen, R. 8, 167, 169, 180
Marx, K. 132, 176-179, 182, 188
McLaughlin, P. 15, 19, 21
Merleau-Ponty, M. 37, 105, 233
Middleton, D. 8-10, 198, 201
Millikan, R. 2, 17-22, 26, 31, 32, 71
Mol, A. 7, 147, 151, 154, 155, 156

Neander, K. 32
Nielsen, K. 9, 10, 224
Norman, D. 113

Olesen, F. 8, 169, 173, 180

Piaget, J. 3, 67, 69, 70, 87
Petroski, H., 125
Pickering, A. 152, 167
Preston, B. 2, 18, 19, 29, 30, 32, 33, 37, 42, 43, 51, 54

Reed, E. S. 72, 75, 82
Ribeiro, G. 10, 11, 121, 225, 229, 230, 232-235

Sapir, E. 104, 105
Schatzki, T. 7, 11
Schiffer, M. B. 51
Searle, J. 30, 45, 46
Sinha, C. 88-93, 98, 103, 105, 106
Smitsman, A. 68
Sørensen, E. 7, 154
Star, S. 7, 173
Suchman, L. 30, 37, 39, 40, 147
Szokolsky, A. 4, 8, 72

Tomasello, M. 51, 54, 69, 87-89, 93, 104, 106

Ungerer, J. 55, 56, 70

Valsiner, J. 53-56, 58, 60
Vermaas, P. 2, 3, 21, 24, 42
Vygotsky, L. 3, 12, 69, 70, 72, 88-90, 95, 101, 104

Walsh, D. 18
Wenger, E. 212
Wertsch, J. 3, 121
Whorf, B. 95, 104
Williams, E. 4, 51, 54, 90
Winner, L. 149, 152, 153, 155

Zukow, P. 73

# Subject Index


activity theory 114, 178
accountability 203, 205
actor-network theory (ANT) 2, 127, 147, 159
affordances 4, 46, 68, 69, 72, 73, 78, 79, 81-83, 88-90, 92-94, 105, 106, 235
agency 37, 52, 152, 154, 167, 178, 189
apprenticeship 9, 10, 209-224
archaeology 1, 127
archiving 8, 9, 193, 198-207
Aristotle on matter and form 175
artefact function 2, 31-35, 37, 39, 41, 43, 45, 47, 127
autism 4, 52-63

beaten tracks 10, 11, 225, 232, 233

canonicality 91-93, 98
categorisation 116-118
classification 7, 8, 32, 171, 173, 188
co-evolution of things and practices 169
cognitive biography 114, 115, 128
cognitive congeniality 6, 119, 124, 125, 127
cognitive ethnography 114
collective action 232-234
computer mediated communication (CMC) 193
computer mediated communication 193, 198, 200
conflict, 140, 144, 158, 203, 205, 223
context 3, 10, 17, 39, 136, 170, 171, 173
conversation analysis 195
coordination 63, 71, 72, 81, 169
craft 221
creativity 23
critical psychology 132, 178
customer's perspective 218

design 12, 13, 18, 20, 25, 31-36, 40, 47, 51-54, 57, 157, 161, 171
disability 6, 142, 143, 145
discursive psychology 8, 193
dualism 1, 62, 176

ecological psychology 4, 45, 67, 68, 82, 90
economy 9, 176, 209-224
education 7, 9, 10, 148, 209, 211, 214-218, 221-228
embodiment 30, 37-41, 68, 90, 105, 119
epistemology 209-212, 218-220
everyday practice 8, 10, 133, 170, 175, 220

fluid ordering 154
formal organization 225
function 2, 3, 15, 16-26, 29-47, 53, 55, 60, 62, 70, 78, 88-90, 120, 127, 132, 137, 172

information processing approach 193-194
intentions 2, 15-26, 30-37, 42-44, 47, 68, 88, 104, 127, 161, 181

language 51, 87-106, 170, 179
learning 9, 10, 53, 54, 62, 89, 90, 105, 113, 136, 209-224, 229
linguistic relativism 104-105

maintenance 6, 11, 23, 122, 158, 206, 212, 232, 235
materialism 175-179
materiality 161, 168, 170, 172, 175, 179, 187, 189, 193
material-semiotic systems 175
means-end relation 36
multifunctionality 19, 22, 31, 82, 93, 105, 137, 138, 144

nature 176, 178, 180
non-discursive ordering 8, 9, 196, 201, 202, 204, 206-7
normativity 36

objectification 133, 139
ordering, 151
organizational remembering 204

participation 212, 221, 222, 226, 234
Piagetian theory 3, 67, 69, 70, 87
plans and planning 2, 3, 29, 30, 33-47, 147, 193
Plato on the designer and user 15
play 4, 6, 7, 55, 62, 67-83, 134
politics of things 152
proper function 2, 3-5, 7, 15-26, 31, 32, 43, 55, 81, 82
properties and their relation to things 2, 7, 8, 87, 95, 167, 171-175, 188
prototype 19-21, 23, 25, 26
purpose 21, 22, 24, 31, 47, 82, 132, 168, 172

rationality 3, 34, 38, 215
regional ordering156
rehabilitation 135, 141, 142, 145

science and technology studies (STS)
selection 2, 17-21, 81
sequencing 197
signs 69, 104, 105, 179, 182
situatedness 30, 37, 39, 40, 88, 90, 142, 167, 171, 174, 180, 188, 189, 212
sociality 8, 193, 198, 200, 201
squatter settlements 228
subject-object dualism 1, 62, 176
sustainability 11, 232, 234-236
system function 2, 15-26

technology 5, 127, 132, 133, 140, 143, 149, 152, 167, 196, 220, 223
teleology 172
theory of mind 3, 4, 52, 62, 67
thing, definition of 171-2

urban making 225 et seq
use plans 3, 35, 36, 37, 41-47

writing 8, 167-170, 174

Zapotec spatial words 96-97